The Brownsville Raid

THE BROWNSVILLE RAID

By John D. Weaver

Foreword by Lewis L. Gould

Texas A&M University Press
College Station

The paper used in this book meets the minimum requirements
of the American National Standard for Permanence
of Paper for Printed Library Materials. Z39.48—1984.
Binding materials have been chosen for durability.

∞

Originally published in 1970 by
W. W. Norton & Company, Inc., New York   ·

Library of Congress Cataloging-in-Publication Data

Weaver, John Downing, 1912–
    The Brownsville Raid / John D. Weaver.
    p.   cm.
    Includes bibliographical references and index.
    ISBN 0-89096-528-5 (paper)
    1. United States.   Army—Recruiting, enlistment, etc.—
History—20th century.   2. United States.   Army.   Infantry
regiment, 25th—History—20th century.   3. United States.   Army—
Afro-American troops—History—20th century.   4. Riots—Texas—
Brownsville—History—20th century.   5. Brownsville (Tex.)—Race
relations.   I. Title.
UB323.A4   1992
355.1'332—dc20
                                                          92–14435
                                                             CIP

For
DORSIE W. WILLIS
Co. D, 25th Infantry
United States Army

Contents

Illustrations

Foreword

AMONG HISTORIANS, it is relatively rare for a single book to change the way that a past event is seen and interpreted. In the case of John D. Weaver's *The Brownsville Raid*, however, the book's publication in 1970 led to a reappraisal of the controversial events of August, 1906, involving African-American troops and the town of Brownsville, Texas. Until Weaver took up the cause of the black soldiers, the accepted version of what happened was that a few of the troops had indeed conducted some kind of shooting episode against the white residents of Brownsville. Responding to these actions, President Theodore Roosevelt ordered that 167 men of Companies B, C, and D, First Battalion, Twenty-fifth Infantry, be discharged without honor because they had refused to identify which of their comrades had committed the crime. Historians agreed that Roosevelt's actions were hasty and unwise, but they did not challenge the finding that some kind of violence had occurred as a result of the deeds of the black troops.

Weaver's book attacked the accepted version at all points. He argued that there was no credible evidence to show guilt by any of the soldiers accused of taking part in the violence. The evidence on which the United States Army and Theodore Roosevelt relied to assign blame to the black troops was weak and melted away under Weaver's searching analysis. The strong possibility that the men of the First Battalion had been framed by the residents of Brownsville pervades Weaver's narrative. As a piece of historical investigation, the book offered the first judicious and balanced appraisal of the case that had been mounted against the accused men.

The Brownsville incident rapidly became a national controversy during Theodore Roosevelt's second term. Having committed himself to the proposition that the black soldiers were guilty, Roosevelt tried constantly to nail down the army's case against critics such as Ohio's senator, Joseph B. Foraker, who questioned the truth of the charges. Weaver demonstrates the extraordinary lengths to which Roosevelt and William Howard Taft, his secretary of war and likely successor, went to establish the guilt of the soldiers *after* they had been dismissed from the army. The president's tactics included the use of private investigators, paid by government funds, to extract trumped-up confessions from some of the soldiers and to collect questionable evidence of their involvement. The Brownsville case is not one of the finer chapters in the political career of Theodore Roosevelt.

Weaver brings out of the historical shadows the crucial role of Senator Foraker. A conservative Republican who disliked many of the economic reforms to which Roosevelt was committed, Foraker had presidential ambitions in 1908. Embarrassing Roosevelt would certainly help his campaign against Taft. But Foraker did not take up the cause of the soldiers simply from political motives. A strong believer in the commitment that his party had once made to black Americans, Foraker (known as "Fire Alarm Joe" for his florid speaking style) became convinced that the men were in fact innocent. He waged a determined struggle to secure justice for them in the Congress and in the court of public opinion. So angry with Foraker did Roosevelt become that he increased his support for Taft's presidential candidacy in 1908. The case became one of the key events in setting up the transfer of power from Roosevelt to

Taft that had such significant consequences for the Republicans in 1912.

John D. Weaver is aware of all these considerations in his book. The interplay among local events in Brownsville, the politics of the army, and the national scene is one of the strongest parts of his story. Weaver is equally good about the black soldiers themselves—Sergeant Mingo Sanders, Private Boyd Conyers, and the other men of the battalion who faced the power of white officialdom without lawyers or legal advice of their rights. The book argues forcefully that the men "were denied the equity of the white man's justice and, dead, the vindication of his Jim Crow history."

Thanks to Weaver, however, the soldiers achieved some degree of belated historical rehabilitation. After *The Brownsville Raid* appeared, African-American members of Congress, led by Augustus F. Hawkins (D-Calif.), urged the exoneration of the soldiers. In September, 1972, the secretary of the army announced that the 167 black infantrymen would receive honorable discharges. One member of the unit was still alive. At eighty-six, Dorsie W. Willis accepted the long-overdue official rehabilitation for his deceased comrades.

But the Brownsville incident is not a closed historical chapter, and it is good to have a new edition of John D. Weaver's book for today's students of black history to read and evaluate. Recent reference works and textbooks on United States history mention the Brownsville case without any reference to Weaver's research. Page Smith in his *America Enters the World* (1985) says that "a black regiment, frustrated and angry at their abuse by local whites, 'shot up' the town." A recent textbook, *Nation of Nations* (1990), asserts that "a few unidentified soldiers had shot up Brownsville, Texas." Finally, in *The Reader's Companion to American History* (1991), the entry for Brownsville states that the soldiers, "in retaliation for discriminatory treatment by local citizens, shot off their guns in Brownsville, Texas, killing one resident." As Weaver shows, the evidence for these statements is dubious at best.

Beyond its careful reconstruction of what happened at Brownsville in August, 1906, and the injustices that were visited on the men of the First Battalion, *The Brownsville Raid* is an instructive reminder that the struggle to achieve civil rights for African-Americans began long before the modern triumphs of the movement in the 1950s and 1960s. The soldiers who felt the wrath of Theodore Roosevelt and the federal government in 1906 were not asking for unusual treatment. They sought only to receive the same rights and guarantees that any other citizen could expect from their government. Instead, they were maligned, spied upon, and disgraced for crimes they had not committed. Speaking on the floor of the United States Senate, Joseph B. Foraker summed up the essence of the case for the black soldiers and the underlying argument of Weaver's excellent book. "They ask no favors because they are Negroes," the senator told his colleagues, "but only for justice because they are men." With the republication of *The Brownsville Raid*, a new generation of readers can understand what John D. Weaver did to help these loyal American soldiers achieve historical justice.

Lewis L. Gould

Acknowledgments

I WOULD LIKE to record my indebtedness to Robert Vosper, Everett Moore, and James Cox of the Research Library, University of California at Los Angleles; Dr. Llerena Friend of the Eugene C. Barker Texas History Center, Austin; Librarian Fred Folmer and Archivist Chester V. Kielman, University of Texas; John M. Kinney, director, Archives Division, Texas State Library; Elmer O. Parker and George P. Perros, National Archives; Roy P. Basler and his staff, Library of Congress; and Richard Haupt, director, and Mrs. Lee Jordan, librarian, Cincinnati Historical Society.

I also wish to thank Ward Colwell for access to the files of the Brownsville *Daily Herald;* Ralph G. Martin for straightening out some questions on Theodore Roosevelt; Stanley D. Solvick of Wayne State University for tracking down an elusive item in the Taft Papers; Carlton Moss of Fisk University and the University of California at Irvine for his storehouse of information on the Negro soldier; and William Weber Johnson of UCLA for the use of his personal library.

"They ask no favors because they are Negroes,
but only for justice because they are men."

The Mystery

———◄•►———

I

*"That Texas mystery . . . sprang out of
the night, baffled the country for years
and died unsolved."*

THE TROUBLE IN Brownsville, Texas, began around midnight on
August 13, 1906, and lasted about ten minutes. The official records list two casualties—a young bartender killed, a police
lieutenant wounded—but the records were compiled by white
men who counted as casualties only other white men, not the
one hundred and sixty-seven black soldiers who were administra-
tratively savaged by order of President Theodore Roosevelt on
the basis of information he had received from a blundering mili-

tary bureaucracy headed by his heir presumptive, William Howard Taft.

Although the Brownsville Raid left an ugly stain on the records of two presidents, it has been swept under history's rug. Every schoolchild knows that Teddy Roosevelt stormed San Juan Hill, but not that black soldiers supported his celebrated charge. Every schoolchild knows that Taft was a fat, jolly President who later became Chief Justice, but not that it was his disagreeable task as Roosevelt's Secretary of War to summarily dismiss three black infantry companies, including some veterans of the Cuban adventure.

The men were discharged without honor and without any sort of public hearing. Afterward, some of them appeared as witnesses at the courts-martial of two of their white officers, some gave testimony before a Senate committee and a court of inquiry, but none of the soldiers was ever brought to trial on specific charges and, with the assistance of counsel, given a chance to confront and cross-examine his accusers.

Just one month before the White House and the War Department trampled the civil rights of the black battalion, the French supreme court had finally righted the judicial wrong done Captain Alfred Dreyfus. The Alsatian Jew, like the black soldiers, had been the victim of a military establishment permeated with prejudice. In Paris as in Washington, the generals had blundered into an indefensible position, and had then tried to defend it against repeated attacks of law, logic, and, when Zola took up the Dreyfus affair, literature as well.

The Brownsville soldiers found their Zola in Senator Joseph Benson Foraker of Ohio, who was politically destroyed before he finished arguing their case. At first, along with everyone else, including the Afro-American press, the Senator had not questioned the accuracy of news reports from Texas that the border town adjoining Fort Brown had been shot up by Negro soldiers. Then, with mounting incredulity and indignation, he had begun to study the evidence.

"No, that isn't true," his wife heard him muttering to himself as he dug into the records. "That doesn't follow at all. . . . No, no, there is nothing in that."

"By George! The men's guilt is as clear as day!" Roosevelt snapped, but not one of the soldiers was ever proved guilty of the crime for which all of them were punished.

"That Texas mystery, involving a Negro Dreyfus, sprang out of the night, baffled the country for years and died unsolved," Mrs. Foraker wrote in 1932, and a generation later the mystery remains unsolved, the injustice unrequited.

The Soldiers

2

"I want to kill a couple of them . . ."

The First Battalion, Twenty-fifth Infantry (Colored), had survived Sioux attacks on the Great Plains, jungle rot in Cuba, rebel skirmishes in the Philippines, and four years of garrison tedium in Nebraska only to find itself bushwhacked on a late spring day in 1906 by its own War Department. To the dismay of the outfit's white officers, Companies B, C, and D were ordered to Fort Brown, Texas. En route they were to stop off in Austin to take part in field maneuvers with the state militia. The thought of his black soldiers engaging in mock battle with white militiamen on Texas soil chilled the regiment's commanding officer.

"It is useless to ignore or deny race prejudice which exists in spite of law and justice," Colonel R. W. Hoyt wrote the War Department, "and I desire as colonel of a most excellent regiment to express my disapproval and to inform and warn the authorities of conditions that are certain to arise from an encampment at Austin with Texas Militia."

The authorities heeded the colonel's warning. New orders were issued, directing the three companies to proceed straight to Fort Brown, but Chaplain Theophilus G. Steward, the regiment's only black officer, was still apprehensive. He kept thinking of the bad feeling three years earlier when the Twenty-fifth had run into Texans at a Kansas encampment.

"During my whole experience in the service the only time that I have been assaulted by uncivil and ribald speech by a man in the uniform of a soldier was at Fort Riley, Kansas, and the man who did so was a Texas militia man," the chaplain wrote the regiment's adjutant. His letter ended on a prescient note: "Texas, I fear, means a quasi battle ground for the Twenty-fifth Infantry."

The oldest federal garrison on the Rio Grande, Fort Brown had been built in 1846 on land stolen from Mexico and named for Major Jacob Brown, who died in its defense during the first serious fighting of the Mexican War.* Nineteen years later, a month after Appomattox, a band of Confederate soldiers straggled out of the fort to fight and win the last engagement of the Civil War. Rebels of a more practical stripe had crossed the muddy river to sell their arms and ammunition to Mexican neighbors who were busy killing one another on behalf of Emperor Maximilian and Benito Juarez.

General Phil Sheridan rode into Fort Brown in June 1865 with orders to secure the border against mischief-making southerners fleeing the country and, while he was about it, also to secure the civil rights of the state's two hundred thousand Negroes. Their plight, he found, was "lamentable." They lived in

* "It is a fact," charged Representative Abraham Lincoln of Illinois in 1848, "that the United States Army in marching to the Rio Grande marched into a peaceful Mexican settlement, and frightened the inhabitants away from their homes and their growing crops. It is a fact that Fort Brown, opposite Matamoros, was built by that army within a Mexican cotton-field."

fear of their lives, denied the fruits of their freedom by terrorists "who, recently their masters, now seemed to look upon them as the authors of all the misfortunes that had come upon the land." During the same month that General Sheridan made his appearance at Fort Brown, Captain William Kelly reported for duty. Negroes were no strangers to the young Irishman who was to become Brownsville's leading banker. He had commanded black troops in the closing year of the Civil War.

"Properly officered," he testified a generation later when he was in his sixty-eighth year, "I believe there are no more civil and inoffensive men. Improperly officered, they are a very dangerous element, in my opinion."

Although he was frank to say he didn't always believe them ("I do not think there are many people who would take the word of a Negro against that of a white man"), Captain Kelly considered himself a man without prejudice. The town's other influential white residents felt the same way, he liked to think.

"There is probably less race prejudice in this community than in any part of the South," he declared, but when he was asked to identify the half dozen or so Negroes who lived in the town where he had spent the last forty-odd years, only the name of one old man came to mind. Later he managed to dredge up two other names, but that was all. The blacks were faceless, anonymous creatures of an invisible world apart.

"I know them all when I see them," he said, "and if they were up here, I could probably call their names, but I see very little of them."

There had never been many Negroes in Brownsville, Captain Kelly explained. Before the Civil War, slaveowners had hesitated to bring their blacks to Texas border towns for fear they might emancipate themselves by skipping across the Rio Grande. Since then, it had been a matter of economics. Negroes could not compete for work with the illiterate Mexicans who made up more than three-fourths of the town's population of some six thousand to eight thousand.

Bilingual "Anglos"—ranchers, merchants, customs inspectors, and retired Army officers—boasted of having no prejudice against their dark-skinned Spanish-speaking neighbors crowded into the filthy dirt-floored shacks of the town's tenderloin, but the true state of affairs was blurted out in testimony of a customs officer who had pistol-whipped a black soldier instead of demanding his arrest.

"You have a police force in Brownsville, haven't you?" he was asked.

"Yes, sir."

"Pretty good force?"

"I don't know, sir; they are Mexicans."

While he was stationed at Fort Brown as post surgeon, Captain Benjamin J. Edger, Jr., was free to carry on a private practice in his spare time. Some of his patients lived uptown in white-columned mansions, but most were Mexicans huddled in squalor along the dusty streets and alleys near the old fort. Toward the end of May 1906, when it was first announced that the garrison's white soldiers were to be replaced by Negro troops, the townspeople talked of little else and Mexican women crossed themselves in Christian resignation at the prospect of being raped by black heathen.

"Of the many persons who daily broached this subject to me," Captain Edger recalled, "there was not one who said the colored troops would be welcome, and all were loud in their denunciations of colored soldiers. Many merchants and storekeepers with whom I spoke, and who were my friends, told me how the Mexican population was afraid of these soldiers and how it would interfere with their business."

Captain Edger remembered a conversation with Dr. Frederick J. Combe, the town's mayor, who had once served with black cavalrymen as a medical officer.

"These people will not stand for colored troops; they do not like them," the Mayor had said. "These Mexican people do not want them here."

A first sergeant of the departing Twenty-sixth Infantry heard one of the town's Mexican police officers, Victoriano Fernandez, remark, "I want to kill a couple of them when they get here." Fernandez swore he never made such a statement, but a similar sentiment was attributed to him by another white soldier of the same outfit, who said he was in an Elizabeth Street saloon when Fernandez remarked to a group of townspeople, "The colored fellows will have to behave themselves or we will get rid of them, and all that we will have to do is to kill a couple of them."

"You will get along all right with the niggers," one of the Twenty-sixth's cooks assured the proprietor of the Miller Hotel. "They are pretty good sort of fellows."

Some of the townspeople talked of forming a posse to meet the soldiers' train and keep them from getting off; others favored sending a delegation to Washington. One outraged businessman wrote a letter to Senator C. A. Culberson, who forwarded it to Secretary of War Taft.

"The fact is," Secretary Taft replied, "that a certain amount of race prejudice between white and black seems to have become almost universal throughout the country, and no matter where colored troops are sent there are always some who make objections to their coming. It is a fact, however, as shown by our records, that colored troops are quite as well disciplined and behaved as the average of other troops, and it does not seem logical to anticipate any greater trouble from them than from the rest."

The one hundred and seventy black soldiers, commanded by five white officers, scrambled off the train in Brownsville on July 28, formed ranks, and marched from the depot to their new quarters.

"People were standing along the streets," recalled the battalion's commanding officer, Major Charles W. Penrose, "but there were no smiling faces or anything of that kind, as you might imagine when you are coming to a new post—a little hand-clapping or a little cheering sometimes. There was nothing of that."

Fort Brown, the newcomers discovered, lay sprawled in a sweeping curve of the Rio Grande at the lower end of the town. The main entrance, a black iron gate, opened onto Elizabeth Street, the principal thoroughfare. The enlisted men's barracks were about a hundred feet inside a waist-high brick wall that paralleled Garrison Road, a thirty-foot-wide strip of government land separating the fort from the town.

The battalion's commissioned officers were housed on the opposite side of the parade ground. Their quarters faced the men's barracks, the rear windows looking out on a horseshoe-shaped lagoon. The windows should be left open in summer, the officers soon learned, to catch the merciful evening breeze that rustled in from the Mexican side of the river.

Watching the arrival of the black soldiers, a white sergeant stationed at the Fort Brown hospital was surprised to notice they had brought no prisoners with them. He had never seen an outfit show up at a new post without having somebody under arrest.

"It was a good showing for the battalion," he testified afterward.

While the men were unpacking, they were visited by a delegation from the local black community, such as it was.

"There was about four families of colored people," recalled D Company's mechanic, Artificer George W. Newton, "and these men came in the post and shaken hands with us and told us that the whites, that they said, 'They didn't want these damn niggers' trade down here.'"

Once he had got settled in his new quarters, Newton was given permission to go to town to deposit twenty dollars. His money was accepted by the bank, he found. Captain Lyon's cook, however, had a somewhat different experience when he went into a drugstore and asked for something to allay the irritation caused by mosquito bites. He was given to understand that his business was not wanted. He made no comment, except to remark to the Captain's wife that it seemed funny he couldn't buy things in a drugstore.

When one of the departing white soldiers, Sergeant Alexander J. Levie, joined a group of townspeople on Elizabeth Street the evening before the black battalion arrived, they were criticizing the War Department for foisting Negro troops on the town.

"An old gentleman who was there made the remark that the

first crooked move they would make they would annihilate the whole shooting match," Levie was to testify a year later when the Senate Military Affairs Committee began its investigation of what it called "The Brownsville Affray." * "Someone amongst the crowd made the remark that it might be a hard proposition to do up the battalion of the soldiers. He continued, saying that if there wasn't enough people in Brownsville, they would call in the farmers from the surrounding country."

This was the fourth time in the town's history that black soldiers had been stationed at Fort Brown, the old man told the street-corner loafers. General Sheridan had brought the first ones, he said, and after their Army careers had ended, many of them had stayed on in Brownsville.

"But they are all gone," Levie remembered hearing the old-timer say. "We used to call them wildcat niggers, and occasionally one of them was found dead in the brush, but nothing was thought about it. Of course, in those days we could do just as we liked with niggers. We could handle them."

As the old man reminisced, Levie continued, Police Lieutenant Joe Dominguez and Policeman Genaro Padron happened to stroll by.

"Now," someone said, "you policemen have got to keep your backbones about you. We are going to stand by you, and we don't want you to give those niggers an inch."

Padron pulled a brown-handled knife with a six-inch blade from his sleeve, Levie testified, and passed it among the crowd.

"For cutting purposes," Padron explained.

* The hearings began February 4, 1907, and ended March 10, 1908. Over one hundred and six witnesses were called. Their testimony is to be found in Senate Document No. 402, Parts 4, 5, and 6, 60th Congress, 1st Session (Government Printing Office, 1908). Short-form citation, SMAC-1, 2, 3.

3

". . . this may cause a great deal of trouble."

DURING THEIR FOUR YEARS AT Fort Niobrara, Nebraska, no color
line had been drawn against the black soldiers in local saloons. It
was different when they got to Texas and set out to slake their
thirst. They could drink freely in the town's six Mexican beer
and mescal joints, but not in the three bars on Elizabeth Street.
John Tillman installed a Jim Crow bar at the rear of the Ruby
Saloon, but the soldiers were refused service of any sort at
H. H. Weller's and at the Crixell brothers' place across the street.

"When they got there, about half an hour after they got into
the barracks," Joe Crixell testified, "there was a crowd of soldiers
came into the place, ten or twelve, and we explained that we had
the officers' trade, and at the time there were some officers in the
back of the saloon drinking, and that we would rather have the
officers there than the soldiers, and that we were satisfied that
they would rather go somewhere else and drink and not mix up
with the officers; so that they took it in good nature and didn't
stop there much more."

"They didn't annoy you?"

"No, sir."

"Did not show anger about it?"

"No, sir."

"Showed no resentment, so far as you know?"

"No, sir."

The men took random indignities in stride. Private August
Williams was walking along a Brownsville street with a fellow
soldier named McGuire, and, as he remembered the incident,
"McGuire was on the outside and passed along by a white
fellow. I guess he kind of pushed up against him; I wasn't paying
any attention. He calls this boy a 'black son of a bitch.'"

As Private William McGuire, Jr., told it, "I was on the outside and he wanted to go between us and I just closed in to the right and let him go on the outside. When he got off apiece, [he] turned around, and said: 'You black son of a bitch; don't you know this is a white man's town?'"

Private James W. Newton and Private Frank J. Lipscomb, both of Company C, were walking down Elizabeth Street about nine o'clock on a Sunday night (August 5) when they came upon a middle-aged customs inspector, Fred Tate, who was standing on the sidewalk with his wife and half a dozen other white matrons of the community.

According to Newton, he and Lipscomb walked single file between the women and a fence bordering the sidewalk, "and as I passed them I said something to Frank—I have forgotten what it was—and when I looked around this way again, why, someone had drawn back, and as I turned that way he struck me with a revolver and knocked me down."

As Tate remembered the affair, the two soldiers plowed straight through the group of ladies instead of stepping out into the street and walking around them. When Newton jostled Mrs. Tate with his elbow, Tate said, he whipped out his .45-caliber Colt six-shooter and struck the man's head with the barrel. The soldier dropped to the sidewalk. His companion disappeared.

In Tate's version, he asked the soldier, "Why did you run over those ladies for?" and the man said, "I didn't know any better." Whereupon Tate inquired, "Do you know any better now?" and the man said, "Yes." In Newton's version, Tate said, "Get up and leave, or damn you I will blow your brains out. I will learn you how to get off the sidewalk when you see a party of white ladies standing there."

Both Newton and Lipscomb swore they hadn't touched a drop of whiskey that night, but Newton * had such a reputation as a heavy drinker that when the incident was brought to the attention of Sergeant-Major Spottswood W. Taliaferro, he shrugged it off. Newton "was a man who drank to excess," he said, "and I

---

* Not to be confused with D Company's artificer, George W. Newton, a teetotaler, who looked on C Company's Newton as "what you might call a habitual drunkard."

thought he was liable to get into trouble most any place, at any time, and I merely thought that he had been downtown drinking and got into a fight down there and got beat up."

"Yes, sir; I drank," Newton admitted, "but not to an excess, sir."

On the Wednesday following the bloodying of Newton's head, Private Clifford I. Adair ran into trouble with one of Fred Tate's colleagues in the customs office. While spending the day on pass in Matamoros, just across the river in Mexico, Adair had paid fifty cents, gold, for a pen. When he got off the ferry on the Brownsville side of the Rio Grande, a customs officer took the pen away from him, refused to let him pay duty on it, and even threatened to report him to his company commander.

"You damned niggers are too smart around here," Adair quoted the man as saying.

Customs figured in still another incident when a mounted inspector, A. Y. Baker, knocked Private Oscar W. Reid into the Rio Grande at about ten o'clock Sunday night, August 12.

"I was on duty down at the ferry landing," Baker testified, "and while I was there these two soldiers came across from Matamoros and they were drunk. I was sitting on the porch there at the custom-house at the ferry landing, and these two soldiers got into a fight down there and began cursing and using indecent language; they kept that up for some time. I went down there. We have an inspectress at that place. I went down to stop them and to make them get away and to stop their racket, and one of them refused to go. That place has a narrow plank walk leading out from the river to the bank, and the river was out of its bank at the time, the water about knee-deep around the plank walk, and this soldier, when he refused to go, I shoved him down from the walk. As he was drunk, he fell into this water."

In C Company's orderly room next morning Reid reported the incident to Captain Edgar A. Macklin, his company commander, who jokingly inquired whether he'd had a hard time getting out of the river. "He laughed and told me that he thought he had gotten just what he deserved," Captain Macklin remembered. He had seen no reason to dignify the dunking with an official inquiry.

On Friday, August 10, the day before the men were to be paid, two enterprising soldiers of B Company opened a beer joint at Sixteenth and Monroe, diagonally across the street from the garrison's northeast corner. The saloon was owned by Private John Hollomon, who had set himself up in business as the battalion's moneylender, and operated by Private Ernest Allison, who was about to be honorably discharged. Later they became partners in the undertaking.

Two of the Crixell brothers, Joe and Teofilo, helped them get started. Along with their Elizabeth Street saloon, the Crixells were distributors for several breweries. They not only furnished Allison and Hollomon the customary ice chest, counter, and backbar they provided any new customer opening a saloon, they also advanced part of the hundred-and-twenty-five-dollar malt-liquor license fee.

The Negro beer joint was packed on payday, but there were no drunken fights, no police incidents. The next evening—Sunday, August 12—Major Penrose had a friendly chat with Mayor Combe, who was filling in for Captain Edger as the post's attending surgeon. Dr. Combe commented on how well the Major's men had behaved the day before. He had grown up in Brownsville, he said, and never had he experienced a quieter payday.

"It was the quietest payday I ever saw," agreed Victoriano Fernandez, the policeman who had been heard making homicidal threats against the soldiers before their arrival.

Every day, and sometimes part of the night as well, Fernandez walked a beat that included John Tillman's Jim Crow bar on Elizabeth Street, and not once had he seen a Negro soldier drunk. "They used to go to the saloon and have drinks in the back there, and they never said a word and would go out," he later told the Senate Military Affairs Committee. The black soldiers, it seemed to him, were better disciplined than the white troops they had replaced. Never had he been called on to place one under arrest.

"There were no arrests made," recalled a white hospital corpsman at the post, "until the shooting up happened."

The shooting up happened around midnight, Monday, August 13.

Monday morning Mayor Combe learned of an attack made the night before on Mrs. Lon Evans by a man she described as a Negro soldier. He had seized the woman by the hair and thrown her to the ground, then darted off, leaving her frightened but uninjured. The Evanses lived in the lower part of town, outside Dr. Combe's social sphere, but he had met them, he knew who they were.

"They were entirely respectable people?"

"Oh, yes, sir; yes, sir. They did not go out in society, but they were respectable people."

Dr. Combe asked the chief of police to look into the matter, then went on about his affairs. Meanwhile, the story was passed with mounting indignation among the post office gossips, the Elizabeth Street saloon philosophers, and the businessmen who banked with Captain Kelly. Two or three troubled citizens dropped by his office at the First National Bank to ask him to use his influence to have the Negro troops transferred.

Sometime between four and five o'clock the Brownsville *Daily Herald* hit the streets with the headline:

INFAMOUS OUTRAGE
Negro Soldier Invaded Private Premises
Last Night And Attempted to Seize
A White Lady

While the townspeople supped on this horror ("The light was shining brightly through the back door of the house and Mrs. Evans saw plainly that the man was a Negro dressed in a soldier's uniform"), Lon Evans burst into the Mayor's office, highly perturbed.

"Doctor," he said, "as mayor of the city, we want you to go with us into the post to interview Major Penrose and report this outrage on my wife."

"How many citizens do you want to go with you?" the Mayor asked.

"At least fifty."

"No; I will not go with fifty citizens," the Mayor said. "I see no necessity for that. You and I can go down and effect just as much. I know Major Penrose, and if this is true, he will do all he can to find out the guilty parties."

Dr. Combe drove Evans to the post in his carriage. They went first to the administration building, where they were told they could find the Major at his quarters. On their way to his quarters, they spotted him on the walk bordering the parade ground. It was around five-thirty, Major Penrose testified at his court-martial, when Dr. Combe stepped down from his carriage with a man he introduced as Mr. Evans.

"Mr. Evans then told me that the night before, about nine o'clock, that his wife had been assaulted by a colored man whom she was positive was a Negro soldier. As I recall it, he said he and his wife were returning from the train, and they met a friend of theirs, who was riding Mrs. Evans' pony, and this friend insisted on Mrs. Evans getting on her own pony and riding home; so he assisted her to mount, and she went on ahead, and Mr. Evans with this other man—I presume he mentioned his name; I don't recall it—they walked on slowly behind. He said his wife went home, entered their house, or the back gate—she had dismounted—opened the gate, and that when she was near the steps and near an ash can or an ash barrel she was seized by a man from behind by her hair and was thrown violently to the ground, and that she screamed and that the man then fled."

The man was a large Negro wearing a slouch hat, blue shirt, and khaki trousers, Mrs. Evans had told her husband. Major Penrose said he had a great many large dark men in his command and asked Evans if his wife could provide a more detailed description. No, Evans said, she had been too frightened to observe anything else about the man's appearance.

Why had he waited some twenty hours to report the attack, the Major asked, and Evans said his wife had been so upset he'd been afraid to leave her. ("Mrs. Evans," the Daily Herald reported, "is feeling quite shaken up today, though suffering no bodily injury beyond a very sore place where her hair was grabbed, and also her neck, which was twisted by the brute in jerking her from the steps.")

After expressing his regret, Penrose assured Evans he would offer every assistance in helping to locate the assailant. He was certain, however, that the man was not to be found among the members of his command. None of his men had ever been accused of such a thing before, he said, and in a dry reference to the town's hospitable supply of Mexican prostitutes, he pointed out that in Brownsville rape was "particularly unnecessary."

As Evans started to leave, Dr. Combe drew Penrose off to one side and suggested: "Major, don't you think it best for you to keep your men in the post tonight? For I am afraid this may cause a great deal of trouble."

"Doctor," the Major assured him, "I have already made up my mind as to that. I would rather anything in the world would have happened than this very thing, and while I don't think it was one of my soldiers, still they will undoubtedly have the blame for it. I shall keep them out of town, and I shall send out and have them all brought in before dark."

Captain Macklin, the officer of the day, was ordered to see that the men were notified at retreat that all passes were to be canceled as of eight P.M. and no one was to leave the post after that hour. Macklin was also directed to send three patrols into town to round up stray soldiers. Under no circumstances were any of the men to be out on the streets that night.

"All passes have been cut off, and the men are all ordered to be in barracks by eight o'clock, and none allowed to leave after that hour," Sergeant-Major Taliaferro was told when he sat down to supper with C Company.

"What is the matter?" he asked.

"It is reported that some soldier frightened a white lady on a horse down town, and the people are very angry, and there is likely to be trouble."

A couple of hours later, when the mail orderly returned to the garrison from the post office, Taliaferro asked him if everything was quiet in town. "He said no; that there was a crowd around the post office that tried to engage him in a conversation concerning the newspaper reports of this assault on Mrs. Evans, and he said that he told them he didn't know anything about it, and tried to get rid of them as best he could, and they seemed to want trouble, and finally, just as he was leaving, one of them said to him, 'It is a good thing that your commanding officer has ordered you all in tonight, because some of you were going to get killed tonight . . .' "

After supper Corporal Edward L. Daniels sat on the front porch of B Company's barracks, resting from a twelve-mile practice march that morning followed by an afternoon of work on some topographical sketches. An old campaigner, he had fought with the Twenty-fifth in Cuba and at the end of each enlistment period his officers had given him an "excellent" character rating.

"No, sir," he said, when asked whether many of the men of his company had sat with him. "Directly after supper everybody right out of the dining room came on the porch. After that some go to the exchange, some go upstairs, and others into the library. Some engage themselves in cards—and they distribute themselves in that way. As a rule a private don't hang around a noncommissioned officer but very little."

Between ten and twenty men had engaged themselves at separate tables, John Hollomon found when he got back to the barracks shortly before eight o'clock. Since it was the Monday night following a Saturday payday, the price of a stack of twenty chips or beans must have been pegged at one dollar, he supposed.

"Do you remember how heavy the betting was that night?"

"No, sir; just about as it always would be round payday. A fellow might bet two or three blue beans or three or four red ones, just depends on how much he had in front of him and how much he had in his pocket to back it. Usually the gambling was high round paydays."

"About how long would it last after payday?"

"It lasted until two or three men got most of the money."

Private Ernest English, the room orderly, put an end to the card games at nine o'clock when he doused the lights. He went to bed about fifteen minutes later. Some of the men were sitting outside on the lower and upper porches of the barracks, smoking and talking.

"There was no excitement whatever in quarters," English said afterward, "and no indication that there would be any."

Making his rounds in the early part of the evening, Captain Macklin noticed nothing out of the ordinary. A few families had taken their customary sunset stroll through the grounds, stopping to watch the men on retreat. Some boys were fishing in the lagoon; others were playing baseball on the post diamond. A playful mood seemed to have settled over the two-storied barracks facing the parade ground.

"The men all seemed to be having a good time, laughing and joking among themselves, a good many of them playing pool, and everything seemed to be perfectly quiet and satisfactory," Macklin testified.

Sometime around eight o'clock Corporal Samuel Wheeler of D Company, one of the corporals of the guard, asked the officer of the day for permission to speak to him.

"What is it, Corporal?" Macklin asked, and, as Wheeler recalled their conversation, he said, "Everything is very peaceable; the men are not drinking—not acting ugly or anything. Why is it you are so particular about their being in at this hour?"

When told of the assault on Mrs. Evans, Corporal Wheeler said he knew a retired black cavalryman's daughter who worked in the boardinghouse where Mr. and Mrs. Evans lived. He thought he might be able to get some additional information from her about the affair.

"I wish you would try to find out," the Captain said, and at his court-martial he gave the substance of Wheeler's report.

"It seems that this Mrs. Evans lived in the tenderloin, or in the vicinity of the tenderloin district, and he reported to me that she leaned over the fence and some man came down the street, and put his hand on her head and said, 'Hello, pet,' or something of that kind and passed on."

4

"Come out, you black sons of bitches . . ."

CAPTAIN MACKLIN sent five patrols into town between seven-thirty and nine-thirty to round up any stragglers who had not yet heard about the eight-o'clock curfew. He posted one of the men on guard duty at the wharf to apprehend anyone going to or from Matamoros and then covered some fifteen blocks of the town himself. He returned to the post satisfied that "all the men were in, with the exception of two or three who were on pass, and they could not be found."

At eleven o'clock, when taps sounded, the post was dark and still. The three noncommissioned officers in charge of quarters reported their companies present or accounted for. Two men of his own outfit—Company C—had not been tracked down by the patrols, Macklin learned. Both men had been given twenty-four-hour passes that morning, and were presumed to have taken the ferry to Matamoros. The officer of the day wasn't worried about them.*

After leaving word with the musician of the guard to call him for reveille (he was an unusually sound sleeper), Captain Macklin dropped by his company's quarters to see whether Acting First Sergeant Samuel W. Harley had carried out a recent order to keep the men sitting out on the back porches of C Company from talking so loud that they kept the other men awake. While he was in the rear of his company's quarters, Macklin ran into the only incident of the evening worth remarking.

"When I got up near the west end of my quarters, I saw up in front of the gate what I thought was a couple struggling, which

---

* There was no need to worry. Sergeant George Thomas was asleep in the arms of Rebecca Collins, about a thousand yards east of the post. He swore that he heard nothing out of the ordinary that night. Private Edward Lee had got back to town from a day in Matamoros and gone to bed with a Mexican woman whose name he hadn't caught.

appeared to me to be a man and woman or two men and two women, so I unhooked my saber and ran up there as fast as I could, and when I got there on the walk between B and D Companies' quarters, I found six or seven or eight children, and they were all huddled together, and a big black dog that belonged to B Company was there growling at them, and they were frightened, and what I took to be their struggling I found was their moving around with each other, because they were all very much frightened, and some of the little girls were crying. I took these children and went out onto the middle walk with them and halfway across the parade ground, and asked the oldest one of them where they had been, and they told me they had been at a party over at Mr. Cowen's house, which was in the vicinity of the garrison. This was about 11:35 then—a little after 11:30."

The sentinel patrolling the barracks area saw the officer of the day come to the children's rescue and watched him start across the parade ground in the direction of the officers' quarters, disappearing into the night. The moon had set at least two hours earlier, and only the stars remained.

Captain Macklin left his saber on the front porch of his quarters, then went into the back room he used as his sitting room. He took a bottle of beer out of the ice box, his second bottle of the day. He had drunk one earlier in the evening with Lieutenant Lawrason. After glancing at the headlines of a Houston paper that had come in the evening's mail, he blew out the lamp on his quartermaster desk, picked up his lantern, and went upstairs to the back bedroom, bare except for two or three chairs and a white enameled bed. He put the lantern down behind the door so it wouldn't shine in his eyes, removed his blouse, and set his alarm clock. He took note of the time. It was ten minutes to twelve.

Major Penrose had gone to bed about eleven-thirty, but was still awake, chatting with his wife, when he heard two shots fired close together. He took them to be pistol shots. They were followed almost at once by six or seven shots fired, it seemed to him, from somewhere in back of C Company's quarters. He had no doubt that these shots came from high-power rifles. Mrs. Penrose interpreted the shooting as a fire alarm.

"I am afraid it is something worse than fire," the Major said, mechanically reaching for the glasses he had worn for the last thirty years. They were always at the side of his bed on a table or chair.

He pulled a pair of trousers over his pajamas, slipped his bare feet into his shoes, and, without stopping to tie the laces, grabbed a blouse and darted downstairs. As he swept up his hat and pistol in the hall, someone began to knock on his door. He flung it open and found himself face to face with a startled sentry, Private Charley Hairston of B Company.

"They are shooting us up," Hairston exclaimed, and the Major ordered him to go to the guardhouse and tell the sergeant of the guard to sound the call to arms.

As he ran across the parade ground toward the men's quarters, Major Penrose heard the rattling of the post scavenger's mule-drawn cart. At the moment, the familiar sound seemed less significant than it would appear later, when Matias G. Tamayo took the witness stand in San Antonio as a key defense witness at the Major's court-martial.

He had been cleaning the guardhouse sinks, the scavenger testified, when he heard the clock strike the half hour at eleven-thirty. A few minutes before it was to strike twelve he stepped inside B Company's barracks to get a drink of water and casually glanced at a sentry walking his post on the town side of the men's quarters. After he got his drink, Tamayo returned to his cart and drove around to the kitchen. He had just finished emptying an ash can and was standing on the left-hand side of the cart, facing the garrison wall, when he heard the first shot.

"Where was this first shot fired?"

"In town."

In the next minute and a half, he continued, he heard about twenty more shots. He saw no one and no flashes of guns, but got the impression that shots were coming from the mouth of an alley between Elizabeth and Washington Streets, where the Louis Cowen family lived. Tamayo put out his bull's-eye lantern, jumped on his cart, and drove off toward the administration building.

Tamayo's flight was observed by Private Joseph H. Howard, standing guard at the No. 2 post, patrolling the area occupied by the enlisted men's four barracks.* At the moment the first shots rang out, Howard was midway between B and C Companies, on the side of the barracks facing the town.

"First I heard two or three shots down the road toward the vacant set of quarters," he testified, "and I looked over in that direction and could not see anyone, and in about half a minute or so after I heard these first shots a fusillade of shots was in this alley right across there from the right where I was at. About that time I called the guard No. 2, and about the time I called the guard the scavenger was at B Company's rear, and he drove off on his cart, and I went between the interval to the front side, to the parade ground, and gave the alarm, discharged my piece three times, and called the guard."

"He shot right up in the air," said C Company's artificer, Charles Edward Rudy, who could see the sentry from the south end of the front porch of the barracks, where he had been sleeping. "There are some trees in there, and he just elevated it right up."

After the sentry fired his piece, the artificer crossed the barracks to the back porch overlooking the garrison wall and the town.

"I could hear voices saying, 'Come out, all you black nigger sons of bitches, and we will kill every one of you.'"

Company B's first sergeant, Mingo Sanders, was asleep with his wife in the quarters reserved for married noncommissioned officers when he was awakened by a hammering on the door. "What is the matter?" Mrs. Sanders asked, and was answered by her next-door neighbor, Sergeant Frazier's wife. "There is a fire

---

* The barracks most distant from the river, reserved for Company A, was vacant. Company A was in Wyoming keeping an eye on the Washakie Reservation Indians while settlers took over part of their land.

out here or something." Mrs. Sanders leaped from her bed and ran to the door, her husband at her heels. He heard the trumpeter of the guard sounding the call to arms.

"Why, that is not any fire," he said, and began to scramble into his uniform, not bothering with his leggings.

As he raced the five hundred yards to his barracks, he was certain he could hear bullets passing ten or twelve feet above his head. A veteran of both Cuba and the Philippines, he had no trouble identifying the sound of Winchester rifles. He was pretty sure he heard Mausers and perhaps a Remington. He also heard pistol shots, which he took to be .45's. Neither the Army's old Krag-Jörgensen nor its new Model 1903 Springfield rifle was involved in the mixed fire. He was positive about that.

"There could have been some of the old Springfields, .45," he testified, "but none of the new model his battalion had been issued some months before when they turned in their Krag-Jörgensens at Fort Niobrara.

When he reached B Company's barracks, Sanders darted into his office, grabbed his rifle and a roll of his men, then rushed back out to the parade ground. He snatched the lantern Sergeant George Jackson was holding and ordered the company to fall in. Shooting could still be heard on the town side of the garrison wall, he remembered.

Sergeant Sanders shared the married noncommissioned officers' quarters with Sergeant Darby W. O. Brawner, who was C Company's noncommissioned officer in charge of quarters on the night of the raid, and Jacob Frazier, D Company's six-foot four-inch first sergeant, who had just started his fifteenth year of soldiering. Frazier and his wife, Hattie, were awakened by two shots that seemed to him "to be out in the town, just below the post, between the road and the post." He jumped up, slipped on his trousers and shoes, and then left without his blouse or his hat.

His company commander, Captain Samuel P. Lyon, had already reached D Company's barracks when Sergeant Frazier got there.

"Sergeant," Frazier remembered the Captain saying, "get the men downstairs and get them in line as quick as possible."

Upstairs, the men were groping their way to the gun racks, which had been quickly unlocked by the noncommissioned officer in charge of quarters. Rifles in hand, they tumbled downstairs and assembled in front of the barracks. They were deployed in a skirmish line along the garrison wall facing the town, and then Captain Lyon ordered Sergeant Frazier to get a lantern and call the roll.

"I just only had a few steps," Frazier stated, "and I stepped back in the orderly room, got the lantern, and called the roll very carefully; started in at the right, and I was in a position where I could see where any man would come in and join the company after that."

"Did anybody join your company?"

"No, sir."

Captain Lyon stood beside the First Sergeant as he called the roll, he stated, "and we went back and forth from point to point, so as to be sure every man who answered to his name was actually the man to whom the name belonged." Two men were on pass, Corporal Charles Hawkins and Private Walter Johnson. Everyone else was present or accounted for.

The shooting lasted about ten minutes. By the time it ended the men of B and D Companies had been armed and assembled. C Company's response, however, was less agile. No one took charge. The first sergeant was in Oklahoma for a rifle competition and the company commander, Captain Macklin, who was serving as officer of the day, had failed to put in an appearance even though Major Penrose had dispatched a sentinel to his quarters.

The initial confusion in C Company's quarters was brought home to members of the Senate Military Affairs Committee by Private William Mapp, who was sleeping on the parade ground side of the barracks when he was awakened by the shots and the bugles. He pulled on his trousers and, still somewhat dazed, sat down on his footlocker and began to put on his shoes.

"The shooting was then still going on," he said, "and while I was putting on my shoes I heard a voice cry out aloud, 'Come out, all of you black sons of bitches.'"

The men were milling around in the darkness, shouting, "Why don't you open these gun racks?" Then Mapp heard Major Penrose's voice: "Why don't you men hurry up and fall out?" Artificer Rudy called back, "We are not going to fall out without our guns to get killed." "Why don't you get your guns?" the Major demanded, and when it was explained to him that the noncommissioned officer in charge of quarters refused to open C Company's racks, he said, "Get them open some way." A minute later, Mapp continued, somebody came upstairs with an ax and began opening the rack nearest him.

The noncommissioned officer in charge of quarters was Sergeant Brawner, who had spent fourteen years in the Army. It was his responsibility to open the gun racks when call to arms was sounded. Instead, he ran downstairs to ask Sergeant Harley what he should do.

Acting First Sergeant Harley had devoted nearly sixteen of his thirty-seven years to soldiering (he had been wounded in Cuba). He knew that a first sergeant should assemble his men when he heard the call to arms, but, unfortunately, he swore he never heard it. He refused to budge on this point even when confronted with testimony that his company's two musicians had sounded the alarm in the barracks where he had been sleeping in the first-floor orderly room.

"I was woke up by the firing," Sergeant Harley testified, "and I dressed as soon as possible and run out of the door from the orderly room, and come around about the stairway, and I met Sergeant Brawner. He says, 'Sergeant, shall I open the racks?' I told him, 'No, wait for orders,' on account of I didn't hear the call to arms blowed by the orders of the commanding officer."

"You thought the post was being attacked?"

"Yes, sir."

"What difference did it make whether you heard the call to arms or not if you were under fire and in charge of sixty armed men?"

"Well, I didn't think I had any business to order the racks open without proper orders."

With his re-enlistment riding on his answers, Harley was given one more chance to explain why he had delayed forming the company simply because he had not heard the musician of the guard or his own company musicians.

"What difference did it make whether you heard the call to arms or not if you really believed you were being fired on by an enemy?"

"Well, I didn't think in a place like that we had any enemies. We weren't supposed to have any enemies. We weren't in no hostile country . . ."

Four of the five white officers in residence at Fort Brown responded immediately to the commotion. When the fifth, Captain Macklin, failed to show up an hour after the shooting, Major Penrose feared the worst. The two men had been friends ever since Macklin's days as an enlisted man at Fort Apache. When Macklin made second lieutenant in the summer of '98, Penrose had asked to have him assigned to his company in the Eleventh Infantry. Subsequent assignments had separated them, but in 1904 they had been reunited in the Twenty-fifth Infantry. Knowing the man so well, Penrose was afraid he had leaped the garrison wall at the first sound of trouble and run straight toward it. He was that kind of officer.

"I thought possibly, as he was officer of the day, he had heard this shooting, had jumped over in the road, and some harm had come to him, and I directed Captain Lyon then to take his company immediately and go along that road and look through the lower part of town."

As the soldiers marched up Madison Street to Twelfth, they found themselves facing an armed mob milling about in front of the county jail.

"It looked like there was forty or fifty, or maybe more, men there," Artificer Newton testified, "and they all had 6-caliber guns, shotguns, and so forth, and Captain Lyon halted the company and asked them what was these men and they said, 'Officers of the law! Officers of the law!'"

No inspection was made of the lawmen's guns to determine whether they had been fired recently, nor did anyone remark at the time that the twelve members of Brownsville's police force carried revolvers, not rifles and shotguns.

The Townspeople

---•••>---

5

*"Oh, everybody generally claimed that the
nigger soldiers had done it."*

IN HIS TWO YEARS AS Mayor of Brownsville, Dr. Fred Combe
had cleaned up the streets, reformed the police force, and re-
duced the amount of casual gunplay, especially along the "Firing
Line," as the road separating the town and the garrison had come
to be called. Most of the townspeople still had a deer rifle, a
shotgun, or a six-shooter within easy reach at home, but the
weapons were no longer displayed so conspicuously in public,
and the shooting scrapes between policemen and soldiers had
become less frequent.

The local constabulary at the time Dr. Combe took office had been a slovenly and predatory cadre of illiterate Mexicans who spoke little or no English and looked on the American soldier as a source of unending money and merriment. At night they delighted in swooping down on their prey, cracking his skull, tossing him in jail, and then tapping him for a two-dollar fine and costs. Costs usually came to ten dollars.

Mayor Combe ordered an end to this banditry. He fired some of the more repacious lawmen and tried to instill a professional pride in the men by dressing them in smart new uniforms. In winter they wore double-breasted blue coats with brass buttons and soft blue felt hats with cords around them. In summer they were dressed in khaki and wore wide-brimmed hats about the same color as those used in the Army. At night, summer or winter, it was not always easy to distinguish a policeman from a soldier.

By day two policemen sufficed to maintain law and order. At night, when the citizenry and the soldiers did their drinking, gambling, whoring, and fighting, the force was quadrupled. On the night of the raid, despite the provocative front-page headline in the *Daily Herald* and the curfew ordered at the post, Mayor Combe and Police Chief Connor saw no need to put extra policemen on duty. Lieutenant Ygnacio Dominguez (his friends called him Joe) was assigned the usual complement of eight men.*

The Mayor, a native of Brownsville, had never known the town to be quieter than it was that night when he walked home around ten o'clock. He lived on the corner of Ninth and Elizabeth Streets with his elderly father and his brother, Joe, both of whom were also doctors. After reading for about an hour and a half, the Mayor went to bed on the back porch, or "gallery" as it was called in that part of the country.

He had just dozed off when he heard the first four or five shots. In his opinion as a lifelong hunter and a combat medical

---

* Genaro Padron, Dioniso Lerma, Rafael Galvan, Vidal Rivas, José Coronado, Felix Calderón, Macedonio Ramirez, Cesario Leal. The three policemen not on duty were Victoriano Fernandez, Joaquin Treviño, and Marcellus Daugherty. Two other officers—José Garza and Florencio Briseño —were abroad that night but not on duty. They were special policemen who served only when a substitute was needed.

officer, they were pistol shots. They were followed by irregular rifle fire. "Joe," he called upstairs to his brother, "there is shooting down the street. I am going down to find out what it is" (or, he told the senators, trying not to mislead them, he may have said "to stop it"). He left the house by the Ninth Street entrance and walked to the corner, looking down Elizabeth Street in the general direction of the garrison.

His brother joined him and they began to run toward the center of town. They had gone about a block or so, just beyond the post office, when Dr. Joe Combe called out, "Fred, hug the wall. They are shooting down the street." The Mayor followed his brother's advice, and when he reached the Eleventh Street corner, he took out his pistol to signal the police.

"One of the signals for the call of a policeman," he explained, "is, when a pistol is not used, to give three sharp raps on an iron lamp post. It gives a sound which can be heard a long ways. I attempted to give that signal with my revolver, but the metal did not give the sound that I expected."

He ran another block, then stopped, picked up a brickbat, and began to beat against one of the iron posts supporting the porch of the Salaya Building. It produced a fine ringing sound.

As the two brothers moved on down the street, getting as far as Putegnat's drugstore or Rutledge's jewelry store, a man darted around the corner from Twelfth Street. They covered him with their revolvers and ordered him to halt. It turned out to be a policeman, Genaro Padron.

"Do not go down any farther," Padron said, placing a hand on the Mayor's shoulder. "You will be shot."

The Mayor turned and noticed a dark spot on the mesquite-block pavement. It was clearly visible in the illumination provided by the street lamp on the corner of Twelfth and Elizabeth and by the acetylene light in the jewelry-store window. He stooped over and put his hand on the stain and then moved closer to the light to examine it.

"Joe," he said to his brother, "this is blood. Somebody has been hurt. Follow the trail and see if you can locate who it is."

While Dr. Joe Combe followed the trail of blood, his brother continued south on Elizabeth Street. The shooting had stopped by the time he reached the Crixell brothers' saloon and spotted a man with a gun. The Mayor halted him, then saw that it was José Garza, one of the town's special policemen who served when the need arose. Garza was not on duty that night and had obviously been drinking.

"What are you doing with that gun?" the Mayor asked and, without waiting for an answer, he confiscated it and marched Garza into the saloon, where Joe Crixell identified the weapon as a Winchester he had taken in on a bad loan six months earlier. Garza had borrowed it from a brother of Crixell's who ran a small drinking and gambling establishment in the Market Square called the White Elephant.

"It doesn't work," Crixell said, and when he tugged at the bolt to show that the ejector wasn't functioning, the Mayor noticed an exploded shell in the magazine. "Because the ejector would not work it out," the saloonkeeper explained. It had probably been there for months, he said, and the Mayor took his word for it.

Monday night had started quietly at Crixell's. In the billiard room in back of the bar Joe Crixell was playing cards for the drinks with Martin Hanson, a contractor; Edward Daugherty, assistant postmaster; Leo Wise, a commission merchant, and Hal Shannon, foreman of the *Daily Herald*.

"It was about ten minutes to twelve that I heard four or five shots," Joe Crixell testified. "I got up from the table, ready to throw my cards down on the table, and I says, 'There is some shooting, boys,' and Martin Hanson told me, he says, 'Joe, go ahead and play your game; that is nothing but torpedoes.' I picked up my cards again and sat down, and just as I was about to play a card, here comes about ten or more shots, one after another, and then, of course, we all got up, and I says, 'That is not torpedoes. That is United States rifles,' judging by the direction and the sound of the shots."

"Joe and I got up and closed the door," Hal Shannon stated in an affidavit some months later. "I had a bicycle leaning against a post at the saloon, and when I went out to get it, a bullet hit the post. Naturally, I was frightened, and Joe came to the door and said, 'Come back in here, you fool; you'll get killed there,' and as I went to step back several more shots were fired."

"We ran to the front door of the saloon," Crixell continued, "and, of course, by that time there was shooting all the time. So I told my porter, I says, 'Joe, let's close the doors up quick.' Right in front of my place, at Tillman's place, the Ruby, there was a bartender and four or five other parties standing right at the sidewalk, and I hollered at them, and I says, 'Close up your doors, boys, here comes the niggers.'"

Paulino S. Preciado, a local bookbinder and editor of a Spanish-language newspaper, *El Porvenir*, was seated at a table in the rear courtyard of the Ruby Saloon about to have a beer with its proprietor, John Tillman, and two friends, Nicolas Sanchez Alanis and Antonio Torres. Tillman had just put his lantern down on the cistern, while the three men were filling their glasses (they had made do with two bottles) when they heard the first shots. Preciado followed Tillman to the front entrance, arriving in time to hear Crixell's warning from across the street and to watch the Ruby's young bartender, Frank Natus, close the doors and secure them with crossbars.

"The door of the alley is open," Natus said. "I am going to close it."

He took a pistol from under the counter of the bar and started toward the courtyard. Preciado was six or eight steps behind him. As Natus drew near the cistern, Alanis came out of the toilet in the back part of the saloon and shouted to the bartender, "Don't go out! A noise is heard in the alley."

"At this moment," Preciado testified, "a group of five or six armed men appeared and fired."

"*Ay Dios!*" Natus cried, and fell dead.

After closing his front door, Joe Crixell put out all the lights save one, locked his safe, took the money from the register and stuffed it in his pocket; then he removed two six-shooters he kept in a drawer under the counter. He gave one to Martin Hanson and kept the other. When Louis Cowen came in from the Chinese restaurant located in the same building and asked for a gun, Crixell had none to lend him.

"I want to go home," Cowen said, and expressed great concern for his wife and children.

"You haven't any business out in the street now," Crixell told him. "If you go out, you will get hurt."

When the saloonkeeper suggested they would all be safer upstairs, Cowen readily agreed.

"It will be a good idea," he said, "because in case those soldiers get here, the first place they will break into will be the bar."

As they crossed the yard and filed up the back stairs, it seemed to Crixell that the shooting was getting closer, coming from the alley behind the Ruby Saloon. He had hardly got upstairs before he had to run back down to the bar to answer the phone. He thought it might be his brother. It turned out to be Frank Kibbe, the city attorney.

"Joe, what is all that shooting?" he asked, and Crixell told him, "The niggers are shooting up the town."

"On the night of the shooting, immediately following the shooting," the saloonkeeper was asked several months later, "in hearing persons speaking of the shooting, did you hear any other expression of opinion but what it was the colored soldiers who had done the shootings?"

"Oh, everybody generally claimed that the nigger soldiers had done it," Crixell replied, although he admitted that he had not seen any Negro soldiers do any shooting that night. "Under oath," he said, "I would not say it was the nigger soldiers; but outside of that I could put my neck on it that it was the nigger soldiers."

Lieutenant Joe Dominguez was sitting on the market-house steps waiting for the schoolhouse bell to ring at midnight when he heard the first shot. The report of the gun had a strange sound, he thought, not like the Winchesters so commonly used around Brownsville. He mounted his large gray horse and set off at a fast trot down Washington Street. At the Fourteenth Street corner he saw Genaro Padron standing in the middle of the street, staring toward the house of Louis Cowen. It was only one block from the garrison and its backyard opened onto an alley that ran past the Miller Hotel.

"What does all this shooting mean?" Dominguez asked, and Padron said, "The soldiers are shooting up Cowen's."

"When you speak of seeing soldiers," Padron was later asked, "how do you know that they were soldiers?"

"Because they wore the uniform of soldiers—yellow."

"Are you sure that they had the soldiers' uniform and were soldiers?"

"The uniform was the uniform of soldiers. More than that I cannot say, whether they were soldiers or not."

Dominguez had no doubt about the identity of the raiders. He had seen eight of them as he rode across the Cowen-Miller Hotel alley.

"I saw them very plain, and they were colored soldiers," he said, and judged them to have been about twenty-five feet away at the time he spotted them.

Ohio's skeptical Senator Foraker questioned the witness' ability to distinguish the raiders as black soldiers at such a distance in a narrow, unlighted alley, the mouth of which was flanked by a two-story frame building and a three-story brick hotel.

"It was not only a dark night," the Senator pointed out, "but probably there was not a darker place in all Brownsville at that particular time than was that particular spot."

It was all the more remarkable that the identification should have been made in the moment it took the Lieutenant's horse to race across an alley twenty feet wide.

"I crossed," Dominguez testified, "and went on on Thirteenth Street toward Elizabeth Street, hollering to the people at the Miller Hotel to escape themselves, and to put out their lights, because the colored troops were shooting the people."

Aside from his inability to stand "against fifteen or twenty men," he explained, he thought it best "to alarm the hotel, because that was a large hotel, and there were people coming from all over the United States stopping there with their families, and there were women and children, and I thought that was the best judgment I could use, not to stop and try to arrest them, but to go on and make an alarm, so that they could escape themselves."

After shouting to the people inside the hotel two or three times, the Lieutenant continued down Thirteenth toward Elizabeth, his back to the raiders. As he turned the corner, heading north, his horse stumbled, then fell dead. The firing went on while Dominguez struggled to get out from under the horse. Once free, he stumbled up Elizabeth Street as far as Twelfth, where he met two Mexicans.

"They knew me, and they asked me if I was riddled all with bullets, and I told them no, but I got my arm broken, and I said, 'If you have a handkerchief, I wish you would tie it,' because I was getting weak."

As the two Mexicans helped the Lieutenant make his way to the drugstore, they passed the Ruby Saloon and Dominguez remembered hearing some shots in back of the place. Then he lost consciousness.

6

"Children, it is the soldiers."

LOUIS COWEN's one-story frame house on Fourteenth Street, only a block from the fort, was crowded with children Monday night. In addition to the five young Cowens, some three dozen guests had turned up between seven and eight o'clock for a surprise party the Cowens were having for one of their daughters. It was a warm night and Mrs. Anna Cowen didn't feel well. A stout, nervous woman whose emotional seams were loosely knit, she had come undone early on and left her daughter's guests to her husband. By ten-thirty he felt he'd had enough.

"I think I have done my duty entertaining those kids," he told her. "Let somebody else take their share now, I am going up-town."

"If you are going uptown," he remembered Anna saying, "get me a couple of sandwiches and a bottle of beer."

Cowen crossed the street to the Leahy Hotel, he later told the Senate Military Affairs Committee, and spent about an hour at the front gate, chatting with the thirty-seven-year-old widow who ran the place. The senators neglected to ask him what they talked about, but when Katie Leahy was called to testify, she said they were not standing at the gate, they were sitting on her gallery with Judge Parks, and they were discussing the attack on Mrs. Evans.

"Mr. Cowen said that if any one of those niggers ever touched or insulted his wife, one of his children, or one of his lady friends, that he would take his Winchester and go down and kill them."

"Was he pretty violent in his talk?"

"No, sir; that is all he said."

"He only said he would kill them?"

"Yes, sir; and any other man would say the same thing; you or any other man."

After leaving Mrs. Leahy, Cowen said he walked up to the Chinese restaurant adjoining the Crixell brothers' saloon. He ordered his wife's sandwiches, then crossed the street to Weller's, the only place in town that carried Schlitz, Anna's favorite beer. At Weller's he bumped into a railroad man named Porter, who suggested they get something to eat.

"Well, I am hungry enough to eat something, I guess," Cowen said, and when he had finished eating he walked through the restaurant into Weller's bar and picked up his bottle of Schlitz. He had just paid for it and put it in his pocket when the shooting commenced. Weller's clock showed six minutes to twelve.

Cowen started to run out of the saloon, but changed his mind and stayed there for a couple of minutes. During a lull in the shooting he walked fifty feet down the street to the Ruby Saloon, where young Frank Natus was tending bar. He asked Frank for a gun, and the bartender said he had only one, a small nickel-plated Smith & Wesson. It was in Natus' hand when he died.

Anna Cowen was alone with her five children and Amada Martinez, the servant girl who had been with the family for twelve years. Still fully dressed, Mrs. Cowen was in the rear of the house, seated at the head of the dining-room table, waiting for some hot water she had asked Amada to bring her. The student lamp on the table and the Rochester lamp hanging in the hallway illuminated not only the dining room but also the two other small rooms on either side where the children were dropping off to sleep. The kitchen door was open, casting some light on the backyard.

"I told my eldest daughter, I said, 'Gertrude, do not go to bed; I do not feel well. Stay up with me. Somehow I am nervous'; and she said to me, 'I will not go to sleep, mamma; I am just lying here, and when the girl comes in with the water, I will get up and help you.' Just then she came and stood alongside of the table, and she was partly undressed, and the servant girl came in with a little pitcher of hot water, when we heard the very first shots.

"Well, at the very instant the little children, of course, ran to me, you know, and they said, 'Fire, mamma, fire.' They all thought it was fire. I am quite familiar with the sound of Army guns, because I have lived there twenty years of my married life, and I am perfectly familiar with the sound, especially during the Spanish war that they would have these sham battles, you know. Nothing could fool us or make us not know that it was the Army guns. You could not but know that they were. The sounds were loud, you know; and then in the empty garrison, you know, we had heard the first shot, and then one, two, three, four, five shots, you know, and in the meantime the little ones all gathered around me, and I said, 'Children, it is the soldiers.' "

She thought the soldiers and the police had got into a shooting scrape, as used to happen frequently in the old days, before Mayor Combe cleaned up the police force and before the Negro soldiers came. They had arrived at the post while Mrs. Cowen was in San Antonio taking care of a sick son. When she got home, she said, she'd been delighted to discover how orderly they were and how kind to her children.

"Oh, Mr. Louis is not at home!" Mrs. Cowen remembered saying to the servant girl when the shooting began, and Amada said, "Madam, it is best that he does not come, because he would never get here alive."

"In the meantime," Mrs. Cowen continued in a torrent of testimony that flooded the Senate committee room, "the back part of the house was completely thrown open, blinds and windows and doors and everything, and I was inexperienced, I didn't blow out my light, I didn't know that they would give me any more trouble, I never thought of anything, and the shooting kept on coming closer and closer, and the children all the time stood gathered by me, and when I heard that they were right on us, I said, 'Children, get under the bed.' They followed me into the bedroom, and I said, 'Get under the bed, and pray God to save your lives. If we are alive tomorrow, we will all go and thank God in church.'"

Amada was standing at one of the back windows trying to close the shutters when she saw ten men coming down the alley toward the house, "five in front and five behind." She was only three feet from them, she said, and she was sure not only that they were soldiers, because of the way they were dressed ("In yellow; that yellow uniform"), but also that they were Negro soldiers.

"They were black. I saw them well."

"Were they any blacker than a good many of the Mexicans are who live at Brownsville?"

"Yes."

"You are not mistaken about that?"

"No, sir. I saw them."

"Were they any blacker than the policeman, Padron?"

"Oh, yes."

As Amada turned from the window the raiders started firing into the house. They shot out the lights and splintered a mirror. Amada crawled along the floor toward her mistress in the back bedroom.

"Madam," Anna Cowen remembered the girl saying, "I believe it is the day of judgment. The soldiers are going to kill us."

Bernard Kowalski, one of the teen-age guests at the Cowen party, was undressing in a second-floor room of his family's Elizabeth Street home when the shooting began. He went to the door and called to his mother, who had not yet gone to sleep, "Mamma, those are the Negroes doing the shooting." Then, before awakening his father and his seven brothers, he told his mother a story he hadn't mentioned to anyone at the party and never considered worth repeating until he was called to testify before the Senate Military Affairs Committee nearly a year after the raid.

Toward the end of the birthday party, young Kowalski said, he was sitting on the windowsill looking out at the alley. He saw four to six Negroes in Army uniforms staring at the laughing, chattering children packed into the Cowen cottage and heard one of the men say, "They are having a fine time in there, but in about half an hour they will not have such a nice time." Just then Gertrude Cowen and another young lady called to him that refreshments were being served the older children, so he left the window and thought nothing more about the remark until he heard the shooting nine blocks away.

"When did you first tell somebody about this, beside your mother?" Bernard was asked.

"Well, my mother told my father about it," he said. "I did not care about being a witness, and I thought that my testimony would not be needed, they had so many better ones than mine."

Katie Leahy, having undressed and wound her clock, was about to go to bed in her first-floor bedroom when the shooting started. It seemed to come from the garrison and from high-powered rifles. She heard the first four shots and then, watching from a second-floor window of her annex, facing Fourteenth Street, she heard the next five shots and, she was willing to swear, she could also see flashes of gunfire coming from the rear galleries —upper and lower—of the barracks second from the river. This was B Company's quarters.

"They were shooting indiscriminately then on the galleries, and it seemed to be between the wall and the barracks," she testified, indicating the area where the post scavenger had been working and Private Howard standing guard. Both swore the shooting came from the other side of the garrison wall.

Like many soldiers and townspeople, Mrs. Leahy mistook the shooting for a fire alarm. Out of curiosity and concern for her property, she went downstairs and stepped out into the middle of Elizabeth Street. She could see flashes of gunfire near the main gate of the garrison and hear bullets overhead.

"The first volley sort of stunned me for a moment," she said. "It surprised me. When the second volley came, I realized that the town was being shot on, and I went back and went upstairs into this window and watched them still shooting off the barracks and heard them shooting in the post."

Two policemen, moving along at a leisurely pace, called up to her, "Where is the fire?" She ran downstairs, bundled them into the hotel, shut them in the bathroom, "and told them under no penalty to leave there until I told them, for no reason whatever to leave there, it did not matter who came in; to stay there until I let them out; which they did."

"Did they want to know why you wanted to put them in the bathroom?"

"I told them the Negroes were shooting up the town."

"Don't you think they ought to have gone out and looked after that trouble?"

"No, sir. They were but two men, with six-shooters, with probably half a dozen shots, and I knew the Negroes were well armed. I knew the Negroes would not come out to shoot up the town without they were well armed."

At the time she hid the two policemen, Mrs. Leahy had seen flashes of gunfire, but she had not seen anyone doing any shooting. Not until she returned to her second-floor window did she get her first glimpse of the raiders. A party of sixteen men ("I counted them") came toward the corner of Fourteenth Street and the alley behind the Cowen house.

The men stopped at a mudhole in front of the Cowens', then walked around it, moving into the alley. Something apparently happened to one man's gun, and as another turned to help him with it he noticed Mrs. Leahy at the window upstairs. He touched the other man on the shoulder and said something the widow couldn't hear. She did hear the other man's reply, however. He glanced up at her and said, "Mrs. Leahy. Keep straight to the front and shoot ahead."

About ten men continued to fire during this brief exchange, she said. They seemed to be firing up in the air. They were in khaki uniforms. The only faces she could make out were the two that had turned up toward her, and both of these faces were dark. One was quite dark, the other light, with spots on it. ("I could not see distinctly, spots or pimples or something, I could see spots on his face.")

The men were standing at least thirty-five feet from her in an unlighted alley. The widow insisted she had no trouble recognizing them as Negroes even though the night was so dark that when the roll of D Company was called Captain Lyon had to use a lantern to identify men he knew well.

From the time the men entered the alley Mrs. Leahy saw and heard no more shooting in the garrison. The firing was still going on as the men disappeared up the alley in the direction of the Miller Hotel.

"Oh, Katie, my God, they have shot into my house and we are frightened to death," Anna Cowen called to her from a rear window.

"Where is Louis?" Mrs. Leahy asked.

"He is downtown."

Two hotel residents, Judge W. N. Parks and Herbert Elkins, escorted Mrs. Cowen, the children, and Amada Martinez into the hotel. A few minutes later, Mrs. Leahy stated, she saw six soldiers heading back down the alley toward the post. Thirty minutes had elapsed since the shooting broke out, she estimated.

It was perhaps an hour later that Captain Lyon marched D Company back to the post after making a hurried search for Captain Macklin. Mrs. Leahy said she was standing with young Elkins at her front gate, five or six feet from the soldiers. She recognized one of the two men she had seen in the alley, she said, and identified him as the very dark one. She was positive it was the same man.

"If you knew that man in Captain Lyon's company, when he went back to the fort, why didn't you point him out and have him arrested?"

"Because I was never asked to do so, sir."

Elkins testified that he, too, had seen men firing from the barracks and heading back toward the post after the shooting ended. Like the Widow Leahy, he recognized them as Negroes, even at a greater distance (sixty-five feet instead of thirty-five). Later, when the soldiers marched past the Leahy Hotel with their white captain and Mayor Combe, Elkins said he was standing at the gate with Mrs. Leahy and recognized a black man he had seen in the alley at the time the Cowen house was fired on.

"We will come back tomorrow and kill the rest of the God damn son-of-a-bitches," he swore he heard the man say.

7

"I am afraid our men have done this shooting."

ONCE THE SHOOTING HAD ENDED, Mayor Combe left Joe Crixell's place and was about to start down Elizabeth Street toward the garrison when he got a disturbing report from his chief of police. Four policemen were missing, and one of them, Lieutenant Dominguez, was rumored to have been killed. The other three missing men were Macedonio Ramirez, Florencio Briseño, and José Coronado. Happily, it developed later, Ramirez had succeeded in running away from the raiders, and the other two men had been safely tucked away in the Widow Leahy's bathroom.

As the Mayor continued down Elizabeth Street he came upon what looked like four or five bodies piled up on the sidewalk at the Thirteenth Street corner. Moving closer, he saw that it was a dead horse.

"Mr. Mayor," someone called to him, "do not go out there in the street. They can see you from the garrison."

Dr. Combe ignored the warning, crossed to the Miller Hotel, and shouted from the doorway, "Does anybody know anything about this firing?" A frightened citizen, the cashier at the Merchants National Bank, darted past him without stopping to answer. The Mayor cautioned residents of the area to go no nearer the garrison, which was less than two blocks away. He started back up Elizabeth Street to the commercial center of the town.

"The people were running in, running in from all parts of town, armed with whatever they could find," he recalled. "They were all excited; everybody running and calling out, 'The soldiers have shot up the town . . .'"

"Was that the universal expression at the time?"

"There was not a man that said anything else, or that seemed to have thought anything else, at the moment. . . . Everybody was clamoring and standing around there with these guns, and saying, 'Let's go down to the post' and 'Let's go down and do those fellows up.' I don't remember the exact language they used, in the excitement of the moment, and I saw that the excitement was getting intense, and Judge Parks was standing to my left, and I said, 'Get me a box or something to stand on,' and they brought me, I do not remember whether it was a box or a barrel, and I got up and I appealed to the people, first, as an ex-Army officer, and I told them, 'I have served with those troops and I know them to be as efficient troops as there are in the world. They are splendidly armed, and if you go down there, many a valuable life will be lost. Besides that, you are within the law. Remain so, and we will get justice.'"

Judge Parks, who was standing at the Mayor's side, had been sent uptown from the Leahy Hotel to find Louis Cowen and bring him back to his wife and family. Anna Cowen was crying and carrying on, much to the annoyance of Katie Leahy. "I haven't any sympathy with a woman in hysterics," the widow said at the Senate Military Affairs Committee hearing, and when one of the senators asked if she had been afraid at any time during the raid, she snorted, "I do not know what fear is."

Returning to the hotel after his first futile attempt to locate Cowen, Judge Parks reported that two policemen were missing and feared killed. Katie Leahy gulped. In the excitement, she had completely forgotten the two men sheltered in her bathroom for the last couple of hours. They were still there, she found.

"Was the door locked?"

"No, sir; just closed."

"They could have come out at any time?"

"Yes, sir; but I had instructed them not to do so."

At the start of the raid Louis Cowen ran from bar to bar pleading for a gun so he could rush home to defend his family, but an hour and a half after the shooting ended he was still uptown hanging around the fringes of excitement. There was a dead man to look at, eyewitnesses to listen to, and large talk of marching on the garrison and wiping the niggers out.

"I started to go home," he explained, "and somebody would come up and say something, and then somebody else would say something else, and I just delayed going home."

It was around two A.M. when Katie Leahy met him at her front gate. Along with Anna's sandwiches and bottle of Schlitz, he had half a pint of whiskey, Mrs. Leahy said (Cowen denied the whiskey, but Joe Crixell swore he'd sold it to him).

"In what condition was he?" the widow was asked. "Had he been drinking or not?"

"I would hate to say, sir, because he talked about suing the Government for fifty thousand dollars for damages to his house and family, and I got tired of listening to it, and I went out to my room."

Cowen testified that after he rejoined his family at the Leahy Hotel, he lit a lantern and walked across the street to his house to see what damage had been done. "I did not make a close examination. I saw that the looking-glass was broken—the plate glass in the wardrobe—and I went in the children's bedroom and

I saw the beds all messed up and the bullet holes all around, and splinters all over everything." He picked up his rifle, went back to the hotel and sat up all night in a side yard.

"Did you put him on guard?" a senator asked the Widow Leahy, and she exploded, "Oh, Senator, don't ask such ridiculous questions, please. . . . Why should I want that man, after I had sent for him and brought him back where I was taking care of his wife and children, to guard me?"

To calm the mob forming in the heart of his constituency, Dr. Combe promised to seek out Major Penrose, who could be depended on to punish the guilty soldiers and prevent a recurrence of their terrorism. At first the Mayor spoke of crawling within hailing distance of the sentries guarding the garrison, but he was talked out of taking the risk of being shot before he could identify himself.

Finally, sometime around 1:15 A.M., when D Company was about to head back to the garrison after looking in vain for Captain Macklin, the Mayor gratefully accepted Captain Lyon's invitation to use his men as an armed escort. Both Combe brothers went marching down Elizabeth Street at the head of the column. As they neared the main gate, Lyon asked the Mayor if he'd seen anything of Ed Macklin, and Dr. Combe said no.

"We cannot find him in the post anywhere," Lyon said, "and we are afraid that he has been done away with in town."

"Oh, bosh!" the Mayor snorted. "That is nonsense."

At his court-martial, Major Penrose recalled meeting the two Combe brothers: "I met them right at the gate. Dr. Fred Combe introduced me to his brother, Dr. Joe Combe, the first time I had ever met him at all, and we stepped up, I suppose, halfway between the gate and the line of barracks. He said to me, 'Major, one man has been killed.' I understood him to say, 'The chief of police has been wounded and his horse killed, and it has been done by your men.' I said, 'Doctor, I can't believe it.' He says, 'Yes; they have been seen by several people; there was a party of five in one and a party of three in another.' I said, 'I can't believe it, Doctor. I have had a roll call, and the men are all present;

every intimation I have seems the other way—coming the other way.' He says, 'It isn't so; our men have seen it.' "

Then, both men agreed, the Mayor warned Major Penrose to confine his officers and men to the post. No one would be allowed in or out except the Mayor, Penrose promised, and shortly afterward, Dr. Combe testified, "Captain Macklin walked up to Major Penrose and saluted him, and said, 'Sir, I report.' Major Penrose said, 'My God, Macklin, where have you been? We have been looking for you everywhere.' Macklin said, as near as I can remember, 'I have been asleep in my quarters.' "

A few hours later, around three-thirty A.M., Penrose sent Companies B and D back to their barracks.

"What orders did you give—specific orders—at this time to the company commanders?" the Major was asked at his court-martial.

"I told them I wanted them to see personally that the arms were locked in the gun racks. As soon as it was daylight in the morning I wished an inspection of arms made, and I ordered them to verify their ammunition."

Leaving Captain Macklin and C Company to guard the post, Major Penrose picked up his wife at Captain Lyon's quarters and took her home. Mrs. Penrose was nervous and excited, he found, so "I sat up in a chair alongside of her until a little while before daylight." Once it was light enough to make an examination, he checked all four barracks for bullet holes or scars. He found none.

The men stood reveille at five-thirty A.M., just two minutes before sunrise. They had never been subjected to a more rigid rifle inspection. None of their pieces showed any sign of having been fired, but Lieutenant Lawrason ordered seven men of B Company to step aside. Major Penrose walked over to the company commander to see what he'd found.

"Major, I am not quite satisfied with these rifles," Lieutenant Lawrason said. "I don't think they have been fired but would like to have you examine them."

"I examined those rifles very carefully myself," Major Penrose testified. "The sun was shining, so I could see into them well, and I put my handkerchief in next the bolt so I could get a reflected light in them. The guns were not clean. Captain Lyon was standing near the end of his barracks and I called him over and asked him to examine these rifles. He examined them, and I said, 'Have they been fired?' He said, 'I think not.' Then we called a noncommissioned officer and had him bring some clean rags, some wiping rags, and we ran a rag with the wiping rod through each one of these guns. We examined them very carefully, smelled them; there was no indication of having been fired; there was oil in there, and a little dust that had accumulated."

Every gun assigned to C Company was inspected by Captain Macklin, along with the rifles of the men on guard.

"Did you find any guns that were powder-burned?" he was asked.

"No, sir; none at all."

Captain Lyon testified that his inspection of D Company's rifles began around 6:20 A.M., after the men had breakfasted.

"I inspected the rifles in the usual manner of inspecting a rifle," he said, "except that the rifles which I found were not perfectly bright in the barrel I put to one side and made another inspection of those special guns."

"How?"

"With the barrack cleaning rod and a piece of white cloth for each rifle—a piece of cleaning cloth for each rifle."

"Were you satisfied at the time as to whether these rifles had been fired, any of them?"

"I couldn't find any trace or any indication in any rifle that it had been fired."

The three company commanders not only inspected the men's rifles and found them clean, they also verified their ammunition. It was intact, every cartridge accounted for. But shortly after daylight Captain Macklin had left the garrison and on the town side of the wall, at the mouth of the Cowen alley, he had scooped up a handful of spent cartridges (six to eight, he thought) and turned them over to Major Penrose, along with five or six clips, each capable of holding five rounds of ball ammunition. The cartridge shells and the clips had been manufactured for the Army's new Springfield rifle, Model 1903.

"Well, Macklin," the Major had concluded, "I am afraid our men have done this shooting."

The Investigators

———◆◆◆◆◆———

8

*"I would give my right arm to find out the
guilty parties."*

RENTFRO B. CREAGER, a young attorney who served as United
States Commissioner and deputy clerk of the United States District Court for the Southern District of Texas, had fled the heat,
mosquitoes, and monotony of a Brownsville summer, taking refuge at Point Isabel, a summer resort twenty miles down the Gulf
Coast. He knew nothing about the raid until he got to town
around eight o'clock Tuesday morning.

"My first information of the shooting came to me from a
Mexican hack driver. I was accustomed to drive in from the station to my office, passing by the post office to get my mail each

morning, on reaching town, and this morning, on getting into my hack, the driver, in a rather excited manner, began at once to tell me of the occurrence of the night before, saying that the Negroes had broken out of the post and had, he told me, killed three men. He was still, and a good many others were, under the impression, I found, up until nine or ten o'clock, that more people had been killed than really were killed."

While armed and angry men converged on the center of town, their women and children huddled behind locked doors and bolted windows. Some fled across the river to Matamoros. Anna Cowen took refuge at a friend's ranch three miles from town ("I just felt like I was unjointed"), but stopped at a church along the way to make good her covenant with the Lord.

The men gaped at the bloodstained courtyard of John Tillman's saloon, inspected the damage wrought on the Cowen house, leaned against Elizabeth Street lamp posts trading rumors, and sat on the market steps calculating how many shots the soldiers had fired (estimates ranged from a hundred to three hundred). They marveled that so much flying lead had produced only one death and one wound (a third man—Preciado—had been grazed by a bullet).

The Fred Starck family reported the narrowest escape. Bullets had thudded into the walls of their Washington Street home, ripping a hole in the mosquito bar covering their three little girls. Death had come within eighteen to twenty inches of the children and might have come to their parents as well if they had been standing in their bedroom.

The Starcks lived next door to Fred Tate, the customs officer who had roughed up Private Newton. The soldiers had intended to take vengeance on Tate and had fired into the wrong house, the town's self-appointed Pinkerton men deduced at once, and refused to part with their theory even when it was learned that Private Newton could have taken no part in the shooting. He was on guard duty Monday night. When the raid began, he was in the guardhouse, asleep.

Commissioner Creager had hardly reached his desk when the phone rang. It was someone at Fort Brown asking him to please come down to Major Penrose's office to discuss the raid. At the post office no one had questioned the identity of the raiders as Negro soldiers, but when he got to the garrison, Creager noticed that the Major said, "*If* my men did the shooting . . ."

The two men had met once before when the Commissioner had paid what Major Penrose had taken at first to be a social call. After chatting for a while about tarpon fishing at Point Isabel, however, Creager had pointedly worked the conversation around to the pistol-whipping Fred Tate had given the Negro soldier accused of jostling Mrs. Tate and some other white women.

"We got on the subject of Negroes in that part of the country," Major Penrose recalled, "and he said the Negroes, of course, can not expect to do as much in that part of the country as they could North. I said no, I suppose not, but as long as the Negroes in my battalion were behaving themselves, committed no offense, I should certainly insist on the people of the town treating them with proper respect. If they overstepped this in any way, I should be glad to punish them, and I would be glad to know of any occurrences of that kind if they happened."

Major Penrose had sent for the United States Commissioner the morning after the raid, he explained, because he thought Mr. Creager could be helpful in advising him how to conduct an investigation, but "I found after a very few moments' talk that he was so biased and prejudiced and so thoroughly convinced in his mind that the Negroes in my battalion had done this shooting that I soon saw he could not be of any benefit to me at all— could not help me at all; he was not a broad enough minded man for that."

Before their talk ended, they were joined by Mayor Combe, who produced some empty shells, a live round of ball ammunition, and a cartridge clip, all of which he had picked up between two and three A.M. in the alley back of the Miller Hotel. The shells and the clip, like those found by Captain Macklin, had been made for the Army's new Springfield rifle.

"Major Penrose, what do you think of that for evidence?" the Mayor said. "Your men did this."

"Combe, this is almost conclusive evidence; but who did it and how they did it, I do not know," Major Penrose replied, and said nothing about the shells and clips Captain Macklin had brought him earlier that morning.

Later Dr. Combe testified that when he collected the empty shells he hadn't taken the trouble to sniff them for the telltale odor of sulphur. It also developed that neither Major Penrose nor Captain Macklin had tested the Cowen-alley shells to see if they had been fired recently. Thus, for all anybody knew, both batches could have been fired days or weeks before the raid and saved as souvenirs by local gunslingers. The Army's powerful new rifle fascinated them, as white soldiers of the Twenty-sixth Infantry had discovered to their profit before leaving town.

"They were peddling cartridges on the street there every day they could get somebody to buy them from them," Joe Crixell told the Senate Military Affairs Committee.

Private Otis C. West, called as one of Major Penrose's defense witnesses, testified that on the day the men of the Twenty-sixth departed Fort Brown to make way for the Negro soldiers, he was working as a teamster, hauling the battalion's freight from the garrison to the depot. Mexican women and boys were swarming over the barracks, he said, scooping up discarded hats, shoes, leggings, exploded shells, and live cartridges. He remembered one youngster in particular, a Mexican boy of twelve or fourteen who was clutching a hat containing fifty or sixty cartridges.

"My curiosity was excited, and I said, 'Kid, what are you going to do with those shells?' and he said. 'I am going to take them down town and sell them to kill niggers with.' "

The newfangled Army cartridge lay outside the professional ken of Captain Kelly, a Grand Army of the Republic veteran who had spent two years in the ranks of the First New York Mounted Rifles before receiving his commission in '64.

"My firearm was loaded with a ramrod," he told the Senate Military Affairs Committee.

"And you bit the cartridge off with your teeth?"

"Bit it off with my teeth; yes, sir."

The Captain was not an eyewitness to the raid. He had heard the shots while reading in his library and had attributed them to the firecrackers, or *cuetes,* of a Mexican procession celebrating some saint's day. Not until he got to his bank around eight-thirty Tuesday morning did he hear the town's version of what had happened. There was never any doubt in his mind, then or later, that the Negro soldiers had done the shooting.

"Any other proposition is extremely absurd—and worse than absurd," he snapped.

Along with other old-timers in Brownsville, Captain Kelly had watched the town change during the last two years, since the coming of the railroad. A new element had moved in, bringing with it the passions and prejudices of cotton-growing states where a generation of white men had grown up to the sound of night riders using the rope and the shotgun to keep black men in subjection.

All Tuesday morning angry southerners ranged the length of Elizabeth Street, drawing heavily on the assault on Lon Evans' wife and on the spectacle of the three little Starck girls cowering in terror while black brutes fired into the open window of their bedroom. Captain Kelly sympathized with the newcomers, because they were "accustomed to Negroes committing all sorts of outrages," but the old Union veteran snorted his contempt for their tall talk of marching on Fort Brown with weapons they kept around the house to shoot doves and deer.

"They were very valiant, and would have done a whole lot of things," the Captain grunted. "One man told me he could take fifty men and go and clean out the whole Negro outfit. That man had never been a soldier."

Mayor Combe came across the same sort of ranting. "I do not want any of this talking," he told Al Billingsley. "I will arrest anybody who keeps it up." Then he ran into Sam Wreford, the man who had protested to Senator Culberson in late May, when the town first learned that Negro troops had been assigned to Fort Brown. "He was elocuting the same way," the Mayor said, "and I laid the law down to him . . ."

After talking with Major Armstrong ("one of our most prominent Republicans") and Mr. Goodrich ("an old Grand Army man"), Dr. Combe decided to hold "a mass meeting of the thinking people of the town." The meeting was called for eleven o'clock in the courtroom of the Federal courthouse.

"I think that nearly all the respectable citizens of Brownsville were at that meeting," Captain Kelly testified, and estimated the peak attendance at five hundred persons, a charitable way of writing off more than ninety per cent of the town's population as not respectable.

"I took the chair and I addressed the people," Mayor Combe explained to the Senate Military Affairs Committee. "I told them what had occurred last night, as they knew it by this time, and went on to say that I agreed with them that unquestionably it had been done by some ruffians of the battalion now stationed at Brownsville, but that we should not condemn all the men and all the officers; that so far they had deported themselves as good citizens, and I appealed to them and requested them to continue to do so; that we would appeal to the highest authority in the land, if necessary, but under no circumstances to take the law in their own hands, because it would lead to trouble and maybe the ruination of Brownsville."

Captain Kelly, it was decided, should choose a committee of citizens to investigate the raid. He made a point of selecting "mostly northern men, who had no special animus against Negroes as such." Along with Mayor Combe, the committee included the sheriff (Celedonio Garza), the chief of police (George Connor), the county judge (John Bartlett), the city attorney (Frank W. Kibbe), a wealthy alderman (James A. Browne), an old Federal soldier who voted a Republican ticket (E. H. Goodrich), the editor of the *Daily Herald* (Jesse O. Wheeler), and a Mexican who had made good as a banker and anglicized his name (John G. Fernandez).

By the time the committee had been chosen, hunger was setting in and several members wanted to go home for lunch, but their chairman said, "No, there is no time like the present. We will go at once to see Major Penrose." They found him in his office in the administrative building.

Captain Kelly described his meeting with the Major: "At first he said, 'It cannot be.' He said, 'I have got the best battalion in my regiment. I know my men. They could not be guilty of such an outrage.' I said, 'Well, who did the firing?' He said, 'Well, I think it was an attack on the barracks from the town.' I said,

'Yes? Have you examined your barracks and buildings? They run right along here, and nothing could be shot from the town without hitting them.' "

Major Penrose had to admit that no trace of gunfire had been found inside the post, but neither he nor the two officers who were in the room with him, Captain Lyon and Lieutenant Grier, appears to have suggested that the raiders may have deliberately tried *not* to hit any of the Army buildings. They may have set out to frighten the garrison, not conquer it.

Instead of exploring this avenue, however, the three officers let the delegation continue along its predetermined course. Its members were in no mood to delay their lunch to hear any nonsense about the soldiers' possible innocence. Dr. Combe interrupted Captain Kelly's presentation of the town's indictment to produce some shells he had been given since his earlier meeting with the Major that morning.

As the Mayor recalled their conversation, he began by saying, "Major Penrose, your men did the shooting; here are the shells, and no one else has those arms or that ammunition'; and he said to me, what he said in the morning, 'I am afraid that is true.' Those are not his exact words, but that is the substance of what he said. He said, 'Gentlemen, I do not understand this at all. I do not know how my men could have done it.' With tears in his eyes, he said, 'I would give my right arm to find out the guilty parties.' "

On his desk Major Penrose had the affidavits of Tamayo, the post scavenger, and Private Howard, the sentry guarding the barracks when the shooting began. Both men swore they had seen no soldiers in the barracks area, nor had they observed any shooting inside the military reservation.

Along with these two affidavits, the Major had received the sworn statements of three soldiers who, as noncommissioned officers in charge of quarters, had been responsible for the rifles in the three occupied barracks. They were men he had no reason to distrust.

Sergeant George Jackson of B Company, mustered into the

Army in the summer of 1898, had re-enlisted in December 1960, with a "very good" character rating. Sergeant Darby W. O. Brawner of C Company had re-enlisted three times since joining the Army in the spring of 1893, and had always been rated "character excellent." Corporal David Powell had received the same rating both times he had signed on for another hitch.

Sergeant Jackson swore that when B Company returned from its practice march between ten and eleven o'clock Monday morning, the fifty-two rifles for which he was accountable had been returned to the racks and the racks had been locked. He had issued six rifles to the men on guard duty, then relocked the racks. B company's racks had not been opened again until after call to arms had been sounded, when he personally had unlocked them. He also stated that he had not left the barracks at any time during the period the forty-six rifles had been locked in the racks and that at the eleven-o'clock check roll call of the company he had found all the men present.

Sergeant Brawner was responsible for fifty-seven rifles, four of which were in the hands of C Company's men on guard duty. The keys to the racks were constantly in his possession, he stated in an affidavit taken by Captain Lyon, and none of the racks was opened at any time except once, about two-thirty that afternoon, when he had procured a rifle for the supernumerary of the guard who was replacing a sick sentry.

Corporal Powell locked D Company's rifles in the racks when the men got back from their practice march about nine-thirty Monday morning, he stated. He opened the racks around ten o'clock to allow five men of the guard to get their rifles, then he locked the other fifty-two rifles in the racks, where they remained until sometime after midnight when he unlocked them. "I did not leave the quarters at any time during the day or night," he continued, and concluded by stating, "I took check roll call at eleven P.M. on the 13th, and all the men of the company were present or' accounted for."

Major Penrose weighed the sworn word of his men against the physical evidence of the exploded shells and Springfield clips found in the path of the raid. Sometime that morning, not yet convinced of his men's guilt and in error as to the rank of the police officer shot by the marauders, he sent a telegram to the Military Secretary, Department of Texas, San Antonio:

"Regret to report serious shooting in Brownsville last evening, in which one civilian was killed and chief of police so seriously wounded that right arm will have to be amputated. Brownsville officials claim shooting was done by enlisted men of this command, and are borne out in their opinion by empty shells and clips picked up in the streets."

Later that day, he advised the Military Secretary: "After further investigation, I am convinced the killing of a citizen and wounding of the chief of police at Brownsville last night was done by from seven to ten men of this command, abetted by others in post."

9

"We know they were Negro soldiers."

AFTER LUNCH THE Citizens' Committee buckled down to work in a borrowed law office, with Captain Kelly and City Attorney Kibbe asking most of the questions. No women were called, no oath was administered, and no effort was made to achieve impartiality. As Captain Kelly explained, "We just called the people up one after another and asked them, 'State what you know about this attack of the Negroes on the town.'"

"We are inquiring into the matter of last night with a view to ascertaining who the guilty parties are," Charles S. Canada was told when he took the stand. "We know they were Negro soldiers. If there is anything that would throw any light on the subject, we would like to have it."

Canada, a newspaperman from North Carolina, obliged by stating that when the shooting started, he left his third-floor room at the Miller Hotel and descended to the gallery on the floor below. He hadn't seen the raiders, he said, but after watching a policeman stagger and fall (it was Joe Dominguez, he learned afterward), he had heard their voices and had concluded that they were Negroes.

"I was raised among them and know their voices pretty well," he explained.

Canada made his identification on the basis of three monosyllables, "We got him." S. C. Moore, the hotel's proprietor, heard someone shout, "There goes the son of a bitch! Get him!" The voice was "very coarse," which led him to believe the raiders were Negroes. C. C. Madison came to the same conclusion after hearing someone say, "Halt."

"Did you see any soldiers?" Madison was asked, and he said, "No."

Dr. Thorn, a middle-aged dentist who lived with his mother near the Miller Hotel, heard the voices of two men. One said, "There he goes" (or "There they go" or "There he is"); the other said, "Give them, or him, hell" and, still louder, "God damn him!" He told the committee, "It was a Negro's voice." The following spring, when he appeared before the Senate Military Affairs Committee, he was still satisfied that the men who did the shooting were Negroes.

"You entertained no doubt of that?"

"No doubt, whatever."

José Martinez, who lived just behind the telegraph office, said, "I hear the noise like somebody—big crowd—jump the fence." He was referring to the garrison wall, thirty-six feet away.

"Were they Negroes or white men?" he was asked.

"Negroes."

"Did you see their uniforms?"

"No; I saw their—what you call it?—bulk."

George W. Rendall, a mechanical engineer who lived near the fort's Elizabeth Street gate, said he was awakened around ten o'clock by "pistol shots" fired close to his house, about sixty feet inside the garrison wall. When he and his wife went to their front window, he could see men moving back and forth inside the military reservation.

"They were shooting," he said. "One man in particular. I watched the shots, seeing the fire leave the pistol, and it was elevated up in the air."

After seeing these flashes of gunfire, which may have been the sentinel's warning shots, Rendall said he heard someone say, "There he goes," and then the men made a move toward the wall and passed from view. He could not tell whether they had guns in their hands, but he didn't hesitate to say they were soldiers. It turned out afterward that he had made this identification at a distance of a hundred and fifty feet, a remarkable achievement for a man of seventy-two who was totally blind in one eye, had impaired vision in the other eye, and could never remember whether he had paused on his way to the window to put on his glasses.

The Citizens' Committee testimony was taken so hurriedly and transcribed so inaccurately that Victoriano Fernandez had to disavow virtually every statement ascribed to him. The policeman who covered Elizabeth Street by day was quoted as saying, "They shot at me the third time—three men with big guns. I shot back. They were dressed in khaki pants." Actually, he told the Senate Military Affairs Committee, he had not seen three men with big guns, nor had he fired at them, and he had never told Captain Kelly's committee that they had been wearing khaki pants.

"I know they were soldiers, because they were in their uniforms," said Genaro Padron, the policeman who had been patrolling the midtown beat. Later a senator asked whether he had been able to recognize the raiders as white or black men. "I could not tell," he said, "in view of my surprise, as they were firing at me."

James P. McDonnel, who lived on Adams Street near the Garrison Road intersection, was expecting trouble, he told the Citizens' Committee. "I knew there was bitter feeling in town and thought that if they caught any Negro soldiers uptown they might do them up. So I laid awake; never pulled off my shoes."

He jumped up when he heard the first shots and headed down Fifteenth toward Elizabeth Street, where the shooting seemed to have originated. He got as far as the alley between Washington and Elizabeth, when "the shooting commenced again just inside the garrison wall." He saw about twenty men assembled on the town side of the wall near the telegraph office, he continued, and had no idea where they had come from. He had not seen any of them come out of the gate or climb over the wall.

"I think they were in trousers and shirts," he said. "I don't know whether they were Negroes or white men, but they were United States soldiers."

If the soldiers tried to repeat "the dastard outrage," the Brownsville *Daily Herald* declared, they would find themselves dealing with a "people fully prepared to defend themselves." Sale of firearms had been brisk since the raid, the paper noted, and estimated that "there are at least four hundred Winchester rifles, besides countless pistols, shotguns, etc., now in the hands of men here who know how to shoot them, and will not hesitate to do so, should the occasion arise."

Convened in a lynching atmosphere, with armed men patrolling streets their womenfolk feared to venture out into, Captain Kelly's posse of high-minded citizens needed less than two days to arrive at a truth no right-thinking man in town had ever doubted. The results of this "most diligent inquiry" were incorporated in a telegram dispatched to President Roosevelt. It reached him at his home in Oyster Bay where he was worrying about Cuba, simplified spelling, and Mr. Hearst's chances of becoming Governor of New York.

The telegram informed him that between twenty and thirty soldiers, "carrying their rifles and abundant supply of ammunition," had emerged from Fort Brown a few minutes before midnight August 13, and, after firing about two hundred shots, had returned to their quarters, having killed one citizen and wounded "the lieutenant of police, who rode toward the firing." (Actually, he had ridden the other way.)

"We find that threats have been made by them that they will repeat this outrage," the telegram concluded. "We do not believe their officers can restrain them, there being but five commissioned officers. Our condition, Mr. President, is this: Our women and children are terrorized and our men are practically under constant alarm and watchfulness. No community can stand this strain for more than a few days. We look to you for relief; we ask you to have the troops at once removed from Fort Brown and replaced by white soldiers."

In the absence of Secretary of War Taft (he was on holiday in Canada), it devolved on the Military Secretary, Major General F. C. Ainsworth, to break the August 19 sabbath by drafting two telegrams. One went to Oyster Bay, advising the President to move the Brownsville soldiers a hundred miles up the Rio Grande to Fort Ringgold; the other to Major Penrose at Fort Brown: "Have you any doubt as to your ability to restrain troops from further violence?"

As he indicated by his reference to "further" violence on the part of the black battalion, General Ainsworth had already pronounced the soldiers guilty of the raid. The only question in his mind that weekend was not whether the Negroes had shot up the town but whether their five white officers could keep them from vaulting the garrison wall and doing it again.

"Have no doubt of my ability to restrain troops," Major Penrose replied. "Everything quiet in city, but very bitter feeling exists in both city and surrounding country."

Meanwhile, on Saturday night, Major Augustus P. Blocksom of the Inspector General's Department had come to town to look into the situation. "Troops under proper control," he reported next day, "although town people are still very much excited, and men all carrying arms." Monday, less than forty-eight hours after his arrival, he was able to state as fact the assumptions with which he had begun his inquiry.

"Causes of disturbance are racial," he telegraphed the War Department. "People did not desire colored troops here and showed they thought them inferior socially by certain slights and denial of privileges at public bars, etc. Soldiers resented this."

Between nine and fifteen soldiers carried out the raid, Major Blocksom reported. They fired seventy-five to a hundred and fifty shots in a period of from eight to ten minutes. In passing, he mentioned a rumor circulating in the lower part of town that neither he nor any of the community's leaders took seriously: "Claim made that citizens fired first, but I believe without foundation."

"Lest newspaper items concerning the trouble at Brownsville, Tex, between colored troops and citizens of town may cause you some concern," General Ainsworth telegraphed Secretary Taft on August 24, ten days after the raid, "will say that I have kept in close consultation with President. . . . Believe no occasion for any anxiety on your part. If you would like to see full official history of case, will send you copies of messages, reports, etc."

"I think you might send me the papers and the telegrams by mail," Taft replied.

In the material bundled off to the Secretary's Pointe Au Pic hideaway was a telegram signed by both Texas senators asking him "to transfer the disorderly Negro troops." In a follow-up telegram, Senator Culberson had reminded Taft of his earlier warning of the risks involved in stationing Negro soldiers in Texas, "especially in Brownsville," he added.

"Citizens of Brownsville," agreed the Army's commanding general in Texas, "entertain race hatred to an extreme degree . . ."

"Our position is misunderstood," the town's leading citizens complained in a second appeal to the President. "We can not convince our women and children that another outbreak may not occur at any time. . . . Many of our citizens have removed and are removing their families elsewhere. A Texas town should not be left unaided in this condition."

Heavily armed special deputies took turns standing watch on the town side of Garrison Road. On the Army's side, separated from the townspeople by a waist-high brick wall, the deputies counted sixty-five soldiers on guard. Armed sentries had been stationed at ten-foot intervals, and with each sentry stood three unarmed men from different companies.

"At present all is quiet, and it is considered quite probable by those in authority that no further outbreak is likely," the *Daily Herald* announced in its news columns, but editorially it denounced the Governor and the Adjutant General for dismissing the attack as a "drunken riot or spree." Quite the contrary, the editorial writer insisted, "it was a premeditated plot to massacre the families of certain citizens." Austin, however, persisted in treating the local citizenry as "a lot of silly, hysterical, timid creatures. Yet here is a town practically in a state of war . . ."

The attack inspired a Texas bard to compose a poem, which, the *Daily Herald* confidently predicted, was "destined to take its place in literature":

"Our daughters murdered and defiled,
    Black fingers crooked about fair throat,
The leering fiend—the tortured breath—
    Where's time for laggard red tape now,
When moments may mean life or death?"

The town's most distinguished citizens gathered at the depot Tuesday evening, August 21, to welcome the white soldiers of Company H, Twenty-sixth Infantry, who had been pulled off maneuvers at Camp Mabry and rushed to Fort Brown to replace the black troops.

"It had been planned to have a band of music out," the *Daily Herald* reported, "but it was deemed wiser not to do so, as some disorder might result."

Captain John F. Preston's men moved into the vacant barracks which had been reserved for the black battalion's Company A. By coincidence, some faceless paper-pusher in the War Department had pushed papers directing Company A to Fort Brown just as Companies B, C, and D were packing to get out of town. Major Penrose managed to stave off this act of bureaucratic lunacy.

He had also persuaded Washington to cancel orders for the black troops to march upriver to Ringgold. Each step along the hundred-mile route would have been an open invitation to violence. Instead, the troops were now to be transferred beyond the borders of Texas to Fort Reno, Oklahoma.

Earlier that same Tuesday, unbeknownst to Brownsville

citizens, President Roosevelt's secretary had advised Acting Secretary of War Ainsworth that Fort Brown was to be "temporarily closed." Instead of sending a full company, the President wanted only enough soldiers to "take care of and ship supplies." A full company had already been sent, General Ainsworth replied, but "it will be made plain that on completion of this work company will be withdrawn and Fort Brown temporarily abandoned."

The President's decision came to Senator Culberson's breakfast table in an Associated Press story. He lost no time getting off a telegram to the War Department: "It would be regrettable that this fort should be abandoned because the people of a border city like Brownsville object to Negro troops under circumstances of raid and murder . . ."

The Senator's telegram had been shown to the President, General Ainsworth was advised the next day, and he had decided to proceed with the "order previously given for temporary abandonment of the post." If a pack of border ruffians had staged the raid, as some newspapers were beginning to suspect, they had overshot their mark. They had succeeded in ridding the town of white soldiers as well as black.

10

"The guns he carried were almost half his size, and helped him, proportionately, to the publicity he craved."

THE New York *Times* scorched the War Department's thick bureaucratic hide for its "incredible folly" in posting black soldiers in a Texas town. "If there must be Negro troops, which is far from evident," the *Times* noted, "it would seem to be the part of wisdom to station them elsewhere than in Texas, or anywhere in the South."

In New York the raid was treated routinely as another explosion of racial violence on a hot summer night in a small southern community. It got only four inches on page three of the *Times* and even less coverage in the *World*. But in Texas the story was splashed across the front pages, which made it inevitable that Captain Bill McDonald of the Texas Rangers should bob up in Brownsville, packing a pair of six-shooters and an automatic shotgun.

"The guns he carried were almost half his size," a Brownsville resident recalled, "and helped him, proportionately, to the publicity he craved."

In the history of the Texas Rangers no one had ever moved more swiftly to capture a horse thief or a headline than Captain McDonald. His services to law and order and the cattlemen's associations were memorialized by Albert Bigelow Paine in 1909 and resurrected a generation later by Walter Prescott Webb in *The Texas Rangers* (1935), which depends entirely on Paine's puffery for its account of the Brownsville affair. In his original draft, Dr. Webb spoke of McDonald's "courageous" investigation of the raid, but on second thought he deleted the adjective. He also ran a pencil through the characterization of the Ranger Captain given him by Harbert Davenport, a Brownsville antiquarian.

"I have never found a Border man who had the slightest respect for Bill McDonald," Davenport had written. "He was, to them, a troublemaker, an advertiser, a teller of tales of which he was himself the hero, inclined to act—and act violently—on false or doubtful information, vain, and self-important."

On the night of the shooting, Bill McDonald was in Dallas, serving as sergeant at arms for the Democratic state convention. When day after day went by without a single black soldier being marched off to jail, he applied to the Adjutant General for some state militiamen, so he could "go down and settle that Brownsville business." To his disgust he was told he had no authority to investigate the conduct of Federal troops.

"Why them hellions have violated the laws of the state, shooting into the people's houses and committing murder," he bellowed, and took the next train to Brownsville.

In Corpus Christi he was joined by District Judge Stanley Welch, a small, voluble, one-armed patriot (he had lost the arm firing a Fourth of July salute), who assured him he had all the power he needed to track down the raiders. The train pulled into town around six o'clock Tuesday evening, August 21, and McDonald immediately presented himself to Mayor Combe and Captain Kelly.

After dressing them down for having wasted a week shilly-shallying, McDonald left to get in touch with two Rangers who had preceded him to Brownsville. The quality of their investigative work can be inferred from a lead one of them had already passed along to Captain Kelly who had solemnly entered it as evidence in the transcript of his committee's deliberations.

"I am a state ranger," Blaze Delling had testified right after the raid. "I have come into the possession of some information this morning, which I got from this soda-water man, who sells soda-water. He told me that this soda-water man had been told by a saloon man who keeps a saloon in the edge of town that some shooting had been done last night, and that Company C could have taken the whole town if they had wanted to, and that they could take the whole damn state."

The two Rangers had discovered that on the night of the raid the town's new Negro saloon had closed early. This was interpreted as a "suspicious circumstance." No one, apparently, had told the Rangers about the eight o'clock curfew imposed on the soldiers that night. The new Negro saloon had closed early because its customers had left early.

Captain McDonald went to the county jail to question Mack Hamilton, a black ex-cavalryman who insisted he knew nothing about the shooting. He had spent the evening at home, he said, chatting for a while with one of the soldiers, Corporal Willie H. Miller, who happened to be his first cousin. He was in bed when the shooting started, Hamilton continued. He had got up, gone out to see what the trouble was, and ended up in jail.

"He was evidently lying to shield himself," McDonald concluded in reporting his interview with Hamilton.

While at the jail, McDonald also talked to the Sheriff, who told him that "a company of soldiers came to the jail immediately after the shooting and demanded to know who had been put in jail and claiming that the citizens had fired on the post." The Sheriff was referring to Captain Lyon's men, who had been sent to look for Captain Macklin.

"My impression," McDonald advised the Governor, "is that Capt. Lyon and his companies [sic] part was to go and finish up the job."

Pleased at having got off to such a promising start on his first night in town, McDonald decided he was ready next morning to march on Fort Brown. He shrugged off warnings that he would never come out of the place alive. Accompanied by a sergeant armed with a Winchester repeating rifle, he advanced on the Elizabeth Street gate, his automatic shotgun poised to spray the file of twenty black soldiers who halted him.

"I'm Captain McDonald of the State Rangers," Paine quotes him as saying, "and I'm down here to investigate a foul murder you scoundrels have committed. I'll show you niggers something you've never been use' to. *Put up them guns!*"

To the Captain's admirers on the American side of the border, the confrontation substantiated a popular saying along this stretch of the Rio Grande: "Bill McDonald would charge hell with one bucket of water." In this instance, however, hell was not quite so formidable as the mythmakers made it appear. McDonald was charging a group of Negroes standing on Texas soil facing two heavily armed white men who claimed to be state officials. They let the white men pass.

Swaggering into the administration building, McDonald proceeded to question Major Penrose and Captain Macklin. The Ranger captain, in Paine's lapidary prose, became "a fox—his ears alert, his nose sharp, his eyes needle-pointed." Where was Corporal Miller on the night of the raid? McDonald asked, and the man was brought to him for interrogation.

He had gone to Matamoros on a twenty-four-hour pass, Miller said, and when he got back to Brownsville, he had looked in on his cousin, Mack Hamilton, and had then repaired to a Mexican saloon. In later testimony, Miller swore that he was playing cards in the saloon when he heard the first shots and, sensing there might be some sort of investigation, he had taken the precaution of showing his pass to the proprietor, who had agreed to testify that Miller was in his place when the trouble occurred.

McDonald questioned some of the other soldiers and, according to Paine, found their stories "confused, contradictory, and full of guilt." The Captain was particularly curious about Private C. W. Askew, whose cap had been found in the street the morning after the raid and identified by the initials C. W. A.

"Tell us about that cap," Askew was asked six months later, and he replied: "I gave the first sergeant one of my old caps when I was at Fort Niobrara, and there was a box of old caps that was shipped down to Fort Brown, and when they got down there they opened that box of old caps, and some of those *muchachos*, I suppose, found them and got them and carried them away; and I think that is the way they got the cap."

McDonald regarded both Penrose and Macklin with scorn and suspicion. They were hiding something, he felt—especially Macklin, who kept insisting he had slept through the raid.

"I couldn't help thinking Macklin must have been out with the coons who were committing murder and trying to kill ladies and their children," he reported, and Paine quotes the old fox as barking at Major Penrose, "When I came here, you told me you couldn't find out anything. I've been here a half an hour and I've found enough, with what I got last night, to warrant me in charging a bunch of your men with murder. How do you explain that?"

"You have had more experience in such matters and understand better how to go at it than I do," the Major is supposed to have replied.

"You are sorrier than these niggers," McDonald continued, addressing both Penrose and Macklin, "because you, as their officers, and as men of the United States Army, ought to be first to hunt out the guilty ones, instead of trying to hide them."

The following morning, Thursday, McDonald returned to the garrison with bench warrants issued by Judge Welch for the arrest of twelve enlisted men and the ex-soldier, Allison, who had opened the new Negro saloon. Major Penrose agreed to commit the soldiers to the Fort Brown guardhouse (Allison, a civilian, was headed for the county jail), but he was planning to leave town that night and balked at the prospect of abandoning McDonald's suspects to what passed for due process of law in Cameron County.

"I do not believe these men will have unbiased trial here," Penrose advised Brigadier General William S. McCaskey, commanding general, Department of Texas. "An effort, in my opinion, should be made to have them tried elsewhere. I also fear for their safety if turned over to civil authorities, in case of mob violence . . ."

General McCaskey suggested to the War Department that the twelve prisoners be transferred to Fort Sam Houston in San Antonio. Major Penrose could drop them off on his way to Oklahoma, the General pointed out, and his proposal was passed along to Oyster Bay with departmental approval.

"We think it unsafe to leave accused at Fort Brown, with only one white company of forty-eight men to protect them," the President was informed. "We also fear that turning them over to civil authorities now or in immediate future would be disastrous to them. Train is now waiting at Brown to take battalion Twenty-fifth Infantry to Fort Reno, Okla. We strongly recommend that battalion take accused men with it to San Antonio and turn them over to military authorities there, to be confined and guarded until they can be turned over to civil authorities safely. Battalion to proceed to Fort Reno immediately upon delivering prisoners at San Antonio."

"I entirely approve of the action you propose to take," the President replied, and directed the Department to "act immediately."

The orders were sent to Major Penrose in a confidential telegram which seems to have been delivered simultaneously to Captain McDonald. The telegram reached Fort Brown a little after five o'clock. Half an hour later McDonald burst in on Penrose, demanding custody of his twelve prisoners. The Major refused to release them. He was acting under orders of his commander-in-chief.

"The President himself directs the action herein ordered,"

the telegram stated, and it cautioned both secrecy and diplomacy. "This movement of accused men should not be announced in advance, and should be made so as to avoid attracting or bringing on conflict with civil authorities. There is no intention of taking these men beyond jurisdiction of State of Texas or of withholding them from civil authorities a moment beyond time when they can be turned over safely. It is not believed safe to leave them at Fort Brown."

In the flurry of telegrams flying between Brownsville, Washington, Austin, and Oyster Bay, no one remarked on the irony of the situation. The townspeople were pleading with the President to save them from the fury of the black soldiers and the President was ordering the black soldiers whisked away in order to save them from the fury of the townspeople.

In keeping with his promise to inform Judge Welch of any change of orders regarding the twelve prisoners, Major Penrose went to the Judge's office that evening and showed him the telegram. Captain McDonald demanded that he be permitted to read it too, but the Major refused. McDonald turned angrily toward Judge Welch.

"Judge, those niggers are not going to be moved from here. They are my prisoners, and I'm going to hold them. I'm going to wire the Governor."

The military authorities were "trying to take our prisoners away from here for the purpose of thwarting justice," he informed the Governor, and asked for assistance to prevent the outrage. "The officers are trying to cover up this diabolicle [sic] crime that I am about to uncover."

While waiting for a reply from Austin, Captain McDonald sent Major Penrose a formal demand for "the delivery to me of the men of your command that I yesterday gave you warrants for and also the other soldiers of your command that were connected with the murder of Frank Natus and wounding of M. Y. Dominguez."

The Major again refused, making it clear that the men would be delivered to civil authorities for trial only when their safety had been assured. "After a most careful investigation," Penrose continued in a passage McDonald could interpret only as further evidence of his efforts to conceal the guilty hellions, "I am unable to find anyone, or party, in any way connected with the crime of which you speak."

A meeting was held that night in Judge Welch's office. Mayor Combe was present, along with the District Attorney, Congressman John Garner, and James B. Wells, the town's most prominent lawyer (he handled the legal affairs of the King Ranch). When McDonald marched in, making a conspicuous display of his automatic shotgun and threatening to shoot it out with the United States Army, Jim Wells tried to calm him.

"You are zealous," Dr. Combe remembered him saying, "you are a good officer, and you think you are doing right, but if you attempt to interfere with those soldiers down there, this matter will break out anew and we will lose a great many lives here. You must remember our wives and children."

McDonald became even more indignant, Dr. Combe continued, when Judge Welch ordered him to return the bench warrants he had issued for the arrest of the twelve soldiers.

"I do not remember all the the conversation," Dr. Combe said, "but they got a little excited—McDonald got excited. Welch was a one-armed man, a man about my size—a small man—and he said, 'You will return that bench warrant to me,' and he did."

"Feeling ran very high when it was first generally understood that Major Penrose refused to surrender the prisoners and would leave here with them at midnight," the *Daily Herald* reported, "and there were scores of citizens who were ready at a moment's notice to back Captain McDonald on his demand for their surrender. Cooler counsel prevailed, however, and after the warrants were revoked things quieted down."

"No," Captain Kelly snapped when asked if McDonald had helped the Citizens' Committee ferret out any criminals, and Mayor Combe explained that the Ranger captain "had been accustomed to handling Negroes in some parts of the state, and I suppose he thought that he could come down there and handle the situation better than we could."

Some weeks later, when Judge Welch was murdered in a

neighboring town, Jim Wells wired the Governor, urging him to rush a company of Texas Rangers to the scene of the crime.

"Be sure and send Captain John R. Hughes and his company if possible," the message stated, "but do not think of sending anyone but Captain Hughes or Captain Brooks. You will understand why it should be either Captain Hughes or Captain Brooks."

Brownsville, in short, wanted nothing more to do with Captain McDonald.

II

"Some of these men are undoubtedly innocent . . ."

THE BLACK SOLDIERS left Brownsville Saturday morning at six-thirty. It was the Mayor's idea to drop the original plan for a midnight departure and put them on an early-morning train.

"If any person is unkindly disposed towards your command and wants to commit an act of violence, they can do it very easily under cover of the darkness," Dr. Combe had pointed out to Major Penrose.

At daybreak an enlarged police force of fifty or sixty civilians stood guard along the route the soldiers were to take to the depot.

"I met Major Penrose myself," the Mayor recalled, "and placed myself at the head of the command, or near him, at one side. The sheriff had command of one flank of my force and I of the other, with instructions that if any citizen made any demonstration whatever, or interfered with the departure of the troops, he was to be arrested, and if a citizen fired a shot, or anything of that kind, he was to be shot."

A *Daily Herald* reporter was on the scene. "Not a word was spoken by the men as they left and only the briefest commands given by the officers as they marched through town. By coincidence, a church bell was tolling as they left."

Later that morning the reporter ran into Captain McDonald, who told him "it was a bitter dose to see those Negro soldiers march out of Brownsville this morning, knowing that at least a score of them were murderous 'thugs' who were guilty of the bloody outrage against Brownsville."

The troops made it to San Antonio "without the slightest trouble or demonstration of any kind," Major Penrose advised the War Department. The twelve prisoners were bundled into an army ambulance and whisked off to Fort Sam Houston while the rest of the battalion left immediately for Fort Reno. Their train pulled in the Oklahoma depot at twelve-thirty A.M., Monday, August 27, exactly two weeks after the men had been awakened by gunfire somewhere in the dark corridor between Fort Brown and Brownsville.

As the soldiers pulled out of Texas, Brownsville was shuddering at what the *Daily Herald* called another "diabolical plot against the town." About three o'clock Saturday morning, just a few hours before the three companies left town, a Fort Brown teamster, William Forster, claimed he had surprised three men trying to break into the post arsenal. The men were after gunpowder, the *Daily Herald* deduced, and left its readers to ponder what new outrages might have been perpetrated if Forster had not frustrated their scheme.

"I came out on the porch and I seen three men there at the arsenal door," Forster testified the following spring. "I asked them what they were doing, and they started to run."

"Were they colored men or white men?" a senator asked.

"Two of them were colored men—had soldiers' uniforms on—and one had citizen's clothes on."

Forster said the white man in citizen's clothes appeared to be his former boss, Wilbert Voshelle. The vague identification not only cast suspicion on a man Forster didn't happen to like, but it also helped him land a new job, driving the town's street-sprinkling cart. Forster was one of the first men in Brownsville to rise in the world by coming forth with damaging new evidence against "the nigger soldiers."

"That the raiders were soldiers of the Twenty-fifth Infantry can not be doubted," Major Blocksom reported on August 29, after spending eleven days in Brownsville. "The evidence of many witnesses of all classes is conclusive. Shattered bullets, shells, and clips are merely corroborative."

Without question, Blocksom stated, Mrs. Evans "was seized by the hair and thrown violently to the ground by a tall Negro soldier." He substantiated the statement by citing the second of six enclosures, a letter from Major Penrose to the Military Secretary in San Antonio. But instead of corroborating Mrs. Evans' story, the Penrose letter cast doubt on the attempted rape because "prostitutes are too common in the town."

Blocksom was convinced that, along with the scavenger Tamayo, at least three soldiers were lying—the sergeant of the guard, the sentry patrolling the barracks area, and B Company's non-commissioned officer in charge of quarters, who swore he had neither heard nor seen any shots fired from his barracks. To believe that these men were telling the truth was to believe that no rifles were fired inside the military reservation except the sentry's warning shots, and that no soldiers sneaked past a cooperative chain of sentinels and took their place in ranks after the raid was over.

Never doubting for a moment that the town had been attacked by soldiers, Major Blocksom could only conclude that those witnesses whose testimony was most persuasive of their innocence must be lying. If these particular soldiers had not taken part in the raid themselves, he reasoned, they certainly knew who had, and by their silence they were conspiring to protect the assassins.

Most of the men Captain McDonald had rounded up were probably guilty, Major Blocksom believed, but "there is little prospect of conviction on evidence thus far obtained." The evidence sought by Captain Kelly's committee, by Captain McDonald, and by Major Blocksom had been confined to material which would support their assumption that the raid had been the work of soldiers. They refused to interpret their inability to fix the blame on a single soldier as an indication that perhaps the men were telling the truth and someone in town was lying.

"Too preposterous to merit further attention," the *Daily Herald* snapped when the Corpus Christi *Crony* suggested the raid might have been pulled off by "persons disguised in uniforms, which are easily purchasable, and using government ammunition, which is no less easy to be secured."

Before Captain McDonald's twelve prisoners were transferred to Fort Sam Houston (Allison remained in the county jail), Major Penrose visited them at the Fort Brown guardhouse.

"If you men had told what you knew about the shooting, you would not have been in confinement," Private Howard remembered him saying.

"Did you or the others ask him to tell you how you could prove that you did not know anything about it except by saying you did not know anything about it?" Senator Foraker asked Howard at the Senate Military Affairs Committee hearing.

"No, sir," Howard replied.

"Has anyone else ever told you how you could prove that you were innocent, except by denying it?"

"No, sir."

General McCaskey, who presided over the Army's Department of Texas, reminded the War Department that Judge Welch had abrogated the warrants under which the twelve men had been arrested. Thus, there were no longer any charges pending against them. Instead of ordering their release, however, Washington directed him to "cause military charges to be formally preferred against said soldiers."

The battalion adjutant at Fort Sam Houston promptly obliged with both charges ("conduct to the prejudice of good order and military discipline . . .") and specifications (". . . did singly or in company with other party or parties unknown take part in a disturbance in the streets of Brownsville, Tex. . . ."). The battalion's commanding officer doubted that "the allegations as set forth can be substantiated."

Eight of the twelve prisoners "can apparently prove an alibi," Lieutenant Colonel Leonard A. Lovering, Inspector General, Southwestern Division, reported after interviewing the Brownsville soldiers in Oklahoma. But he made no recommendation that the prisoners left behind in Texas should be returned to their regiment. A month after the raid the men were still behind bars. They didn't know why. Neither did General McCaskey.

"The reasons for the selecting of these men, or the manner by which their names were procured, is a mystery," he informed the War Department. "As far as known there is no evidence that the majority of them were in any way directly connected with the affair. It seems to have been a dragnet proceeding."

Judge Welch, the peppery one-armed jurist who had issued the bench warrants for the men's arrest, was on hand in September when the Cameron County grand jury met in Brownsville to investigate the raid. In his charge to the jurors, the judge denounced the "unprovoked, murderous midnight assault committed by the Negro soldiers" and declared that "fiendish malice and hate, showing hearts blacker than their skins, was evidenced by their firing of volley after volley from deadly rifles into and through the doors and windows of family residences, clearly with the brutish hope on their part of killing women and children, and thus make memorable their hatred of the white race."

The grand jury spent three weeks listening to a procession of indignant townspeople, many of whom had already told their story to Captain Kelly in Jim Wells's law office. The jurors never doubted that the soldiers had done the shooting, but as United States Commissioner Creager explained, "the evidence did not point with sufficient certainty to any individual or individuals to justify or warrant them in bringing in an indictment . . ."

When the grand jury adjourned without returning any indictments, Judge Welch notified the military authorities that the Army's twelve prisoners were "entitled to release," but the War Department saw nothing wrong in continuing to hold the men for no reason other than a lawman's unsubstantiated hunch that they might have had something to do with the disturbance.

Two years before the Brownsville Raid, when some white soldiers had been involved in a shooting spree at Athens, Ohio, Secretary Taft had taken an avuncular interest in their case. They were rather like wards of the Government, he felt, and had made sure the men were given legal assistance. But no War De-

partment lawyers were sent to San Antonio to protect the rights
of the Government's black wards rounded up by Texas Ranger
Captain Bill McDonald.

While the twelve prisoners stared at the guardhouse walls
in Fort Sam Houston, the rest of the men were penned up at
Fort Reno, forbidden to leave the post. When they weren't marching up and down the drill field, they were working at fatigue or
walking a guard post. At night when they they crawled into their
bunks, they never knew just when they might be awakened by a
surprise inspection after the regular eleven-o'clock check roll call.

"Those men took all that without a murmur or a complaint of
any kind," Major Penrose later testified.

Throughout the battalion's dreary confinement at Fort Reno,
only five men were charged with breaking out of quarantine. All
five were court-martialed and dishonorably discharged. One of
the men who sneaked into town was a noncommissioned officer
who tried to beat the rap.

"He told me perfectly frankly what he went in town for,"
Major Penrose recalled, "and he begged to get out of it, and said
that he was anxious to stay in the service; and I said to him,
'Well, now, Corporal, I have but one rule in these matters, and
that is charges; but if you will tell me any man, or if you can find
out any man, or if you can get any clue that will lead to the
identity of any man or men connected with this deed, I will tear
these charges up. They will not be preferred against you.'"

"I swear before Almighty God I do not know anything about
this thing," the Corporal said, tears coming to his eyes.

Some of the battalion's officers, having been won over to the
official view of the soldiers' guilt, now began to wonder whether
the men might be telling them nothing simply because they had
nothing to tell. Major Penrose, however, still was unable to shake
off the nagging feeling that a small group of his men had banded
together to commit the crime. Finally, in late September, he
made what seemed to him a drastic proposal.

He suggested the lifting of all restrictions and the assignment
of a black detective to each of the three companies in the hope
that the men would relax, drink a few beers in town, and start

talking among themselves about the raid. If this stratagem failed to uncover the names of the raiders, the men should then be advised that the criminals among them would have to be identified by a certain date or twenty per cent of the three companies would be discharged. Thirty days later, if the guilty men were still at large, another twenty per cent would go. This process would continue until only twenty per cent of the men remained in uniform.

"The discharge of eighty per cent of the present strength is deemed excessive," General McCaskey thought, but on October 4 the Army's newly appointed Inspector General, Ernest A. Garlington, was ordered to deliver an even more extraordinary threat.

Unless the enlisted men with guilty knowledge "of the facts relating to the shooting, killing, and riotous conduct" of the black battalion reported "such facts and all other circumstances within their knowledge which will assist in apprehending the guilty parties," every soldier serving at Fort Brown on the night of the raid would be discharged without honor and would be forever debarred from federal employment in either a military or civilian capacity. This ultimatum, based on a recommendation by Major Blocksom, came directly from the President of the United States.

The Inspector General assumed from the outset that the shooting had been the work of a group of soldiers.

"You did not waste any time trying to find out whether or not someone else might possibly have done it?" he was asked some months later, and he replied, "I wasted no time; no sir."

After stopping off in Oklahoma City to discuss the case with Major Blocksom, the General proceeded to San Antonio to interview the prisoners at Fort Sam Houston. "I found several of them had lived in localities with which I was more or less familiar, one having lived at my own home,* and then subjected them to a rigid examination. As soon as the subject of the trouble at Brownsville was introduced the countenance of the individual being in-

* Private James W. Newton, C Company. The town was Greenville, South Carolina.

terviewed assumed a wooden, stolid look, and each man positively denied any knowledge of the circumstances connected with or individuals concerned in the affair."

A native South Carolinian, Garlington fancied himself something of an authority on Negroes. "I lived with them, played with them as a child, was brought up on large plantations with them," he liked to point out, and when he came to prepare his report, he drew on his expertise: "The secretive nature of the race, where crimes charged to members of their color are made, is well known."

"Now," Senator Foraker asked, "I would infer from your statement that the man who is himself charged with crime is secretive, if he be a colored man. . . . But why should another colored man, who is not charged with crime, who holds no responsibility for it, and who is being injured by it, be secretive about it?"

"I do not know why. I cannot explain that."

If a few soldiers, angered by acts of violence and discrimination, had jumped the garrison wall and shot up the town, as General Garlington believed when he arrived at Fort Reno, their comrades were obviously lying to him when they all insisted they had heard no barracks talk of retaliation against the townspeople. To some investigators, the men's unanimity on this point might have been interpreted as an indication of their innocence, but to this well-born white southerner it suggested "a possible general understanding" among the men as to the position they would take on the Brownsville affray. They had joined a "conspiracy of silence."

"They all insisted they had no knowledge?" Senator Foraker asked.

"Yes, sir."

"They all insisted that they had taken no part in the shooting?"

"Yes, sir."

"They all insisted that they did not know of anybody who had?"

"Yes, sir."

"Now, if they had been absolutely innocent, as some people are simple-minded enough to think they were, would you have expected them to say anything other or different from that which they did say?"

"Granting—yes; assuming the proposition as you state it: yes, sir."

When the soldiers failed to provide the information he needed to substantiate his assumptions, the Inspector General assembled all three companies on the Fort Reno parade ground for a showdown. It was Saturday morning and he intended to head back to Washington the next evening. Standing in the hollow of a U-shaped formation, he appealed to the men's pride in their regiment and in their individual service records, then concluded his remarks by reading aloud the orders he had received from the President.

Until nine o'clock the following morning, he announced, he would be available to any man who cared to come tell him what he knew about the raid. Only one soldier showed up. First Sergeant Mingo Sanders of B Company presented himself to the Inspector General to disclaim any knowledge of the affair and to declare his inability to gather any information about it. He had brought his enlistment records with him.

He had joined the Army in May 1881, when young Lieutenant Garlington was doing his bit to keep the Dakotas safe from Indian uprisings. "Character excellent; a faithful and reliable soldier," the records indicated when Sanders signed up for his second hitch in 1891. He had fought in Cuba and the Philippines, advancing from buck private to first sergeant in the company to which he had devoted twenty-six years of his life.

"Now, I am a poor man," Sanders said, pleading for a chance to serve out his time (two and a half years) and retire on three-quarters pay. "I served honest and faithful for the government . . ."

General Garlington was sympathetic but unyielding.

"They appear to stand together in a determination to resist the detection of the guilty; therefore they should stand together when the penalty falls," he declared in his report, and recommended that all the men be discharged without honor, including Sergeant Sanders.

"The men of long service and the good men seemed very

much cast down at the prospect of discharge without honor, but some of the younger ones didn't appear to care," said B Company's Private English. "The old men said it was tough to lose so many good years put in the service of the Government when they hadn't done anything, just because of a lot of scoundrels who had made all the trouble. I am sure there were plenty of us who would have told in a minute if they had even suspected any soldier of doing the shooting. Even at Fort Reno I could hear of neither gossip, rumor, nor suspicion directed against any man, and nothing could be found out."

As it developed later, when General Garlington testified before the Senate Military Affairs Committee, it really hadn't mattered what the soldiers said to him. He wouldn't have believed them anyway.

"Do you think colored people, generally, are truthful?" he was asked.

"No, sir; I do not."

"You would not believe their testimony ordinarily, even under oath, would you?"

"Where their own interest, or some special interest, was concerned. It depends entirely upon the circumstances."

"You think a colored man might testify truthfully about the weather, but that he would not testify truthfully about a crime?"

"He might have some difficulty in testifying about the weather."

12

". . . turned loose like mangy curs . . ."

THE GARLINGTON REPORT started through channels to the White House on October 22. It had been established "beyond reasonable doubt," the Inspector General stated, that soldiers had fired "into the houses of the citizens of Brownsville" and had subsequently failed to take advantage of their opportunity "to tell all that it is reasonable to believe they know concerning the shooting." Their punishment, innocent and guilty alike, should serve as "a forceful lesson" to fellow soldiers and as assurance to private citizens that "men wearing the uniform of the Army are their protectors, and not midnight assassins."

Ten days later, on the eve of the 1906 off-year elections, the report lay on the President's desk while he crunched the frost-covered ground around Pine Knot, Virginia, and bagged his first wild turkey ("I killed it dead," he wrote his son, Kermit, "and felt mighty happy as it came tumbling down thru the air"). Secretary Taft was out west, inspecting Army posts, campaigning for Republican congressional candidates, and giving local party leaders a chance to size up the affable mountain of a man who had come to be looked on as Roosevelt's hand-picked successor.

Taft still yearned for the center seat on the Supreme Court, but his wife saw no reason why he should bypass the White House on his way to the bench. While her mildly reluctant candidate stumped the west, Nellie Taft kept an eye on the President, a man she never learned to trust. To her distress, as she lost no time in informing her husband, Roosevelt had mentioned to her the probability of his having to back Charles Evans Hughes, currently a four-to-one favorite to become the next Governor of New York.

"Dear Will," the President wrote when he returned to the White House, "Mrs. Taft could not have told you that I might probably have to support Hughes for the Presidency. I do not think there is one chance in a thousand of it. What I said to her was that you must not be too entirely aloof because if you were it might dishearten your supporters."

On the same day—Monday, November 5—the President directed the War Department to carry out General Garlington's recommendations for the dismissal of the black battalion, but his decision was not made public until the following evening, after voters had elected Hughes and a Republican Congress. They had also returned Roosevelt's son-in-law, Nicholas Longworth, to the House of Representatives by a majority of about three thousand. Princess Alice's charming husband would not have made it back to Washington if half of the thirty-two hundred black voters in his Ohio district had voiced their outrage by defecting to the Democratic candidate.

"Negroes are not fools, at least not all of them, and this after-election order is well understood by them," declared the black editor of the Washington *Bee*, and he was echoed by the Waterville, Maine, *Sentinel*, "The picture of a President whose chief merit is supposed to lie in his fearless bravery dodging an issue like this one, until after the votes are counted, is not pleasant to look upon, even though it stamps him as a clever politician."

"The action was precisely such as I should have taken had the soldiers guilty of the misconduct been white men instead of colored men," Roosevelt stoutly maintained, but in Richmond, Virginia, black readers of the *Planet* were asked in a widely re-printed editorial to speculate on what would have happened if white soldiers had been charged with shooting up a Negro community. The editor doubted that they would have been booted out of the Army for failing to produce the culprits.

"If the troops had been white troops, nothing would have been said about my action," Roosevelt contended, and accused the Brownsville battalion of having taken a precipitate course "which cannot be tolerated in any soldiers, black or white, in any policeman, black or white, and which, if taken generally in the Army, would mean not merely that the usefulness of the Army was at an end but that it had better be disbanded in its entirety at once. Under no conceivable circumstances would I submit to such a condition of things."

Booker T. Washington, given advance notice of Roosevelt's decision, had tried to talk the President out of making what he felt to be a "blunder." Two weeks after the dismissal order was announced, the Tuskegee principal advised Secretary Taft, "I have never in all my experience with the race experienced a time when the entire people have the feeling that they now have in regard to the Administration."

"The Afro-American people present an unprecedented phenomenon of unity and resolution—their alienation from the President, once their idol, has been spontaneous, bitter, and universal," declared the New York *Age*, and from the pulpit of the Abyssinian Church of New York came the angry advice of the Reverend Charles S. Morriss, who urged his congregation to avenge the Administration's insult by working to elect a Democratic President in 1908. "Thus shall we answer Theodore Roosevelt, once enshrined in our love as our Moses, now enshrouded in our scorn as our Judas."

Roosevelt, as every black American knew, had got his accidental presidency off to a controversial start in the fall of 1901 by inviting Booker T. Washington to dinner.

"The most damnable outrage which has ever been perpetrated by any citizen of the United States was committed yesterday by the President, when he invited a nigger to dine with him at the White House," roared the Memphis, Tennessee, *Scimitar;* and the Richmond, Virginia, *Times* somehow got the notion that "it means the President is willing that Negroes shall mingle freely with whites in the social circle—that white women may receive attentions from Negro men."

"When Mr. Roosevelt sits down to dinner with a negro, he declares that the negro is the social equal of the White Man," declared the New Orleans *Times-Democrat* in a curious display of typographical prejudice, and "Pitchfork Ben" Tillman of South Carolina was quoted as saying, "The action of President Roosevelt in entertaining that nigger will necessitate our killing a thousand niggers in the South before they will learn their place again."

When the incident became a campaign issue in 1904, President Roosevelt welcomed the support he got on the hustings from Ohio's Senator Foraker, a Civil War veteran who felt that "the American people, instead of rebuking a man who had courage enough to recognize the equal rights of American citizens, would uphold and sustain and encourage him." No such sustenance and encouragement came the President's way. After making a halfhearted show of defending his high moral ground (he insisted he would have Dr. Washington "to dine just as often as I please"), Roosevelt quietly abandoned it. Never again did he ask a black man to break bread at the White House.

Roosevelt, Foraker wrote in his memoirs, "had relatives and friends in the South, and had a great admiration for the chivalric character of the Southern people, and no doubt felt keenly their almost universal criticism and the apparent loss of their friendship and good-will. No one can say this had anything to do with his action in discharging the colored soldiers, but it was doubtless quite agreeable to him to see his fierce enemies suddenly become warm friends."

"President Roosevelt is right," beamed the Atlanta *Constitution* in editorial approval of the punishment meted out to the black battalion. It would serve as "a warning to that racial instinct which has done so much to stir up strife and retard the progress of the Negro—the instinct which prompts the average Negro to protect the criminal at the expense of law, order and decency."

"The respectable colored people must learn not to harbor their criminals, but to assist the officers in bringing them to justice," Roosevelt solemnly warned.

Respectable colored readers of the Boston *Guardian* were given a somewhat different appraisal of just what it meant for one black man to turn another over to white authorities. "In the South it is to be an accomplice in the murder of one's own race until the South stops lynching and grants colored men fair trials. In the North it is unfair and ridiculous. Everywhere it endangers the personal safety of innocent colored persons. The President has put all law-abiding colored people in danger by giving presidential prestige to the notion."

Several editors, black and white, commented on a homely irony in Roosevelt's handling of the Brownsville affair. Only a few weeks before the soldiers were dismissed for not informing on their comrades, Theodore Roosevelt, Jr., had found himself in a similar fix in Boston. He and a fellow student at Harvard had been fleeing two policemen on the Common, when Roosevelt's companion had collided with one of the officers, broken the man's nose, and then escaped. Hauled off to the police station and asked to identify his friend, young Roosevelt had refused. His father, it was then suggested, would advise him to name the fugitive.

"I don't think he would," the youth had replied.

After sampling War Department reactions to the President's dismissal of the Brownsville soldiers, a Washington correspondent of the New York *Times* reported that most Army officers agreed "the men have only themselves to blame and are without ground to complain of injustice." None of the officers would say it out loud, the reporter continued, but many of them made whispered references to the change that had come over the Army's black regiments in the five years since the President had asked the olive-skinned Tuskegee principal to come have dinner with him.

"There is plenty of comment on that change," the *Times* man noted. "It is usually described as a strange development of 'cockiness' on the part of the men. It has occurred in each of the four Negro regiments, and has caused a lot of talk among Army officers."

The White House calmly accepted a hint of this sort of talk when it appeared in the closing line of Major Blocksom's report on the Brownsville Raid: "It must be confessed the colored soldier is much more aggressive in his attitude on the social equality question than he used to be." But the President exploded when the views expressed in the privacy of officers' club lounges cropped up in the public prints in the form of an interview attributed to an infantry colonel who had no use for Negro troops.

"I never liked them and the farther away from me they are kept the better it pleases me," Colonel William L. Pitcher, Twenty-seventh Infantry, was quoted as saying. "For the life of me, I cannot see why the United States should try to make soldiers out of them."

Roosevelt sent a newspaper clipping of the purported interview to the War Department. If the officer had been correctly quoted, he wrote, proceedings should be taken against him for conduct "but little better than that of the offending Negro troops themselves." Colonel Pitcher denied the statement attributed to him, but, the *Times* suggested, it "would be stamped by a literary critic as genuine on its inherent evidence."

By threatening to court-martial a high-ranking officer at the same time he was dismissing the black enlisted men, the Presi-

dent had given evidence "of his intention to be fair to the colored troops," a Washington *Post* reporter observed. He saw no
difference between the public trial the President was to accord
the officer and the punishment he had inflicted on men against
whom no charges had been filed or substantiated in any sort of
judicial proceeding.

In the report on which the President had based his action,
General Garlington had recognized the fact that the "extreme
penalty" he was recommending would fall on "a number of men
who have no direct knowledge of the identity" of the raiders.
The phrase caught the eye of A. E. Pillsbury, a Boston lawyer,
who doubted that even a Roman emperor would have punished
men "for not disclosing what they did not know, and therefore
could not have disclosed had they been willing to. They are not
punished for not telling who the offenders were, but for not
knowing who they were."

"The foundation of all discipline, either in the Army or Navy,
is justice," said Major General Daniel E. Sickles, a Union officer
who was no stranger to controversy (disobeying orders at Gettys-
burg) or to precipitate action (shooting and killing an admirer
of Mrs. Sickles). "You cannot maintain discipline without a feeling among the men that whatever happens they can expect justice, fair play, a square deal."

"If the Department had allowed the affair to go unpunished,"
explained Acting Secretary of War Robert Shaw Oliver, "the
result might have been disastrous, and the same troops might
again do the same thing."

When a reporter asked why no attempt had been made to get
at the facts of the affray through courts-martial, Oliver replied:
"A court-martial of any of the men was impossible. To try a man
it is necessary to have charges against him. There was no one
against whom direct charges could be filed."

Thus, with no chance to face their accusers or even to discover what accusations had been brought against them, the soldiers were, in the angry words of the Baltimore *Afro-American
Ledger*, "turned loose like mangy curs to go through the world
with the brand of Cain upon their brows."

The Politicians

———◆◆◆———

13

"He is too big a man to play the lackey."

ONCE HE HAD MADE HIS DECISION, Roosevelt went bounding off to Panama to check on the progress of his canal. "Goodbye," he shouted from the deck of the presidential yacht, "I am going down to see how the ditch is getting along." The next day the War Department released Special Orders No. 266 dismissing the three companies and forever debarring the men from serving their government either as soldiers or as civilians.

While the President sat in the aftercabin of the USS *Louisiana* reading Milton and Tacitus, his Secretary of War was out on the hustings absorbing the political shock waves radiating from the Brownsville decree. Kansas was lost, Taft learned from party leaders, and the already disheartening situation in the new state of Oklahoma, where Democrats had shown surprising strength, would now undoubtedly worsen. Local papers along his route carried reports of mass meetings in abolitionist New England and in such crucial states as New Jersey, Maryland, Indiana, and his native Ohio.

On Roosevelt's home grounds, where three newly re-elected Republican congressmen had large black constituencies, the New York County Committee of the Republican Party had agreed on a watered-down but still strongly worded resolution calling on the President to rescind his order.

"To measure the full significance of the County Committee's action," the New York *Age* pointed out in a front-page story, "one must remember that this committee is in a peculiar sense the President's own personal machine, and that its chairman, Congressman Herbert Parsons, is the man in New York State politics who stands closest to him."

The resolution had been presented by Gilchrist Stewart, a black committeeman who echoed editorial comparisons of Brownsville and the Dreyfus Affair when he declared race prejudice in the United States Army to be as pervasive as anti-Semitism in the French forces. Once he had pushed his resolution past the President's friends on the County Committee, Stewart took off for Fort Reno to investigate the raid on behalf of a civil rights organization, the Constitution League of the United States.

"Although rumors had been floating around Washington for several days before I left home that the President might take such drastic action, few believed he would do so," Mrs. Mary Church Terrell, president of the National Association of Colored Women, recalled some years later in her still-unpublished memoirs.

Mrs. Terrell was in New York preparing to take the morning train to Boston when she read about Roosevelt's order. In Boston she called on an old friend of the black people, Colonel Thomas Wentworth Higginson, who had chronicled his experiences with the First South Carolina Volunteers in *Army Life in a Black Regiment* (1870).

"When I commanded them in the South," the Colonel told Mrs. Terrell, "I feared that colored men would never learn to stick together and be loyal to each other, because they were so treacherous to representatives of their own race. But, if the colored soldiers really shot up Brownsville and they can be neither forced nor bribed to reveal who did it, they have taken a long step forward."

When she got back to Washington, Mrs. Terrell was delighted to find that a telephone had been installed in her home, but she didn't realize the strange new device was in working order until Saturday morning, November 17, when it rang around ten o'clock. It turned out to be a long-distance call from New York. John Milholland, the wealthy white sponsor of the Constitution League, wanted her to go over to the War Department and talk to Secretary Taft, who was due back at his desk that day.

Mrs. Terrell waited outside the Secretary's high-ceilinged office in the State, War, and Navy Building while Taft dug into a mass of indignant letters, telegrams, petitions, and resolutions. The unkindest cut of all came from the city of his birth. Cincinnati's Union Republican Club had condemned the President for his "despotic usurpation of power."

Finally, a few minutes before four o'clock, Taft's secretary ushered Mrs. Terrell into his massive presence. She had come on behalf of the colored soldiers, she said, and Taft asked, "What do you want me to do about it? President Roosevelt has already dismissed them and he has gone to Panama. There is nothing I can do."

"All I want you to do, Mr. Secretary, is to suspend the order dismissing the soldiers without honor until an investigation can be made."

"Is that *all* you want me to do?" he asked with what struck Mrs. Terrell as good-natured sarcasm. "*All* you want me to do is to suspend an order issued by the President of the United States during his absence from the country."

As a former federal judge with a hankering to be Chief Justice after he left the White House, Taft was inclined to move more judiciously than Roosevelt, who was not a lawyer. Also, as a leading candidate for President, the Secretary of War had still another compelling reason to proceed with caution. Looking back to the election of 1896, when McKinley beat Bryan by half a million votes, he could appreciate the influence of black Republicans.

If Bryan ran again in 1908, as seemed possible, Democrats stood to make impressive gains in states with large numbers of black adult males: Maryland (60,406), Missouri (46,414), New York (31,425), Ohio (31,325), New Jersey (21,474), Indiana (18,186), and Kansas (14,689). Unlike the retiring President, his heir presumptive was in no position to make white friends in the South at the expense of black votes in the North.

"I do not think he realizes quite the great feeling that has been aroused on the subject," Taft wrote his wife, and asked Roosevelt's secretary to send the President a confidential message. The text was not released to the press and was later withheld from the voluminous Brownsville file the War Department delivered to the Senate Military Affairs Committee.

"New York Republican Club and many others appealing for a suspension of the order discharging colored troops until your return that you may have a rehearing. . . . Much agitation on the subject and it may be well to convince people of fairness of hearing by granting rehearing.* The reports of the officers on which the action was founded will be published early next week."

Sunday, while black preachers around the country were fulminating against the President's decree, Taft was on his way to New Haven.

"Cable President that procedure of final discharge not completed and may be suspended," he telegraphed his private secretary from Baltimore, and from the West Philadelphia station, he sent a second message, "Cable President that discharge hardly begun and that order can be suspended."

* The men had received no "hearing." They had answered a few routine questions put to them under oath by Captain Lyon. Some had been interviewed at various times by Major Blocksom, Colonel Lovering, and General Garlington, but no formal proceedings of any kind had been afforded the soldiers before their summary dismissal without honor.

Both telegrams were sent to Roosevelt by wireless, the secretary reported, but the President had left Panama "some time last night." The next day, on his own initiative, Taft suspended the dismissal order. The New York *Times* could recall no precedent for the Secretary's action. The paper's Washington man took it to mean that "Mr. Taft has enlisted zealously in the cause of the discharged soldiers." He added a wry comment: "How Mr. Roosevelt will view it remains to be seen. He is not fond, as a rule, of having his subordinates cross him."

"Discharge is not to be suspended unless there are new facts of such importance as to warrant your cabling me," the President advised his Secretary of War on Wednesday, November 21, in a telegram from Ponce, Puerto Rico. "I care nothing whatever for the yelling of either the politicians or the sentimentalists. The offense was most heinous and the punishment I inflicted was imposed after due deliberation."

Taft's resignation was rumored in the press. "He is too big a man to play the lackey," declared the Minneapolis *Daily Tribune*, but even before Roosevelt dashed off his cablegram, Taft had decided against a direct confrontation. Deferring to the ancient wisdom of his calling, he had risen above principle after holding out from Sunday, when he suspended the President's order until Tuesday, when he ordered the military authorities to proceed with the discharge of the three companies.

"I think his order is fully sustained by the facts and the evidence, which I have read," Taft wrote Richard Harding Davis, "and it is quite embarrassing to me to have it thought that I differ with him on the subject."

As he had indicated to the President, Taft also released the official documents on which Roosevelt had based his decision.

"Their contents proved surprising," the New York *Times* reported. "It was found that no evidence had been gathered to prove a conspiracy on the part of the members of the battalion. The whole proceeding in fact was based on the assumption of the officers who made the inquiry that those who did not take part in the riot at Brownsville 'must know' who did." As for the Garlington report, the *Times* reporter found it "extraordinary." "Not a particle of evidence is given in the 112 pages of the document to prove that any enlisted man had certain knowledge of the identity of any of the participants in the riot."

"Soldiers in no conspiracy," Gilchrist Stewart wired Taft from Fort Reno, where he had been interviewing the men on behalf of the Constitution League. "Not allowed to present their side and investigation farce."

Inspector General Garlington had talked to only about thirty of the hundred and sixty-seven soldiers to be dismissed, Stewart had learned, and the General's line of questioning had been limited to his own assumptions about the raid, the men declared.

"If we started to say anything that tended to show the innocence of ourselves, he would say: 'All right, that's all for you.' Everybody who heard that shooting knows that there were dozens of shots fired that night that did not come from Army guns."

During Taft's absence from the War Department, the Military Secretary had taken the precaution of ordering a battalion of white soldiers to Fort Reno "under the command of discreet officer" to prevent any disturbance on the part of the black troops when they were discharged. The discreet officer turned out to be Major C. J. T. Clarke, Twenty-sixth Infantry, who had known Major Penrose for more than thirty years (they had gone to school together in Detroit). Clarke arrived at Fort Reno on Sunday, November 11.

The next day, ringed by white soldiers, the black infantrymen were subjected to the humiliating ceremony of surrendering their rifles. Some of the men were in tears, among them B Company's battle-toughened first sergeant, Mingo Sanders, who had carried an Army rifle for more than half of his fifty years.

"I feel sorry for them from the bottom of my heart," one of the battalion's white officers told a New York *Age* reporter. "I know they are innocent of any wrongdoing, and it looks pretty hard to them."

Stripped of their arms and soon to be sent packing, the men were still confined to the post, still subjected to daily drill and fatigue duty. Their appearance, Major Clarke remembered, was "very neat, very soldierly."

"I never experienced such sadness in my life," Private Boyd Conyers testified before the court inquiry. "We were fatigued there every day, and I believe if any man had been implicated in that shooting he would have told something about it. I know I would. If I had knowed anything about the shooting at that time I would certainly have told it, because I never experienced such sadness in my life among all the soldiers."

A snowstorm was raging when the first of the men were summoned to the adjutant general's office in groups of eight or ten, given their pay, their separation papers, and their travel fare back to what had once been home.

"They were orderly and well behaved," the New York *Times* reported, "and not one of them displayed an ugly feeling."

"Were there any actions of misbehavior after these men were discharged that came to your notice?" Major Clarke was asked at Major Penrose's court-martial.

"Not one."

"Did you take particular pains to look for that?"

"I did. Not only in and about the post, on the reservation, but I sent officers almost daily to the town of El Reno, five miles away, to find out if any men after they had been discharged were in the vicinity or in the town, and no disturbance of any kind was reported to me."

For the first time since their arrival in Oklahoma three months earlier, the men were free to explore and enjoy the worldly pleasures of El Reno. They hit town with anywhere from fifty to more than a thousand dollars in their pockets, but, despite the blandishments of loose women and hard liquor, not one of the men was picked up for drunk or disorderly conduct. Quietly they went their separate ways.

The incident was closed, President Roosevelt snapped when he bounded back to the White House on Tuesday morning, November 27, but he kept the Cabinet waiting half an hour while he discussed the case with two black admirers, Charles W. Anderson, New York City's suave, politically sure-footed Internal Revenue Service collector, and Emmett J. Scott, the private secretary of Booker T. Washington. Roosevelt listened attentively

(Scott read from a memorandum his employer had prepared for him), but refused to retreat unless new evidence was brought to him.

"There has been great pressure not only by sentimentalists but by the Northern politicians who wish to keep the Negro vote," he wrote later that day to Silas McBee, editor of *The Churchman*. "As you know I believe in practical politics, and where possible, I always weigh well any action which may cost votes before I consent to take it; but in a case like this, where the issue is not merely one of naked right and wrong but one of vital concern to the whole country. I will not for one moment consider the political effect."

At the other end of Pennsylvania Avenue, however, the political effect had not been lost on Senator Joseph Benson Foraker of Ohio. The President's handling of the Brownsville affair had not only given him a providential opportunity to serve the cause of justice but also a chance to settle his political accounts with Roosevelt, knock Taft out of contention for the presidency, and advance his own claim on the White House.

During the latter weeks of November, just before the Fifty-ninth Congress was to meet for its second session, Foraker was absorbed in the Brownsville case. Years later his widow remembered him "writing, wiring, sending men out to Texas to take sworn testimony, to secure exact details; spending hours and hours in a thickening jungle of newspapers, clippings, letters, and calf-bound books."

"We must not fail to have a full set of affidavits in the Brownsville matter when Congress meets," the President reminded his portly Secretary of War; and, knowing Senator Foraker's skill in conducting a floor debate, he emphatically added, "*Very important.*"

14

"There is more in this contest than a mere discussion of the Brownsville incident."

No ONE IN THE United States Senate was more thorough in preparing an argument or more eloquent in presenting it than Senator Foraker. A big-business lawyer before he became a big-business senator in 1897, he was committed to a philosophy of government that would leave his corporate clients beyond reach of federal interference, free to plunder and to grow. When an assassin's bullet catapulted Vice President Roosevelt into the White House in September 1901, Ohio's tall, silver-haired senior senator found himself in a strange and not always congenial new century.

"It is far pleasanter to go with the tide of public sentiment," he conceded to the crowded galleries one February afternoon six months before the Brownsville Raid, when he was making another forlorn effort to preserve the kind of laissez-faire world in which he had cut such a handsome swath.

To give the Interstate Commerce Commission power to control rates charged by railroads was a revolutionary and unconstitutional proposal, he argued in opposition to the Hepburn rate bill. If this Administration proposal were adopted, he warned, it would eventually bring every other kind of business under the thumb of a government agency. Privately, many of his conservative Republican colleagues shared his apprehensions, but shrank from taking a public stand against their impetuous, short-tempered President, especially on a measure so popular with the electorate. When the bill was finally brought to a vote in mid-May, Foraker was the only senator on his side of the chamber to join two Alabama Democrats in saying nay.

Back home, the Cincinnati *Enquirer* praised him for voting his convictions "in an adverse sea." In New York, readers of the

Sun were reminded that the Senator's lonely, losing battle had not been "a pleasant experience for a proud and a sensitive man." "Foraker in the Senate has always been against the people," a muckraker snorted, and it was generally agreed that he had destroyed whatever remote chance he might have had of becoming the Republican candidate for President in 1908.

"He is a very powerful and very vindictive man," Roosevelt wrote Senator Henry Cabot Lodge a few months afterward, "and he is one of the most unblushing servers and beneficiaries of corporate wealth within or without office that I have ever met. It is possible that he has grown to feel so angry over my course, that is over my having helped rescue the Republican party and therefore the country from the ruin into which, if he had had his way, it would have been thrown by the party being made to appear as simply an appanage to Wall Street—that he intends hereafter to fight me on every point, good or bad."

A few weeks after Senator Foraker celebrated his sixtieth birthday, on July 5, 1906, he came across a brief news item about some Negro soldiers who had leaped a garrison wall on the Texas border and shot up the town of Brownsville. He had no reason to question the story's accuracy.

"I knew there was a prejudice throughout the South against colored soldiers," he recalled in his memoirs. "I supposed there had been on this account more or less nagging of the men and that they, in an effort to revenge their wrongs, had been guilty of the outrages perpetrated."

But in November, after the President dismissed the three companies of black infantrymen, Foraker began to examine the testimony on which the decision had been based and found it "flimsy, unreliable and insufficient and untruthful." As he dug more deeply into the case, his wife heard him muttering to himself, "No, that isn't true. . . . That doesn't follow at all. . . . No, no, there is nothing in that . . ."

On Monday, December 3, when the Fifty-ninth Congress convened, it was no secret that Senator Foraker planned to ask for an investigation of the Brownsville matter. Although he had no intention of disrupting the holiday atmosphere of opening day, when custom prohibited the transaction of any business other than the adoption of certain ceremonial resolutions, he happened to have a draft of his proposal in his pocket when he made his way into the Senate chamber. His secretary had handed it to him as he left his office.

When Vice President Fairbanks called the Senate to order at high noon, seventy-eight senators answered the roll call and unanimously agreed that the President and the House of Representatives should be officially notified that the United States Senate was once again in business. Suddenly, to the astonishment of senators and spectators alike, Boies Penrose of Pennsylvania shattered precedent by springing up with a resolution requesting the President to supply "full information" on the dismissal of the Negro soldiers "if not incompatible with the public interests." The bill had been cooked up by the Administration to forestall any more drastic and embarrassing proposal that Foraker might have in mind.

The Vice President hardly had time to recover his composure and ask if there were any objections to considering the Penrose bill before Foraker was on his feet, fumbling through his pockets for the draft of his own resolution, which he now presented as a substitute measure. It was addressed to the Secretary of War rather than to the President and, instead of a polite request to provide material deemed suitable for Senate study, it *directed* the Secretary to furnish *all* of the Brownsville records ("letters, telegrams, reports, orders, etc.")

Foraker clipped and saved a Dayton (Ohio) *Evening News* editorial expressing admiration for the way the state's "wily old Senator" had taken "the bark from under the President and left him hanging by the claws." Had Roosevelt succeeded in putting across the Penrose proposal, he would have dictated just what Brownsville material would be sent to the Senate. By anticipating this gambit, the editorial writer pointed out, Foraker had not only laid claim to all of the data in the War Department's files but had also clearly won the first round of his fight with the President.

Secretary Taft parried by leaking to the press that section of the War Department's annual report which dealt with the dis-

missal of the three companies. No matter what private reserva-
tions he might have about the President's action, Taft now declared it to be "fully sustained by the facts." To a sympathetic
biographer, his reasoning suggested a "temporary atrophy of the
judicial lobes of his brain."

With no facts to prove the involvement of a single soldier in
either the disturbance or the suspected conspiracy of silence to
shield its perpetrators, Taft concurred with Roosevelt in the
opinion that "the only means of ridding the military service of a
band of would-be murderers of women and children, and actual
murderers of one man, is the discharge of the entire battalion."

By arguing the proposition that when no one man can be
proved guilty of a crime, every man in the outfit must pay the
penalty for it, the Administration had raised its standard on
ground already overrun by Dan Sickles. "This country is not
Turkey," the old general had growled. "It is not a place where,
if trouble occurs, everybody in the vicinity is clapped into jail
and the heads of fifty men are cut off in order to be sure to get
the head of the guilty one."

Roosevelt, on December 19, sent to the Senate a message on
the Brownsville affray which demonstrated to Foraker that "he
was irritated and full of the spirit of indignant resentment that
the rightfulness of his action had been questioned." Other senators, according to the Washington *Post*, marveled at its "virility
of language and forcefulness of expression."

As the *Post* made clear, "there is more in this contest than a
mere discussion of the Brownsville incident. A far greater stake
is being played. Should an investigation by the Senate show that
a grave injustice has been done the members of this battalion,
the outcome would lessen the great prestige the President now
has before the country, and would necessarily cause Senator
Foraker to loom as a much greater factor politically than he is
today."

The significance of his attack lay in the power it might give
him when the Republicans met to choose their presidential nom-
inee for the 1908 campaign. Even if he had no hope of getting the
nomination himself, Foraker could conceivably use Brownsville

to maneuver himself into a position that would enable him to prevent Roosevelt from naming his successor.

"The Negro vote cast in a Republican national convention is the greatest asset a politician can have," explained the New York *Times*. "The Negroes will insist upon representation in every Southern delegation. Where they are denied they will contest. Their full representation would give them a larger vote than New York and the New England states combined."

The bare-knuckled, eye-gouging personal nature of the political battle Roosevelt intended to wage was apparent in one of the opening paragraphs of his message, when he commented on the efforts that had been made to discredit the Garlington report because the Inspector General happened to be a native of South Carolina. In a low blow aimed at Foraker, Roosevelt observed that Major Blocksom, the first War Department investigator to pronounce the soldiers guilty of the raid, was "a native of Ohio."

"If there is a man from Ohio in the Army who, unfortunately, beyond any other, was unfitted for this special work, it was Major Blocksom," Foraker reported, and read aloud a letter he had received from a constituent who knew the Blocksom family.

During the Civil War, it seems the Major's father had been one of Zanesville's most outspoken Copperheads. As a young Union soldier, Foraker had seen these Vallandigham Democrats at political rallies, parading their women beneath banners that read: SAVE US FROM NIGGER HUSBANDS. Major Blocksom's background helped explain why he had ended his Brownsville report with a curiously irrelevant comment on the increasing aggressiveness with which black soldiers were pressing the social equality question.

"Major Blocksom's report is most careful, is based upon the testimony of scores of eyewitnesses," the President insisted.

This meant that the Major had drawn on the testimony of at least forty eyewitnesses, but, as Foraker discovered when he counted them, only twenty-one persons had appeared before Captain Kelly's committee of influential citizens. Of these, only eight could qualify as actual eyewitnesses and their unsworn statements seemed to Foraker "loose, conflicting, disjointed, and contradictory." To Roosevelt, the same evidence proved "conclusively" that "the soldiers were the aggressors from start to finish."

"The act was one of horrible atrocity," the President declared, "and, so far as I am aware, unparalleled for infamy in the annals of the United States Army."

Never in the memory of old Senate hands had a presidential message been dissected with such clinical precision and thoroughness. Foraker took it apart statement by statement, as senators on both sides of the aisle sat transfixed. When the House adjourned, Speaker Cannon ambled over to the Senate chamber to hear the closing arguments. Representative Longworth was also there, listening attentively to the neat, surgical dismemberment of his father-in-law's case against the black battalion.

First came the question of whether a few soldiers had banded together to terrorize the town, and then the question of whether others had joined a conspiracy of silence to conceal the criminals. On the first point, Foraker countered the testimony of the town's eight eyewitnesses by citing the sworn statements of the sentinel who fired the first warning shots, the sergeant of the guard who gave the alarm, and the enlisted men who sprang from their bunks, waited for the gun racks to be unlocked, and then answered a roll call taken by their noncommissioned officers under the direct supervision of four white officers, each of whom had run to the area of the men's quarters while the ten-minute spree was still in progress.

"Does any man believe," Foraker asked, "that fifteen or twenty men, who had been off engaged in an excitement of that character, shooting up the town, trying to murder people, rushing back under such circumstances, could get into camp, could join their commands, in the very presence of the noncommissioned officers and the commissioned officers also, and avoid being detected in doing so?"

On the second point—the conspiracy of silence—Foraker simply quoted from the Inspector General's report. General Garlington had assumed from the soldiers' refusal (or "inability," as the Senator argued) to identify the raiders that they had entered into a "possible" understanding among themselves to remain silent, but, he had admitted, he had found "no evidence" of such an understanding. Thus, in dismissing the great majority of soldiers for their participation in the so-called "conspiracy of silence," the President had acted not on the basis of "conclusive evidence," as he claimed, but, as his Inspector General's report bluntly admitted, on the basis of "no evidence."

"People have spoken as if this discharge from the service was a punishment," Roosevelt had reported. "I deny emphatically that such is the case, because as punishment it is utterly inadequate. The punishment meet for mutineers and murderers such as those guilty of the Brownsville assault is death; and a punishment only less severe ought to be meted out to those who have aided and abetted mutiny and murder and treason by refusing to help in their detection."

"Mr. President," Foraker said in reply, "we will agree that, if these men committed this atrocious offense, the punishment of being discharged without honor is inadequate; if they deliberately committed murder, the punishment appropriate is death, as the President says; and if their comrades deliberately were guilty of misprision of felony in refusing to give testimony as to the facts of which they had knowledge, they committed a crime punishable with imprisonment in the penitentiary for three years. So the President is right in saying that the punishment he has imposed is inadequate.

"But, Mr. President, punishment does not have to be adequate to be punishment. It is punishment although it may be grossly inadequate if measured by the character of the offense. If these men committed murder, as charged, the punishment is inadequate. If they were innocent of murder and innocent of misprision of felony, then is the punishment of a discharge without honor grossly exaggerated, harsh, and brutal, for in that case they would not have committed any crime and yet be severely punished."

Roosevelt's secretary, two days before Congress convened, had asked the War Department to look up some precedents for the President's order. Even though the Military Secretary had failed to find one in the history of the Regular Army, the President informed the Senate that "there are plenty of precedents for the action taken." He made irrelevant references to Grant and Lee, neither of whom had operated under existing ground rules. In passing, Roosevelt aimed another low blow at Ohio's senior senator.

"The Sixtieth Ohio," the President declared, "was summarily discharged on the ground that the regiment was disorganized, mutinous, and worthless."

As Roosevelt must have expected, Foraker cried out in rage and pain at this slur on his Highland County neighbors, who had seen some lively action against Stonewall Jackson in the Shenandoah Valley before they were overwhelmed at Harpers Ferry. The survivors had been taken prisoner, then exchanged. While in Chicago waiting to be released from service, some of the one-year volunteers had vented their boredom and frustration in minor disorders, but all had been honorably discharged, Foraker informed the President, and most of them had immediately signed up for a full three-year hitch.

"I knew the men of the Sixtieth Ohio," said the ex-brevet captain of the Eighty-ninth Ohio, who had tried to join the outfit when he was fifteen. "There were no better men in the Union Army."

The day after Foraker delivered his devastating attack on the President's message, Roosevelt went into a huddle with Secretaries Root and Taft, the two ablest lawyers in his Cabinet. Both men, it was understood, advised him to obtain sworn testimony to refute the Senator. Roosevelt responded by ordering Milton D. Purdy, Assistant to the Attorney General, to join Major Blocksom in Brownsville for a more legally satisfactory investigation of the raid.

"He admits that his case needs bolstering," crowed the New York *World*.

Foraker refused to be drawn into a public debate on this new development, but, he pointed out, it certainly lent credence to his contention that the President had proceeded without proper or convincing evidence. Another Ohio lawmaker, Representative Martin L. Smyser, had come to the same conclusion after taking advantage of the Christmas recess to examine the Brownsville testimony. He found it "flimsy and incomplete." If he were defending the soldiers in court, he said, "it would be the easiest thing in the world to secure their acquittal."

The Administration, however, was more intent on acquitting the President than the soldiers. The federal bureaucracy, lumbering to his defense, drew on the resources of three different executive departments. While War and Justice were represented by Major Blocksom and Mr. Purdy, who normally handled antitrust matters, Treasury's Secret Service agents were furtively at work, ransacking Brownsville for proof of what Roosevelt insisted had already been conclusively proved.

"I suppose you noted the fact that the President has sent Secret Service men down to Brownsville to work up the case against the colored soldiers," a Washington correspondent for the Cleveland *Leader* wrote Foraker. "Doubtless he has overlooked the fact that in the appropriation bill passed last winter Congress specified explicitly that the Secret Service men were to be used for the detection of counterfeiters and for protecting the life and person of the President, and for no other purpose. Perhaps he will contend, however, that in using them to strengthen his case against the Negro troopers he is using them to protect himself against you."

While Government investigators in Brownsville were questioning townspeople behind closed doors, giving the accused soldiers no opportunity to confront or cross-examine the witnesses against them, Senator Foraker was at work in the office of his four-story yellow-brick mansion on the northwest corner of Sixteenth and P Streets.

"We haven't a great many friends now upon whom we can lean," wrote the Reverend Francis J. Grimke, thanking Foraker for having extended his strong arm to lean upon." Washington's distinguished black churchman also declared that "any exercise of arbitrary and despotic power on the part of the President ought to be checked," and Foraker agreed that no American citizen, black or white, soldier or civilian, should be convicted of a crime and punished by executive fiat without any sort of hearing.

The Senator was reminded of the reply Festus made to the Jews when they called for Paul's blood: "It is not the manner of the Romans to deliver any man to die, before that he which is accused have the accusers face to face, and have licence to answer for himself concerning the crime against him."

This was the law in the time of Agrippa; it was still the law on the eve of the one thousand nine hundred and sixth anniversary of the beginning of the Christian era, Roosevelt being consul.

15

"The testimony of a great number of witnesses has been rather unsatisfactory . . ."

TWO DAYS AFTER Congress recessed for the Christmas holiday, word came from Fort Reno that Captain Macklin, the officer who had been so mysteriously slow in making an appearance on the night of the raid, had been shot twice and severely wounded by a masked Negro believed to have been one of the men dismissed by the President's order. Again Roosevelt's temper flared up before all the facts had been put at his disposal. White House visitors, the New York *Times* noted, found him in "an astonishing frame of mind," his anger "raised to the white hot pitch" by this fresh outburst of violence.

Later, when Macklin was out of danger, it was learned that his assailant had not belonged to one of the three disgraced companies and the motive had been robbery, not revenge, but by this time the President had been reported ready to invite impeachment proceedings rather than back down on his Brownsville decision. If Congress tried to resore the men to duty, he was heard threatening, he would veto the bill, and if it was then passed over his veto, he would seek some administrative means to block its execution.

Meanwhile, the President was still brooding over a remark let drop by Senator Nathan B. Scott during the Senate debate on the Foraker resolution.

"If I am correctly informed as to the history of the Spanish-American War," the West Virginia Republican had commented, "it is reported that if it had not been for the gallant and courageous action of the Tenth Regiment of Cavalry at the battle of San Juan we might not now have the privilege of having in the White House that brave soldier and 'square deal' and patriotic President of ours. As I understand, had it not been for the gallantry of the Tenth Regiment of Cavalry, a colored regiment, at that battle there might not have been a sufficient number of Rough Riders left to tell the tale."

On Christmas Eve, in a letter "not for publication," Roosevelt informed the Senator that "no incident remotely resembling it ever happened." It was true, he explained, that his regiment had been brigaded with the Tenth Cavalry and the outfits had frequently fought side by side, but "no one of them was ever helped out of a scrape by another."

The next morning the President's famous teeth must have gnashed when he opened the New York *Times* and discovered a front-page story on Mingo Sanders, who, in the opinion of some unnamed Republicans, had "a better record as a soldier" than Roosevelt. The former first sergeant of Company B had come to Washington to apply in person for re-enlistment. He was not invited to the White House, even though he had once placed its illustrious occupant in his debt; Sanders had shared his company's hardtack with Colonel Roosevelt and his men when they met in Cuba on June 25, 1898.

The President and his wife began their sixth Christmas in the White House by sitting on a bed with their children opening presents, as Roosevelt had done in his own childhood. In the afternoon he took a walk with Cabot Lodge, who stayed on for a family dinner. At some time during the day, plotting un-Christian vengeance, the President got off a letter to Booker T. Washington, asking him to send over a couple of politically acceptable blacks. He wanted to use them to bait Ohio's senior senator.

"Can you give me the names of one or two first-class colored men," Roosevelt wrote, "good Republicans and who are in addition men of the highest standard, who live in Ohio, and whom I could appoint to office in that State—men who would, for instance, be up to the standard of an internal revenue collectorship? I should prefer a first-class colored man around Cincinnati . . ." *

Cincinnati was, of course, Foraker's hometown, and Taft's as well.

Roosevelt was acutely sensitive to any suggestion that the dismissed soldiers had been dealt with so harshly because they were black.

"Officers or enlisted men, white men or colored men, who were guilty of such conduct, would have been treated in precisely the same way," he insisted, but not until a month after he had ordered the black enlisted men discharged did the President direct Secretary Taft to make a "thoro investigation" (he was still plumping for simplified spelling) to determine whether their white commissioned officers "are or are not blamable."

A few days later, on December 14, the War Department announced that Major Penrose and Captain Macklin would be court-martialed on charges of having violated the Sixty-second Article of War. The regulation, which covered noncapital crimes, applied to both officers and enlisted men. It also provided for "a regimental, garrison, or field officers' court-martial," but no such trial had been given the enlisted men.

Dishonored and dispersed by presidential decree, the black infantrymen had been denied not only due process but also equal protection of the laws. Two of their white officers were to have their day in court, as Article Sixty-two stipulated, and the other three officers who were at Fort Brown on the night of August 13 (Lyon, Grier, and Lawrason) were to go scot free. In short, a

---

* "The most damaging thing to me anyone can do is to give the impression that in what I have been trying to do for the Negro I have been actuated by political motives," President Roosevelt had advised a member of the National Republican Committee on March 13, 1903.

white company commander was not to be held as strictly accountable for the discipline and conduct of his men as a black first sergeant.

Noncommissioned officers, the President had stated in his first Senate message on the Brownsville affair, were responsible for "the discipline and good conduct" of their men, and as far as discipline was concerned, they filled "a part that the commissioned officers are of course unable to fill, although the ultimate responsibility for the discipline can never be shifted from the shoulders of the latter." But, despite this "ultimate responsibility," three white commissioned officers were to be spared after every black noncommissioned officer had already been sacked.

"The President and I have both assumed," Secretary Taft admitted privately on December 30, "that the noncommissioned officers had opportunities for learning the facts from the men which ought to have enabled them to ferret them out, or at least to give evidence which would have led to their discovery."

But, as Mingo Sanders explained to the War Department, if the men had any incriminating information to hide, they would be just as likely to withhold it from their black NCOs as from their white commissioned officers. To a black youngster from some red-clay country road, power is power, no matter whether it is exercised by a white man who went to West Point or by a hard-nosed black sergeant who fought in Cuba and the Philippines.

"They were excellent," Major Penrose said, when asked about his noncommissioned officers, and Brigadier General Andrew S. Burt concurred. "They were a class of men that you could give an order to and turn your back and not have to observe them at all and you would know that that order would be carried out in the spirit and the letter."

General Burt had commanded the Twenty-fifth Infantry for ten years. He was the regiment's colonel when the men left Missoula, Montana, on a spring day in 1898, the first outfit to be called up for the war in Cuba. Along their embarkation route, skeptical southerners used to ask, "Will those niggers really fight?" Years later, in retirement, the old general's face would flush as he repeated his stock answer, "Fight, did you say? Why they would charge into hell, fight their way out, and drag the devil out by the tail."

On his arrival in Washington Sergeant Sanders went to see his old commanding officer.

"Now, Sanders," General Burt said, man to man, "we are here alone; tell me all about it."

"General, I will tell you all I know," the Sergeant replied. "So far as I know, our men were not in it. I tried to find out. I tried to find out if they were in it, and I am satisfied, sir, that they were not in it. I tried all I knew how."

Later, when asked about Sanders, the General said, "There is no better first sergeant in the United States Army than Sergeant Mingo Sanders. His veracity, as he sees a thing, is beyond question."

Sergeant Samuel W. Harley, C Company's acting first sergeant on the night of the shooting, made a similarly favorable impression on the New York *Times* reporter who interviewed him at the home of the pastor of the Abyssinian Baptist Church in early December.

"He is well set up and soldierly in appearance," the *Times* man noted. "Dressed quietly, in good clothes, he looks a self-respecting man, whose word can be relied on."

The sergeant had spent three years in the Ninth Cavalry before joining the Twenty-fifth Infantry in 1894. In Cuba, at the battle of El Caney, a brass fragment from a Remington bullet had torn the knuckle from one of the fingers of his left hand.

"They said 'we must have known' who made the trouble in Brownsville, but we did not know, and we did everything we could to find out," Sergeant Harley declared, and, speaking as a combat veteran, he agreed with Sergeant Sanders that the gunfire he heard that August night did not have the sharp sound of the Army's new Springfield rifle.

"It was more like the reports of six-shooters and Winchesters," he said.

Any such reference to six-shooters and Winchesters outraged members of Brownsville's Anglo-Saxon minority and the scattering of socially acceptable Mexicans who mingled with them. It

was bad enough for an unoffending town to be the victim of
what the Brownsville *Daily Herald* called "a premeditated, cold-
blooded raid," but it was intolerable to have lived through such
an attack only to be accused of having staged it.

Before Mr. Purdy left his Justice Department desk to spend
the latter part of the holiday season in Brownsville with Major
Blocksom, Secretary Taft drew up a list of instructions for the
two investigators. They were to go about their business as ex-
aminers seeking the truth rather than as prosecutors trying men
under indictment, he said, and they were not to be influenced
by the President's conclusion as to the facts of the case.

"If the President's conclusion in the matter is wrong," Taft
declared, "he earnestly desires to be set right."

Should the President turn out to have erred, however, the
investigators could set him right only by producing evidence that
would clear the soldiers and condemn the War Department for
leading the Administration into a massive political blunder. This
is not what the Secretary of War had in mind, as he let slip in a
letter to Purdy, asking him to check the Miller Hotel room occupied by Hale and Ethel Odin of San Antonio on the night of
the shooting.

The Odins had been quoted in the public prints as having
seen the raiders and identified them as black soldiers. Taft
wanted Purdy to find out just what lights were on in the hotel
at the time, especially in the Odins' upstairs room. "This," he
explained, "is for the purpose of ascertaining whether the Odins
had an opportunity for distinguishing the soldiers." If the Secretary of War had not prejudged the case, he would have asked
Purdy to find out whether the Odins were in a position to distinguish "the raiders," not "the soldiers."

"I have talked with a great many of the prominent citizens
of Brownsville," Purdy wrote the Secretary on Sunday, December 30, after spending three days in town, "and, while they know
nothing concerning the shooting on that particular night, they all
ridicule the idea that it was done by persons other than the
soldiers in the garrison."

Purdy was happy to report that he had already accumulated

"ample evidence to prove that the soldiers were responsible for the shooting up of the town," but, unfortunately, "the testimony of a great number of witnesses has been rather unsatisfactory for the reason that, in most cases, they were so frightened by the shooting that instead of trying to find out who was doing the shooting, they were looking for some place of safety."

In line with Taft's instructions, Purdy collected some seventeen photographs showing the town-fort relationship and establishing the location of the Cowen-Miller Hotel alley and the various buildings struck by the raiders' bullets. He also picked up a certified copy of the coroner's inquest proceedings on the death of Frank Natus, the Miller Hotel guest register for August 13, and a letter written by Judge Parks to his wife on the Wednesday following the raid.

Although Purdy realized the letter "would not be admissible on the trial of a cause in any court of justice," he forwarded it to the War Department because of its "unusual weight and importance." The judge was occupying a second-floor room at the Leahy Hotel annex on the night of the shooting. A couple of weeks later he tumbled to his death from the same window through which he had peered out at the disturbance.

"It is supposed," Mayor Combe explained, "that Judge Parks went over the river and libated too much, and that when he came back he sat in the window to cool himself and fell out."

From this window, Judge Parks wrote his wife, he "saw the whole thing, but could not tell they were shooting in the house, and I had no arms whatever to do anything with, and if I had done anything they would have stormed the hotel and killed everyone in it." Nowhere in his account of this "fearful night" did the judge mention having recognized the raiders as black soldiers. His letter simply reflected the common assumption that some soldiers had shot up the town because they had not been allowed "to drink at saloons beside the white people" and in some instances had been pistol-whipped "for very trivial cause."

Herbert Elkins, the seventeen-year-old confectionery-store employee occupied the room next door to Judge Parks, was certain he had seen "anywhere from eight to fifteen" Negro soldiers. When he was first awakened by the shots, he told Purdy and

Blocksom, he rushed to the window, "but I could not see any-
thing for four or five minutes, then I saw two Negro soldiers."
They were in the alley between Elizabeth and Washington
Streets, just east of the Cowen house.

"And you state positively that they were colored soldiers?"

"Yes. I could see them plainly."

"What light was there in the vicinity of the Cowen house?"

"None, unless there was one at the corner; but it was not
very dark."

The night was so dark that Army officers accustomed to night
maneuvers were unable to identify their men at a distance of a
dozen paces, but not only had young Elkins recognized these two
men and, later, other raiders as Negro soldiers at a distance of
from thirty to forty paces, he had even been able to identify the
color of their trousers (yellow khaki) and, in one instance, a
summer Army shirt (blue).

An editorial writer for the Brownsville *Daily Herald*, who
was within earshot of the raiders, stated that they were "remarkably quiet" and spoke to one another "in suppressed tones," but
Elkins swore he heard their voices distinctly. He particularly remembered the voice of a man who called out a warning to the
others to avoid a mud puddle across the alley from the Cowens'
house.

"Do you know whether or not it was the voice of a colored
person?"

"Yes, sir; it sounded like a Negro's voice, though it was not
as coarse as some I have heard."

Hale and Ethel Odin were occupying a second-floor room at
the Miller Hotel with their five children on the night of August 13. Neither of them had testified before Captain Kelly's
committee or before the grand jury, but Mrs. Odin had signed
a statement which included the line: "I went to the raised window and looked out and saw a number of Negro soldiers, about
twelve in number." Mrs. Odin had also made the demonstrably
false statement: "It was a very bright moonlight night."

Since then, after repeated recitations of what they had seen
and heard, the Odins had adjusted discrepancies in their recol-

lections of the raid. By the time Purdy and Blocksom caught up with them in San Antonio on January 4, they were like seasoned performers who had honed a successful act and saw no reason to change it. They showed up for their interview with a prepared statement and balked at departing from their script.

Finally, Purdy reported to Taft, they agreed "to give their testimony from memory, but it seemed to me that they were anxious to be guided in giving it by the written statement which they had prepared." Mr. Odin struck Purdy as a very opinionated man of extraordinary intelligence who dominated his wife absolutely.

Mr. Odin, as Taft might have expected from such a characterization, was a shade too precise in his account of the raid. It began at 11:55 P.M., lasted "about twelve minutes," and was carried out by black soldiers "dressed in brown uniforms and a broad-brimmed soft hat." One of the soldiers, a large Negro, was freckled. Mrs. Odin had seen the same "speckle-faced Negro." At the time the shooting began, Mr. Odin was "sitting in the alley window." He counted "about sixty shots" before the raiders came into view, and remembered exactly how many men were in the first wave of the attack.

"I counted six Negro soldiers, three abreast in two columns, with one soldier running alongside, who stopped, crossed the alley opposite our windows, and one large Negro soldier gave the order, 'Halt!' and said 'There he goes; shoot!' and they fired a volley. Immediately one other Negro soldier joined them from the same direction from which the other seven had come. Then there were four more Negro soldiers followed and joined the other eight, these four coming also from the direction of Fort Brown through the alley."

Certain details of the Odins' testimony, Purdy confided to Taft, might "impress you as it has impressed me—unfavorably." However, he was satisfied that "the Odins saw and recognized the men who did the shooting as Negro soldiers." No reference was made to a significant point raised by both Mr. and Mrs. Odin. They swore they had seen the raiders using revolvers, a weapon readily available to the townspeople but not to the soldiers.

In reviewing the Purdy-Blocksom material for the President, Taft admitted that "Mrs. Odin's statements bear evidence of being affected by conversations with her husband, and there is somewhat suspicious agreement as to exact details between their two statements," but in his effort to reconstruct the crime, the Secretary of War not only made full use of the couple's testimony, he even distorted it.

"Mr. and Mrs. Odin heard the shooting at the *barracks*," * he stated, intruding an incriminating word neither of them had used.

Mr. Odin testified that the first shots came from "down the alley, toward Fort Brown." Mrs. Odin agreed. "The shooting commenced toward the fort." Nothing was said about "barracks," which would have placed the first shots inside the garrison wall rather than on the town side, where the soldiers swore the shooting originated.

Obviously, if any shots had been fired from a barracks, the men of that company would have known about it. The soldiers of all three companies had denied such knowledge under oath. This body of evidence had to be weighed against the testimony of four or five townspeople who claimed to have seen flashes of gunfire coming from the men's quarters. It took Secretary Taft twelve printed pages to sum up the evidence given by the townspeople. One curt paragraph sufficed to brush aside the sworn statements of more than a hundred and fifty soldiers.

In submitting the Purdy-Blocksom report to the Senate on January 14, 1907, Roosevelt declared that the additional evidence made it "likely that there were very few, if any, of the soldiers dismissed who could have been ignorant of what occurred." The report, in his view, "renders it impossible to question the conclusion on which my order was based." He retreated on only one point. He revoked as invalid that part of his order which had debarred the soldiers from all civil employment with the Government.

Along with sixty-three affidavits gathered by Purdy and Blocksom, the President sent the Senate "a bandoleer, 33 empty

* Emphasis added.

shells, 7 ball cartridges, and 4 clips picked up in the streets of Brownsville within a few hours after the shooting." The bullets could have been fired only by the Army's new Springfield rifle, a weapon which had been in use by American troops for a few months before the raid. This particular rifle, as the President made clear, was "not in the possession of private citizens," but, like his Secretary of War, he paid no attention to the revolvers seen by the Odins and heard on both sides of the garrison wall by, among others, Mayor Combe, Major Penrose, and Sergeant Sanders.

The shells and bullets alone would be conclusive evidence of the soldiers' guilt, the President argued, even if fourteen eye-witnesses had not seen the assailants and identified them as Ne-gro soldiers. One of the fourteen was Paulino Preciado, who had assured Purdy that the men who wounded him and killed the Ruby Saloon's bartender were Negro soldiers, but Preciado had neglected to make such an identification in earlier testimony. In the meantime, however, he had filed a ten-thousand-dollar suit against the Federal Government for the injuries he claimed to have suffered in the raid. Thus, it was to his interest to prove that the shots were fired by the Government's soldiers, not by the town's roughnecks.

The other eyewitnesses included Mrs. Odin, Judge Parks, an elderly man blind in one eye and with impaired vision in the other, a terror-stricken young Mexican girl, and a locomotive engineer who had peeked out of a third-floor window of the Miller Hotel just long enough to recognize a couple of raiders as Negroes. Their black faces could be readily distinguished on a moonless night, he said, but admitted that it had been too dark for him to tell what color clothing they were wearing.

Police Lieutenant Dominguez testified that he had first seen the raiders and recognized them as black soldiers only after he had warned the Miller Hotel guests that the Negroes had broken out of the garrison and attacked the town. Policeman Macedonio Ramirez also saw what he expected to see that night. He had been told by Lieutenant Dominguez that Negro soldiers were shooting up the town before he was able to see—at a distance of about a hundred and twenty feet—that "they were soldiers, because they were dressed in this uniform. It is not a blue uniform; it is a sort of burnt color."

George W. Rendall swore he could hear the men "talking lowly—suppressed sort of voice" at a distance of about sixty feet. J. P. McDonnel saw three shots fired from inside the garrison wall, but they may have been the warning shots fired by the sentry, Private Howard.

José Martinez, speaking through an interpreter, was heard to say he had seen soldiers jumping the wall, but, testifying before the Citizens' Committee a few hours after the shooting, he had said: "I hear the noise like somebody—big crowd—jump the fence." When asked how many men he had seen, he had replied, "I could not see him; I hear."

Fear and confusion ("the firing was so near me and so heavy") fogged the eyewitness testimony of F. A. H. Sanborn, the Western Union manager who lived across from the garrison's main gate.

This left two remaining witnesses who had identified the raiders as black men in Army uniform. Herbert Elkins was a young stranger in town who now cut quite a figure on Elizabeth Street. Katie Leahy was a lively, loose-tongued widow who liked to entertain her guests, especially the young men, with recollections of the raid. So far neither Elkins nor Mrs Leahy had been summoned to a public place, put under oath, and subjected to cross-examination.

16

"The law, Mr. President, is for all."

ONCE THE SENATE CLERK had finished reading the Purdy-Blocksom report, Senator Foraker was on his feet, more determined than ever to press for adoption of his resolution calling for an investigation of the Brownsville affair.

"I want these men who have been accused of murder, mutiny,

and treason to have their day in court, where they may have a chance to defend themselves," he said, and pointed out that the President's new evidence was "all *ex parte* and taken behind closed doors."

In the past, when Roosevelt had been cracking down on corporate predators, he had enjoyed such overwhelming public support that his opponents in Congress had failed to make much headway against him. Now, as the political pundits had spent the Christmas holiday reminding him, the situation was different. Brownsville had made him vulnerable.

On the Republican side of the Senate chamber, Roosevelt could count on the support of his friend Cabot Lodge, but he needed a lawyer with the forensic skill of Senator Foraker, someone like Philander Knox of Pennsylvania or John Spooner of Wisconsin. At first no volunteers came forward. Some Republican senators secretly rejoiced in the mess the President had made of the Brownsville business; others were chary of risking their political skins to defend an exposed position Roosevelt might abruptly abandon once the going got rough.

"The President is not always as bold at the end as at the beginning," said Senator William J. Stone, a Missouri Democrat, and colleagues on both sides of the aisle had reason to agree. They remembered the bitter, protracted fight over the railroad-rate bill, when Roosevelt had betrayed his Republican friends (Knox, for one), embraced the most rabid of his enemies (South Carolina's "Pitchfork Ben" Tillman), and then double-crossed his Democratic allies.

Roosevelt wanted John Coit Spooner, the "fiery midget" (he was the Senate's shortest member), to argue the Administration's case. The stocky, resourceful Republican stalwart, made rich by fees from grateful railroad companies, was a match for Foraker. At the end of the first week in December, when three different Brownsville resolutions were pending in the Senate, Roosevelt's secretary dropped the Wisconsin senator a note, asking if it would be convenient for him to come see the President the following morning before the Cabinet met.

A month later, when the senators returned from their Christmas holiday, Taft began sending him copies of the same reports, affidavits, and other evidence Foraker had requested from the War Department. Judge-Advocate General George B. Davis offered Spooner a lengthy memorandum which sought to prove that, contrary to what Foraker had alleged, "a discharge without honor carries with it no deprivation of the rights and pecuniary allowances which attach to an honorable discharge."

The President's use of a new and little-known administrative device, the "discharge without honor," had caused confusion that still persists in the work of historians and biographers who mistakenly refer to the soldiers as having been "dishonorably discharged." No soldier, then or now, could be dishonorably discharged without being given his constitutional right to counsel and to a fair trial. The "discharge without honor" had been designed for cases where it was inappropriate to give a soldier either an honorable or a dishonorable discharge.

When a man enlisted in the Army, the War Department argued, he entered into a contract which the President was free to terminate at will. In fact, during the preceding two years, three hundred and fifty-two enlisted men in the Regular Army had been discharged without honor.

"In all those cases," Foraker pointed out, "there was no punishment involved; they simply severed connection with the Army, as in the case of a young boy who comes and wants to enlist and misrepresents his age, stating that he is of an age which authorizes him to enlist; but the next day or the next month or six months thereafter his mother comes and says: 'This is my only support. He has made a misrepresentation about his age. Here is the record. He is only sixteen,' or whatever his age may be, 'and he did not have my consent to enlist. I want to have him discharged.' Thereupon, the case going to the Secretary of War or to the President, he is discharged without honor, according to this regulation."

Under the wording of the Fourth Article of War, "no discharge shall be given any enlisted man before his term of service has expired, except by order of the President, the Secretary of War, the commanding officer of a department, or by sentence of a general court-martial." Thus, it was clear that the President and the Secretary of War were empowered to dismiss an enlisted man before his term of service expired, but, Foraker asked, was this power to be exercised only as an administrative convenience or could it be used to bypass established trial procedures and punish a soldier whose guilt might not be susceptible to proof at a court-martial?

The President had emphatically denied that his order was a punishment, and to back him up in this contention the military bureaucracy had made sure that the dismissed soldiers received travel allowances home from Fort Reno, because, as the Judge-Advocate General explained in the memorandum he prepared for Senator Spooner, the law provided for the withholding of such payments only when a soldier had been discharged "by way of punishment for an offense."

Roosevelt's action had undoubtedly involved punishment, Foraker kept insisting, and badgered the War Department to advise him as to just what benefits the soldiers might have lost. In his resolution he had called on the Secretary of War to explain, among other things, whether the men had been deprived of their right to retire on three-fourths pay, to enter a national soldiers' home, and to be buried in a national cemetery.

The Judge-Advocate General gave Senator Spooner the answers to Senator Foraker's questions. Retirement rights were forfeited by any soldier who was separated from the service for any reason before he was eligible to retire, General Davis declared. This meant that men like Sergeant Sanders who had served twenty years or more but had not racked up their required thirty years, even with the extra credit given for service in Cuba and the Philippines, had suffered a real loss in being deprived of their right to retire on three-fourths pay. According to the Judge-Advocate General, however, they would be permitted to live out their days in a soldiers' home and to have their mortal remains committed to a Government grave.

Senator Spooner took the floor on January 15, the day after the Senate received the Purdy-Blocksom report from the White House. The validity of the President's order dismissing the soldiers was now a judicial rather than a legislative question, he argued. If any of the men wished to challenge the authority of their commander in chief, they could go to the Court of Claims and sue for their pay.* As for Congress, Spooner reminded his colleagues, it might properly launch an investigation, but only "with a view to changing existing rules for future operation."

He was not opposed to such an investigation, Spooner explained, but he did oppose any senatorial inquiry into the correctness of the President's action in discharging the soldiers. Personally, he would like to have seen the Brownsville matter brought before a court of inquiry or a board of officers. The President, however, had chosen a different—but nonetheless lawful—course. He had discharged the men not as a punishment, but as an act of discipline for the good of the service.

"One man, without committing a court-martial offense, can demoralize the discipline of a good part of a company," Spooner maintained, raising a point Foraker had already covered.

The great majority of the soldiers *had* been dismissed for a court-martial offense, according to his interpretation of the Sixty-second Article of War, which provided a court-martial for "all disorders and neglects." In General Davis' standard work on military law, Foraker had informed the Senate, "neglect" was defined as "an omission or forbearance to do a thing that can be done or that is required to be done."

From this it followed that if the soldiers had been guilty of omitting or forbearing to identify the men who had shot up the town and killed one of its residents, they had committed an offense for which they should have been brought to trial under Article Sixty-two. In that case, of course, it would have been up to the prosecution to prove knowledge rather than deeds. Most of the men had been dismissed for what they were thought to *know* about the crime, not for having participated in it.

Spooner agreed with Foraker that the President had no power to punish a soldier. He could not "make a charge against an enlisted man, try him before himself, convict him himself, sentence him himself, and execute the sentence himself." But, Spooner argued, no *charge* had been brought against the soldiers and no

---

* Private Oscar W. Reid took that route in an effort to recover $122.26. He carried his case to the Supreme Court and lost. Cf. *Reid v. United States*, 221 U.S. 529 (1909).

punishment, in the legal sense of the word, had been meted out to them. The President had run into the same difficulty that had stumped the Cameron County grand jury, the impossibility of identifying the perpetrators of the crime.

"Now, what was the President to do?" Spooner asked. "Transfer those men to some other southern community? Why take them away from Brownsville and quarter them somewhere else among the people? Why take them from the South and send them to some village in the North? What community would be willing to have stationed in its midst a battalion of troops a portion of whom, undiscovered and undiscoverable, had made a midnight attack upon a city with Government weapons and ammunition?"

Spooner was gingerly picking his way across the thin legal ice on which the President rested his right to dishonor one hundred and sixty-seven men without subjecting them either to any "charges" or any "punishment," when he suddenly felt the prod of Senator Tillman's oratorical pitchfork. The two senators then got into an argument neither of them could win. "Pitchfork Ben" challenged Spooner to justify the President's action in the light of "the fundamental principle of English and American liberty that every man shall be considered innocent until he is proved guilty." Spooner countered with an impassioned attack on the South's lynch law, which Tillman had so often defended.

"No man," Spooner suggested, "can come with very good grace to berate and vituperatively impeach the President of the United States for having discharged men without honor from the Army without trial because he could not identify the guilty and single them out from the innocent, who comes to that accusation from a lynching bee or from justifying one. There ought not to be one law for the white man and another law for the black man. The law, Mr. President, is for all."

After touching briefly and none too convincingly on the evidence against the soldiers ("I incline strongly to the opinion that the heart of the trouble was in Company C"), Spooner ended by giving Tillman a verbal caning for the disservice he and men of his kidney were doing by advocating lawlessness in the South while warning law-abiding white and black neighbors in the North of the race war to come.

"I do not know of a more certain way to precipitate a struggle between the two races in such an environment than to be constantly violently declaring it to be imminent and inevitable," the Wisconsin senator concluded to applause in the galleries.

He spoke for four hours and then hurried home to dress for a dinner party the Tafts were giving for the President and Mrs. Roosevelt.

"John was the hero of the hour—& I came in for a share," Mrs. Spooner wrote in her diary. "We had to stay late because the Pres. always does & I had on my handsomest *Altman* desss—wh. nearly crushed me being so tight, so I got easily fatigued."

The Senate was obviously determined to conduct some sort of investigation of the Brownsville affair. The President was equally determined that any such inquiry should confine itself to the facts of the raid. The senators were not to step across the borders of the legislative branch and invade the executive. No Brownsville investigation should be permitted to question the exercise of his constitutional authority as commander in chief of the nation's armed forces.

"I have had a perfectly comic time with the Senate," Roosevelt wrote an old friend. "They have been hopping about, insisting that they could not desert Foraker, because it would 'split the party'; and I finally told the most active of the compromisers that if they split off Foraker they split off a splinter; but that if they split off me they would split the party nearly in two."

The President met with a few key senators at Cabot Lodge's home on January 20 and, despite Roosevelt's advice to the contrary, it was agreed that Foraker should be permitted to make a public display of party unity by offering an amendment to his pending resolution. The next day Foraker offered the compromise. The Military Affairs Committee was to conduct its investigation, but "without questioning the legality or justice of any act of the President in relation thereto." The resolution was unanimously adopted.

"I was sorry that Foraker was allowed the chance to offer the amendment," Roosevelt wrote, "and it was against my earnest advice that the Senators who were on my side permitted him to do so. But when he 'ate crow' and took the very amendment upon which I insisted, I did not see how I could make any open protest against it. There never has been a more complete case of breakdown and humiliation than this of Foraker's."

Foraker went to his grave protesting that he sought only to establish the facts about the Brownsville case. Once the truth were known, he thought, "the President would in a manly fashion undo the wrong he had done." Although he knew that Roosevelt was "somewhat provoked," he later recalled, he was not prepared for what happened at the Gridiron Club dinner the Saturday night after the Senate agreed to investigate the Brownsville affray.

17

"All coons look alike to me."

As HE MUSHED through a Washington snowstorm to the New Willard Hotel on January 26, 1907, Senator Foraker had no idea that he would be called on to address the Gridiron Club's celebrated guests. He wasn't even sure the President would attend, but when the Senator managed to make his way to his seat, he found Roosevelt on public display at the head table, along with the Vice President, Speaker Cannon, Mr. Justice Harlan, and J. Pierpont Morgan. Both Roosevelt and Foraker were among the forty guests the club had chosen to spoof in its souvenir booklet:

[ROOSEVELT]
"I'm busy with things night and day,"
A Rough Rider was once heard to say,
"Writing views, singing tunes,
Killing bears, firing coons,
Or composing an old Irish lay." °

° Roosevelt's article *"The Ancient Irish Sagas"* had appeared in the January issue of *Century Magazine.* When J. B. Bishop, his future

[FORAKER]

"All coons look alike to me,"
J. B. Foraker, says he, says he,
"Even if they is black as kin be,
An' is dressed in blue or yaller khaki.
All coons look alike to me,
Since 'mancipation set 'em free,
Nigger vote hold de balance,
All coons look alike to me."

As usual, Indiana's affable Jim Watson was on hand for the evening's fun. During his years in Congress he racked up an unbroken record of thirty-five consecutive Gridiron dinners.

"These bright young fellows lay on and spare not in their treatment of public officials, sparing the President really less than anybody else when they once get after him," Watson wrote in his memoirs.

When Roosevelt was called on to speak, he was expected to set the tone with an appropriate *jeu d'esprit*. Instead, he spent nearly an hour delivering what Watson called a "preachment." He defended his administration, attacked Senator Foraker, and lectured big business. All eyes turned toward Morgan's flushed, angry face as the forty-eight-year-old President shook his fist at the sixty-nine-year-old financier and, in his high-pitched, strident voice, called on Wall Street to repent and to give thanks that his reforms were being engineered by a conservative Republican administration; otherwise, the plutocrats would have been forced to swallow even more drastic and distasteful measures forced on them by the spirit of "the mob, the mob, the mob."

Foraker got his lumps when the President, without mentioning the Senator by name, lashed out at the opponents of railroad-rate regulation and then dismissed the Senate debate on Brownsville as an "academic discussion." The legislative branch, he contended, had no constitutional authority to review or reverse an

---

biographer, asked him how he'd found time for the research involved, the President explained, "I have always been interested in the subject, and when this Brownsville row started in the Senate I knew it would be a long and possibly irritating business if I followed it; so I shut myself up, paid no heed to the row and wrote the article."

action taken by the executive branch. He had done what he took to be his duty, Roosevelt shrilled, and he would brook no interference from anyone in discharging the obligations of his office. In conclusion, he made use of the tasteless doggerel his hosts had aimed at Foraker in their satirical *Who's Who.*

"There may have been but two companies of that regiment engaged in that unwholesome business," Jim Watson heard him say, "but 'all coons look alike to me.'" °

"When legal and human rights are involved, all *persons* look alike to me," Foraker retorted when Roosevelt sat down to sparse applause and the club president introduced the Senator with what some guests understood to be the line "Now is the time for bloody sarcasm." The introduction appears in the club's history as "Now is the time to bridge the bloody chasm."

"I did not know when I took the floor where to commence," Foraker wrote his son, Benson, a few days later, while his memory of the evening was fresh.

The Senator's face was "white as a sheet," Champ Clark recalled. In top form, "he gave blow for blow, and behind his blows he put all the steam of which he was possessed." It was a pity, the Missouri congressman felt, that posterity would have no picture of Foraker as he stood facing the President, a handsome, well-proportioned figure, over six feet tall, with "as fine a shock of iron-gray hair as was ever on a man's head."

Resting his opposition to the Administration's railroad-rate bill on constitutional grounds, Foraker bluntly informed Roosevelt that he had voted "according to my judgment and the obligations of my office, which were as sacred and inviolate to a Senator as were the obligations of the President's oath." Then, moving along to the Brownsville incident, he paraphrased a remark of Roosevelt's to the effect that no man in the United States stood so high or so low that, if guilty, he would not be punished

---

° The following Monday, with White House approval and, in all likelihood, as a result of its pressure, the Gridiron Club announced that the President had included the words, "and all white persons look alike to me also." Foraker was among those who failed to hear this part of the statement.

for breaking the law and, if innocent, would not be granted the law's full protection.

"I said I agreed with him entirely in that sentiment," Foraker continued in his letter to Benson, "but stated that I thought he had failed to apply that principle in the Brownsville case, where, according to his own statement of it, there were doubtless many men with splendid records as soldiers, absolutely innocent, yet branded as criminals, and dismised without honor."

After citing the wrong done Sergeant Mingo Sanders, Foraker said he was glad to have an opportunity to deny in Roosevelt's presence the charge made by some newspapers (and the Gridiron Club's lampoon) that he was out to get the Negro vote. His purpose in calling for an investigation had not been political, he said, nor had the Senate debate on his proposal been "academic." The soldiers would now have a chance to be heard in their own defense, "to the end that if it should appear that injustice had been done it might be righted."

Toward the end of his twenty-minute rebuttal, Foraker wrote his son, he reminded Roosevelt of the time "when I loved him as though one of my own family," but this personal feeling could not be allowed "to stand in the way of my differing with the President, when, in my judgment, he was in error." Their differences, however, had always been in the open, he said, and the President "would testify that I had fired no shots from ambush."

Earlier in the evening, Foraker went on, it had been remarked that he was rarely seen at the White House these days. "I said I went there as often as I had any business, that I did not go there frequently because I had no occasion to go unless it would be to discuss questions of difference, and I had never found that either agreeable or profitable; that the President in such conversations always 'had the drop on me'; that, being President, courtesy required me to defer to him, with the result that he generally did all the discussing, and I came away at the end of his conversation with the feeling that I had not accomplished anything."

As Foraker spoke, Roosevelt shook his head, gritted his teeth, clenched his fists. "That is not so," he muttered; "I am going to

answer that; that is not true; I will not stand for it." Three or
four times he would have sprung up and shouted the Senator
down if he had not been restrained by Mr. Justice Harlan. The
three coordinate branches of government came into play when
the elderly judge laid his hand on the arm of the impetuous young
chief executive while the middle-aged legislator declared his
great respect for Roosevelt's high office but demanded that the
President should have no less respect for the United States
Senate.

"I did not come to the Senate to take orders from anybody,
either at this end of the line or the other," Champ Clark remembered Foraker declaiming. "Whenever I fall so low that I
cannot express my opinion on a great question freely, and without reservation or mental evasion, I will resign and leave my
place to some man who has the courage to discharge his duties."

As Foraker took his seat, the banquet room erupted. News-
papermen and their guests leaped up, cheering, crowding around
the Senator and offering their congratulations, while a red-faced,
sputtering President popped up from his chair and appealed for
quiet so he might "make some remarks in answer to Senator
Foraker."

"There was scant applause," Watson noted, when Roosevelt
finally managed to get the floor and further antagonize his audience by subjecting it to still another repetition of the arguments he had used so often in defending his treatment of the
Negro soldiers.

"Some of those men were bloody butchers," he was heard to
say, in effect; "they ought to be hung. The only reason that I
didn't have them hung was because I couldn't find out which
ones of them did the shooting."

"At the end of ten minutes," Watson wrote later, "he strode
out of the hall, leaving no good taste in anybody's mouth and no
good feeling in anybody's heart."

The club president, Samuel G. Blythe, spotted the serene
countenance of Speaker Cannon and, to relieve the tension, he
asked him to make a few remarks. "What in hell can I say about
this mess?" Uncle Joe mumbled to the man seated on his right,

then put aside his cigar long enough to place the distinguished gathering in its proper historical perspective.

"People pay too much attention to individuals anyhow," he said. "If the earth were to yawn here and now and swallow this hotel, with the Vice-President, members of the Cabinet, members of the Supreme Court, distinguished diplomats, senators, and representatives, railroad presidents from all parts of the country— well, tomorrow the newspapers would come out and say that a great calamity had befallen the nation, appropriate exercises would be held in many places and in the residential cities of all those so unfortunately lost; and then the ranks would again fill up, people everywhere would be chosen to take our places right off, the procession would move forward, and in two weeks, well, there wouldn't be anybody give a God-damn."

As Watson recalled the historic evening and its aftermath, Uncle Joe's homily "made Roosevelt madder, when he heard of it, than anything Foraker had said about him, for that anyone should imply that he would be forgotten in two weeks, or that nobody would care about his departure, certainly did not set well with him."

Once Uncle Joe Cannon resumed his seat and his cigar, Gridiron president Blythe called for a chorus of "Auld Lang Syne" and then, around midnight, hastily adjourned the proceedings before most of the guests had eaten. Unaware that Roosevelt had left the hotel, Foraker tried to elbow his way to the head table for a conciliatory handshake, but he was unable to escape the crush of admirers bearing down on him. Even Senator Albert J. Beveridge, who sided with Roosevelt on the Brownsville issue, sent him a card with a scribbled message: "I am against you, but I never so admired you as this instant. You are game, and you are masterful. You were altogether thoroughbred tonight." *

---

* "Foraker ought not to have been called upon to speak," Roosevelt wrote to Beveridge the next day, "but, as he was called upon, I do not blame him much for the speech he did make. I was in two minds what to say in answer; I was inclined to make a Berserker speech myself and go

In Champ Clark's opinion, "the bout ended in a draw, though the sympathy of the majority of the audience was with the Senator because he was attacked by the President and was therefore fighting on the defensive." To Foraker, it was important that his son should understand "that I was not responsible for it, and that I am happy to know from all who heard me that I did not use a disrespectful word, or say anything to be regretted."

"Oh, no," Blythe was reported to have said afterward, when Washington gossips insisted the President had been drunk at the dinner. "He only took a quart of sauterne and a quart of champagne, and what is that between us old sports?"

It was two o'clock in the morning when Foraker got home, "white and fagged, but not defeated," his wife remembered for the rest of her life. The library fire had gone out. "We put on fresh logs; it was oddly symbolic. Everything afterwards served to add to the flame of discord between the Gridiron duelists, once friends."

Two years later, his political career wrecked, his reputation tarnished, Foraker would look back with regret on the day he left his Highland County farm home to enter public life. "Politics has not brought me an hour's happiness," he remarked to an old friend, momentarily forgetting that hour in Washington with Julia, when he had piled a fresh log above the cold ashes of the library fireplace and relived his Gridiron Club triumph.

"The whole town is full of it," Julia wrote her son the following Wednesday. "From all sides the universal verdict is that your father did just right and was equal to the occasion and the feeling is that he is the only man who would have been equal to it."

---

over the whole business, and perhaps this would have been better; but in the few minutes I had to decide I concluded that I would merely make a flat contradiction of what he had said, point out the fact that I and not he would pass judgment upon the case, and that I should absolutely disregard anything except my own convictions, and let it go at that."

The Hearings

———◆———

18

". . . she would add just double what the original story amounted to."

THE SENATE Military Affairs Committee opened its Brownsville hearings in Washington on February 4, 1907, the same day that Major Penrose was brought to trial in San Antonio. His defense would be based largely "on falsehood and fabrication," the Brownsville *Daily Herald* warned, and, to give the lie to any such inventions, a cadre of townspeople descended on Fort Sam Houston to testify for the prosecution.

The soldiers were not formally on trial at the Penrose court-martial, but the guilt of the battalion's commanding officer was predicated on the guilt of his men. He was charged with having neglected his duty to take proper measures to prevent the attack and to detect its perpetrators. Obviously, if his men had not perpetrated the attack, he was not to blame for having failed to restrain them.

The first witness called to the stand by the prosecution was George W. Rendall, the septuagenarian who was hard of hearing and had defective vision in his one good eye (he had lost the other in '66). Despite his physical impairments, Mr. Rendall had managed to hear and see all manner of things on the night of August 13. Each time he had testified since then, however, he had not been quite sure just what he had heard and seen.

Similar contradictions cropped up in the testimony of other townspeople, who, it soon became evident, had edited and embroidered their stories after repeating them to Captain Kelly's committee, the grand jury, Major Blocksom, Mr. Purdy, and various newspaper reporters. The eyewitness accounts recited in San Antonio—and subsequently in Washington—had gained a richness of detail in the six months following the disturbance.

Overnight "the nigger raid" had made celebrities of small-town nonentities who normally would have had to die, preferably by violence, in order to get their names in the paper. Their new importance was measured by the weightiness of their testimony. To become a star of the magnitude of Katie Leahy or young Herbert Elkins it was necessary to have seen the raiders' black faces, heard their black voices, and recognized the sound of their new Springfield rifles. As the lines came trippingly on the tongue in performance after performance, even the bit players began to remember with heightened clarity and conviction certain sights and sounds they had neglected to mention before.

Dr. Thorn, a fifty-year-old bachelor dentist, had not seen anything. "I know nothing except what I heard," he had told Captain Kelly's committee right after the raid. What he said on that hot August day occupies eight lines in the official records. What he said at Fort Sam Houston the following winter sprawls across twenty-four pages.

He had heard shooting and he had heard voices. Having grown up with firearms and Negroes, he was satisfied that he'd heard the Army's new Springfield rifle and the voices of black men. He remembered hearing someone say, "There they go" or "There he goes," and on the basis of these three words—only one of which he was sure of—he could swear the man he heard was black.

"I suppose it is merely a difference in race characteristics," he explained when asked how he was able to differentiate the voices of white and black southerners; "they have different colored skin, they have different hair, they have different voices."

Dr. Thorn's keen ear had also detected the sound of pistol shots, certainly as many as three and possibly five or six. The officer prosecuting Major Penrose acted as though he hadn't heard this embarrassing detail. Pistols were not available to the soldiers, but were so commonplace on the town side of the garrison wall that some of the Brownsville witnesses had shown up at the trial packing their six-shooters. One witness, a real estate man, had left an arsenal at home. After a casual reference to the Winchester he always kept within reach, he was asked what other weapons he had around the house.

"Twelve double-barrel shotguns, two .38 Colt revolvers, two double action .38 Smith & Wessons, and a small rim-fire pistol," he replied, and then recalled that the youngest of his four sons also had "a small .22."

A new witness, making his debut at the Penrose court-martial, was Almas Littlefield, twenty-six-year-old loafer who claimed to have spotted one of the raiders as a tall, slender black man in khaki breeches and a light blue shirt. He hadn't bothered to report this identification to any public official until nearly five months had gone by. Then he had told his story to Commissioner Creager, who, even by local standards, was known to be notoriously hostile to Negroes.

"I had done some work with the chief of police," Littlefield said when defense counsel asked about his employment record.

His work, it turned out, was volunteer service for which he had not been paid.

"Well, before the shooting," he explained, "in going to Mexican dances around there, sometimes I would go out with the police there and I would be there and if the police called on me, I helped them."

By the time he took the stand at Fort Sam Houston, Littlefield was no longer an unpaid hanger-on waiting his chance to help subdue a drunken Mexican. He had been made a deputy sheriff.

"Twenty feet," he said when asked how far he was from the "very black man" he swore he had glimpsed for an instant as the Negro darted down an unlighted alley on a moonless night.

At almost the same moment that night, a twenty-seven-year-old West Pointer, Lieutenant Lawrason, had been trotting across the parade ground at Fort Brown. He had failed to see a soldier running toward him until he was within about two feet of the man.

"I almost ran into him," Lawrason testified. "In fact, I passed him before he called to me."

"How far could you have recognized him, know who he was— by sight, I mean, not by sound of voice?"

"I don't believe I could have recognized him over three feet."

Another young West Pointer, Lieutenant Grier, testified that after leaving his wife and baby at Captain Lyon's quarters he had run about fifteen yards across the parade ground when he heard someone rushing toward him in the darkness. It proved to be Sergeant Harley. The Lieutenant had not been able to see the soldier until "he was in about five or six feet of me." As he explained on cross-examination, "The night was too dark to see anybody until they were right up on top of you; that is to recognize them."

Katie Leahy, peering out of an upstairs window, could not only see black faces, khaki uniforms, and some blue shirts in a dark alley, she could even see one man's freckles and the "blue barrel" of the raiders' rifles. Herbert Elkins looked down at the same black alley and was able to swear the men were firing Springfields, because he could see them operating "a knob."

"Young Elkins was an exceptional witness possessed of a brilliant memory," the San Antonio *Daily Express* reported, and went on to describe him as "by long odds the most remarkable witness appearing before the court-martial."

No one seemed to notice that Elkins had edited his recollections of the raiders. In Judge Wells's law office, when his memory was fresh, he had made a point of describing two of the leaders of the Cowen-alley attack as "small black Negroes, none of them over five feet six." Afterward, when he told his story to the grand jury, gave a sworn statement to Mr. Purdy, and testified for the prosecution at the Penrose trial, he continued to speak of these same two Negroes, but he avoided giving any physical description of the men. Their height, as someone may have pointed out to him, suggested that they might have been Mexicans.

"An interesting witness," the Washington *Post* reported on June 7 after Katie Leahy had cleared up any misunderstandings the Senate Military Affairs Committee might have been harboring about the raid. "She was dressed in a close-fitting white duck suit that set off her well-rounded form to advantage," the *Post* continued, "and the immaculate effect was accentuated by a large white hat, with an impressive plume. Mrs. Leahy was very positive in her answers . . ."

"There is no mistake about the positiveness of her evidence," said Major Penrose's defense counsel in his closing argument. "It gushed forth with that promptness of the overcharged bottle of seltzer—all you need to do was press the button and she did the balance."

"Little or no credence" should be given her testimony, Senator Foraker was advised by Captain Edger, an Army surgeon who had boarded at Mrs. Leahy's establishment for some months during his two-year tour of duty at Fort Brown. She had a tendency "to exaggerate and falsify even the smallest details of anything she may have to tell," the Captain wrote in a candid assessment of the Brownsville witnesses.

"I used to speak with her nearly every morning," he continued when he testified before the Senate Military Affairs Committee, "and she would come to the breakfast table and sit down there and speak about things that I knew about myself, and she would add just double what the original story amounted to."

She was in her own bedroom, alone, preparing to retire, when she heard the first shot at exactly five minutes to twelve, Mrs.

Leahy testified at the Penrose court-martial. Three more shots were fired before she got upstairs to a vacant room in the hotel annex and looked out the Fourteenth Street window toward the post. She reached the window in time to see the fifth shot fired from the balcony of the second barracks from the river, the one occupied by B Company.

The post scavenger, Tamayo, was emptying an ash can on the side of this barracks which faced the town when the shooting began. "In town," he said when asked where it had originated. He saw no soldiers and no flashes of gunfire anywhere inside the garrison. Neither did Private Howard, the sentinel walking his post on the town side of the men's quarters between B and C Companies.

"In about half a minute or so after I heard these first shots," Howard said, "a fusillade of shots was in this alley right across there from the right where I was at."

In this "half a minute or so" between the first shot and the fusillade in the alley, Mrs. Leahy swore she had sufficient time to walk upstairs, peer out the window, go back downstairs, talk to her sister, duck a hailstorm of bullets on Elizabeth Street, and return to the upstairs window, where she watched soldiers moving about and shooting from B Company's galleries, both upper and lower. She spent ten minutes watching this activity, she said, contradicting the principal witnesses from both sides of the garrison wall, who agreed that the entire raid lasted only eight to ten minutes. Mrs. Leahy was positive it began at 11:55 P.M., railroad time, and ended at 12:25 A.M.

It was during the ten-minute period when the guns were supposedly blazing away on B Company's galleries that the enlisted men, their black NCO's, and four of their white officers swore that the three companies were being assembled and accounted for. They took an oath that no gunfire had been heard or seen in the barracks area.

Elkins not only backed up the widow's testimony about the shooting from the barracks, he also added to it. Standing at Judge Parks's window, he said, he had seen shots from B Company's quarters. From his own room next door, the room nearest

the Cowen alley, he swore he had seen one or two flashes of gunfire from C Company's barracks. He was quite sure it was this
particular barracks.

But, as defense counsel quickly established, it was physically
impossible to see any part of C Company's barracks from any one
of the three second-floor rooms of the Leahy Hotel annex. Second
Lieutenant Harry G. Leckie, a mechanical engineer, had studied
the view from all three upstairs rooms. From Elkins' room, he
testified, only about ten feet of the upper end of B Company's
barracks could be seen.

Lieutenant Leckie had also peered out of the window from
which Mrs. Leahy swore she had watched men of B Company
blazing away on both the upper and lower galleries. She had
neglected to mention the orange tree which had blocked her
view of the fort from this window. Only about half of the upper
gallery was visible, Lieutenant Leckie said. The lower gallery was
completely obscured.

"I saw through the leaves," Mrs. Leahy calmly replied when
Senator Foraker asked how she had managed to see men walking
about and shooting rifles on the lower gallery.

The extraordinary feats of nighttime vision reported by the
Brownsville witnesses were tested in experiments conducted at
Fort McIntosh, Texas, by Lieutenant H. A Wiegenstein of the
Twenty-fifth Infantry. To simulate conditions in the Cowen alley
as viewed from the upstairs rooms of the Leahy Hotel annex,
he stationed observers between two lanterns at the top of an
arroyo, then asked them to describe what they had seen and
heard after a firing party of a dozen men filed by some twenty to
twenty-five feet below. It was a clear, starry night, with a moon
about to enter its second quarter.

The "raiders" accompanying Wiegenstein in the experiment
consisted of eight black soldiers, two white Americans, and one
Mexican. The civilians were armed and dressed in dark blue
shirts (one wore black satin), khaki trousers, leggings, and campaign hats. Some of the soldiers wore the same outfit. Others
were in khaki blouses. The Lieutenant had on an olive-drab

uniform, wore a cap, and carried a saber. He also sported white cuffs and a white collar.

One of the observers was Harry A. Stucky, a retired colonel who often hunted at night, sometimes when coyotes were on the prowl, sometimes when he simply felt like going outdoors and banging away with a high-powered rifle in an act of what he supposed was "pure savagery." By chance, he happened to be a house guest at Fort McIntosh the night of the first Wiegenstein experiment. He was delighted to accept his host's invitation to take part in it.

"They led us out back of the fort to where the arroyo was deepest and the shadows most dense," Colonel Stucky testified, "and a squad of men were marched down in there and a number of shots were fired. We had no knowledge of the number of shots or how the men were located or anything else. There were two lanterns placed on the upper banks of the arroyo as points of safety by the lieutenant in charge of the experiments, and we were instructed to stand between those lights and see what we could tell about what would happen."

The "raiders" marched into the simulated alley, fired two volleys, then fired at will. The observers were asked how many shots they had heard. Their estimates ran from twenty to thirty. The correct number was eighty. They were then asked to describe the raiding party. Colonel Stucky said they had been able to distinguish nothing other than a pair of white cuffs.

"Could you yourself make out any of the figures of any of those men?" he was asked.

"None whatever."

"Could you make out the complexion of any of those men?"

"No, sir."

"Could you see the rifles or any part of the rifles of the men, assuming that they had rifles?"

"No sir; I had no idea of what they were firing from; might have been fired from a coffee mill for all I could tell."

Two other witnesses in the Wiegenstein test, Robert P. Harbold and James Blyth, both second lieutenants, followed Colonel Stucky to the stand. "Nothing whatever could be seen of the men, except the black line extending in front of us," Harbold said, and

Blyth declared he had been unable to distinguish the men's clothing, complexion, or weapons.

Later that same night, after the moon had gone down, the test was repeated. The raiders fired from the hip and, as Blyth described it, "when the flash of the first volley came, all that appeared to me was a long row of legs." He had no idea what the men were wearing or what weapons they were using. Harbold had the same experience. "It was impossible for me to state how they were dressed or what they had on; I could see nothing of the rifle or nothing above the hips."

In a subsequent test, conducted under starlight conditions, the lieutenant and six black soldiers wore dark blue shirts, khaki trousers, leggings, and campaign hats. A Negro sergeant, who, as Wiegenstein put it, "would probably be described by a recruiting officer as light brown," wore a white collar and an officer's cap. He was put in command of the firing party.

While Harbold and Blyth watched from a second-floor rear window of the latter's quarters at Fort McIntosh, the Negro sergeant marched his detail past them in broken order on the lawn below. The garrison's street lamp, about a hundred feet away, was behind the men, but, even so, neither of the two observers was able to spot the white officer among the black soldiers. The two lieutenants then moved to a front window, with a light directly in front of them, not more than twenty paces distant. They still could not tell whether the men below were black or white.

"Then we went downstairs and sat on the porch," Blyth said. "The men were marched past in single file on the sidewalk, which was about five paces or five steps from the porch. We were sitting on the steps, so our heads were about in line with theirs, with the light shining on them. We failed to distinguish Lieutenant Wiegenstein, who was in line himself."

When asked how she had managed to recognize the raiders as Negroes, Mrs. Leahy explained, "By the flash of their guns while they did the shooting." Elkins echoed the widow's statement. "The light from his gun," the young man said; "it made a very good light."

According to Colonel Stucky, an electrical-mechanical engineer who had done some research on the sensitivity of the human eye to sudden bursts of light, the gunflashes in the arroyo on the night of the first Wiegenstein experiment revealed absolutely nothing except "a phosphorescent glare," which for an instant disclosed the direction from which the shots were coming.

Lieutenant Wiegenstein, just one step away from a soldier firing a Springfield rifle in a Texas arroyo, was unable to tell from the momentary burst of light whether the man was white or black, but Mrs. Leahy, looking down on a dark alley from a second-story window, swore she could recognize one of the raiders as a freckled Negro simply by the flash of his gunfire. Elkins was equally positive he could see the "knob" of the raiders' rifles at a time when the attacking party was, by actual measurement, eighty feet away.

"In view of the testimony given by the officers who made the experiments as to ability to see and distinguish men and clothing in the night time, the testimony of these Brownsville people is perfectly absurd," Senator Foraker wrote Major Penrose. "Yet, it answers to make up a case with all who want to see a case of that kind established."

"Have you ever thought of illustrating before the Committee just what can be seen at night?" Penrose wrote back. "I would be willing to stake my reputation that, on a moderately dark night, I could form a party composed of soldiers and civilians, white and black, and march them within fifteen feet of the Committee, and they could not tell one from the other, or in what manner they were dressed, and I would not ask for as dark a night as obtained at Brownsville on August 13th either."

Such an experiment, the Major felt, would "go a long way to vindicate the soldiers, and place before the people of the country the utter lack of truthfulness of the Brownsville witnesses."

Some of the townspeople seem to have been consciously lying; others had told their stories so often they may have come to believe the additional details that had crept into their narratives; and still others, like Lieutenant Joe Dominguez, were confused at the time of the raid and even more confused when put on the stand at Fort Sam Houston and asked to swear to what they had seen and heard.

Dominguez testified for the prosecution, but it was the prosecuting officer who artfully led him into the error. "I heard shots fired, *toward* the reservation," the police lieutenant said, and the prosecutor put his statement in the form of a question, "The sound of the shots came *from* the reservation?" * "Yes, sir," Dominguez replied, failing to notice how he had been tricked into suggesting that the trouble had broken out inside the fort. He was in no position to pinpoint the location of the first shots. He was sitting on the market steps, more than three blocks from the garrison wall.

"I started on horseback toward the reservation," Dominguez said, and when he rode down Washington Street as far as Fourteenth, the raiders "got through shooting in the alley, where Mr. Cowen's house is."

"You saw the soldiers at the Cowen house?" the prosecutor asked.

"Yes, sir."

On cross-examination Dominguez explained that he had not actually seen the raiders at the Cowen house. On his way from the market he had been told by one of his men that the house had been fired upon by soldiers. He reached the Fourteenth Street intersection just in time to see the raiders streak across the alley, heading toward the Miller Hotel. He turned around and rode back up Washington Street to Thirteenth, then turned west toward Elizabeth. As he crossed the alley, just before he was hit and his horse killed, he heard someone call out, "Give him hell."

"State, if you can do so," the prosecutor asked, "whether the voice was that of a white man, Negro, Mexican, or otherwise."

"Yes, sir; it was a coarse voice—sounded like a Negro man."

"Is that the only thing made you determine it was a Negro talking—the coarseness of the voice?" the defense counsel asked.

"And the uniform they had," Dominguez answered.

As the Lieutenant wound up his direct testimony, the prosecutor called attention to the emptiness of his right sleeve and

* Emphases added.

asked him to tell the court how he had come to lose part of his arm.

"I was shot by Government colored soldiers," he said.

"How do you know they were Government soldiers?" defense counsel asked.

"Because I saw them—saw them in uniform—and I could see the guns."

"Could you see the color of the men?"

"I could see they were dark—they looked dark at night."

Before Dominguez first laid eyes on the raiders, he had been told that the Cowen house had been shot up by Negro soldiers. Moments later, when he saw someone run across the Cowen alley, he saw what he expected to see—Negro soldiers. They were about twenty-five feet away, approximately the same distance that separated the observers and the firing party in the first Wiegenstein experiment. Next time Dominguez spotted the raiders they were around sixty feet from him.

"I get so confused I don't know whether I am stating right or not," he complained when defense counsel was trying to straighten out his testimony on what he had seen in the Cowen alley.

"Were you so confused that night you didn't know?" he was asked.

"I was when the shooting was going on."

During the eight or ten minutes the shooting was going on, he had been conscious. When it ended, he was lying on a drugstore floor, unconscious.

"Contemptible," the Brownsville *Daily Herald* bellowed in reporting the methods used by defense counsel to clear up the misleading statements the prosecutor had wangled from the police lieutenant. Joe Dominguez was a well-bred, well-liked Mexican, a Mason, and the son of an Army officer, the paper reminded its readers. When funds were being raised to help Joe get back on his feet after the raid, the *Daily Herald* had been delighted to chip in. The paper had been good for two dollars.

19

"... *my men had nothing whatever to do with it.*"

TAKING THE STAND as a prosecution witness at Major Penrose's court-martial, Major Blocksom had to suffer through a reading of the full text of his report on the Brownsville Raid and then try to justify its conclusions in the light of the evidence on which they rested. He had recommended that one hundred and sixty-seven soldiers be dismissed without honor if they failed to produce the criminals he suspected they were harboring in their ranks. Defense counsel asked how many of these enlisted men he had interviewed.

"I interviewed quite a number of them—possibly twenty-five or thirty," he said.

"Did you as a result of your investigation of any of the enlisted men down there, get anything in the nature of a clue?"

"I did not."

"Showing the guilt of any individuals?"

"I did not."

In his report, Major Blocksom had praised Major Penrose for having "conducted himself in a manly way under trying circumstances" but had faulted him for his failure to arrest three soldiers and the scavenger Tamayo "as soon as he believed the criminals were soldiers." The three men selected for immediate arrest were Sergeant Jackson, B Company's charge of quarters, who swore he had neither seen nor heard any shooting from his barracks; Sergeant Reid, the sergeant of the guard who, as Blocksom put it, had ordered the sounding of call to arms "probably too early during the firing to be genuine," and Private Howard, the sentinel who had corroborated Tamayo's testimony that the shooting began on the town side of the garrison wall.

"It is very probable that proper effort would have induced

one or more of these men to tell what he knew," Blocksom had stated in his report, and when he came to testify six months later he said he still felt that Major Penrose "might have gotten a good deal of valuable information if he had used coercive measures very soon after the thing occurred."

When asked just what Major Penrose should have done to the three soldiers (Tamayo, a civilian, had been reported to civil authorities, who had not seen fit to arrest him), Major Blocksom suggested "keeping them in solitary confinement and possibly on bread and water and something of that kind and getting at them by threatening them in some way or another." Blocksom had no idea how such treatment could be made to jibe with Army regulations, but he kept insisting that Penrose would have been "justified in threatening them in quite a number of ways."

Why had B Company's charge of quarters, Sergeant Jackson, been picked as a candidate for coercion? Blocksom was asked, and he sputtered, "There were several witnesses, or at least one—I think I interviewed two—who saw the firing from the porch . . ."

Aside from Mrs. Leahy and Herbert Elkins, the only other prosecution witness willing to swear he had seen shots fired from this barracks was J. P. McDonnel, a middle-aged carpenter whose testimony before the Citizens' Committee the day after the raid conflicted sharply with his subsequent statements.

"I might have been a little confused the next morning," McDonnel said, and when asked just when he had managed to get his facts fixed firmly in his mind, he cheerfully replied, "Oh, immediately, I guess, in a few days."

Having explained, at least to his own satisfaction, why Sergeant Jackson should have been clapped into solitary confinement and put on bread and water, Major Blocksom was asked about James Reid, the sergeant of the guard, who, it seemed to Blocksom, had been suspiciously quick in ordering his trumpeter to sound the call to arms.

"Did you ever ask Major Penrose whether the call to arms was sounded or not; and if so, by whom?"

"I don't recollect whether I did or not," Blocksom replied.

"If he had told you that he ordered the sounding of the call to arms, would it change your opinion as to that particular thing?"

"Why, certainly it would."

Later, appearing before the Senate Military Affairs Committee after Major Penrose had testified that he had, indeed, ordered the sergeant of the guard to give the alarm, Major Blocksom admitted that Sergeant Reid might "have sounded this call through an honest desire to help defend the fort."

"Did he do anything at all, except order the call to arms sounded, that gives you any right to throw any suspicion on him?" Senator Foraker asked.

"No, sir," Blocksom replied; "he did not."

As for Private Howard, the sentry who had joined Tamayo in swearing he had seen no soldiers fire any shots inside the garrison, Major Blocksom would have subjected him to threats and starvation because his testimony had been impeached by four witnesses who "indicated to me that he couldn't help seeing somebody."

The four witnesses were the elderly, one-eyed Mr. Rendall; the confused Mr. McDonnel; José Martinez, who could never remember clearly what he had seen before he put out his light and threw himself face-down on the floor; and F. A. H. Sanborn, the Western Union manager who testified that he had not looked outside until after the shooting had shifted from the vicinity of the fort to the Cowen alley.

Against these four witnesses, only two of whom laid any serious claim to having observed activity inside the fort, Blocksom had the affidavits of forty-one enlisted men who were asleep in B Company's barracks when the shooting broke out. As he explained at Major Penrose's trial, he chose to ignore the sworn statements of the soldiers because he had already accepted the unsworn statements of the townspeople.

"I didn't take any affidavits at all from the people of the town," he said, "because I saw a great many of them, and their evidence was so convincing that the act had been committed by colored soldiers that I thought there would never be any question of it, and I don't see now how there can be any possible question of it."

It was questioned, among others, by General Burt, who had

spent ten years with the black regiment. When he appeared before the Senate Military Affairs Committee, he was asked if some
one hundred and fifty men in three different companies would be
likely to shelter from ten to twenty members of the battalion who
had committed a crime for which they were being made to suffer.

"That would be simply an impossibility," the General
snapped, and, seated in an improvised courtroom in Texas, listening to the Brownsville witnesses and reading the testimony of his
men in Washington, Major Penrose found himself coming to the
same conclusion.

Charles W. Penrose had rounded out twenty-two years of
service, the last three with the First Battalion, Twenty-fifth
Infantry (Colored).

"Now, Major," he was asked when he took the stand in his
own defense, "how does the discipline and soldierly conduct of
this battalion which you commanded compare with that of other
regiments in which you had served?"

"With all due modesty," he replied, "I wish to say I considered it the best drilled and best disciplined battalion that I have
ever seen in the Army."

He was put on trial for his handling of these men during a
twelve-hour period, beginning around five o'clock Monday afternoon, August 13, when Mayor Combe and Lon Evans reported
the town's reaction to the story of the rape attempt on Mrs. Evans,
and ending at daybreak the following morning, when the battalion's rifles were inspected and found to be free of powder stains.

The Major was guilty of "neglect of duty, to the prejudice of
good order and military discipline," on two counts, it was
charged: (1) following Mayor Combe's afternoon visit, he should
have ordered Captain Macklin, his officer of the day, to exercise
"special vigilance" and to make "frequent inspections" to prevent
the soldiers from doing violence to the town, and (2) once the
Mayor had returned to the garrison after the assault and informed
him that some of his men had murdered a young bartender and
wounded a police officer, the Major should have ordered an
immediate inspection of his men's rifles instead of waiting some
four hours or more for daylight.

Cowen alley, where the shooting took place, looking from the garrison wall.

Elizabeth Street photographed from in front of Weller's saloon.

The garrison wall and barracks as seen from Mrs. Randall's room in the Western Union building.

The Miller Hotel, taken from the spot on Elizabeth Street where Lieutenant Dominguez's horse fell.

One of the barracks at Fort Brown.

Allison and Hollomon's saloon.

Senator Joseph Benson Foraker
of Ohio, who demanded a full
investigation of the Brownsville
raid and took up the cause of
the dismissed infantrymen.

Two of the satirical drawings from the Gridiron Club's souvenir booklet
for the dinner of January 25, 1907, when President Roosevelt (left) and
Senator Foraker (right) had a major confrontation about Brownsville.

President Theodore Roosevelt (above) and his Secretary of War, William Howard Taft (left), became involved in the Brownsville affair much against their wills.

HOME AGAIN!

Two views from the white press: New York World, *November 27, 1906, depicts Taft's greeting to President Roosevelt on his return from Panama* (above); Harper's Weekly, *January 12, 1907, comments on the dishonorable discharge of the black troops* (at right).

Two views from the black press: The New York Age, December 27, 1906 (above), and August 1, 1907 (below).

B Company's Baseball Team

1. Harry Carmichael	*5. George Mitchell*	*9. Wade Harris*
2. James Johnson	*6. Charles E. Cooper*	*10. John Hollomon*
3. Edward Daniels	*7. Mingo Sanders*	*11. James Allen*
4. Henry Jones	*8. Isaiah Raynor*	*12. Joseph L. Wilson*

Both charges rested on the War Department's conviction that a dozen or more still-unidentified black soldiers had shot up the town. One of the specifications—failure to take proper measures to stave off trouble—sprang from Washington's curious notion that on a hot summer night in a Texas border town aflame with talk of an attempted rape of a white woman by a black soldier, the threat of violence lay with Major Penrose's men rather than with Mayor Combe's constituents.

As Dr. Combe recalled his conversation with the Major that afternoon, he had said, " 'Major Penrose, this is a terrible thing; the people in town are very excited and it will not be safe,'— I am not positive now whether I used the expression 'it will not be safe' or 'I will not respond for the lives of your men if they go into town,' but I used one or the other."

Major Penrose was not sure of the Mayor's exact words either, but it seemed to him that Dr. Combe had said, "Major, don't you think it best for you to keep your men in the post tonight? For I am afraid this may cause a great deal of trouble." The threat of trouble, as both Dr. Combe and Major Penrose clearly understood at the time, lay on the town side of the garrison wall.

No one, Major Penrose was certain, could have possibly over-heard his conversation with the Mayor, but Wilbert Voshelle, Fort Brown's white corral master, was on his way home to supper between five and six o'clock and, he swore to Constitution League investigators, he heard Dr. Combe tell the Major, "If there is not an arrest made between this hour and eleven o'clock, every enlisted man seen on the street will be shot."

When, in mid-December, Senator Culberson first flashed Brownsville the word that attorneys for the Negro soldiers had confronted the Senate with Voshelle's affidavit, the *Daily Herald* dismissed the man as a dissolute deadbeat who "associated with Negroes and the lower classes of the tougher, most disreputable Mexican element."

Dr. Combe, Evans, and Penrose joined in repudiating Voshelle's rendering of the Mayor's warning. What Dr. Combe remembered saying, he advised Senator Culberson, was: "It is a terrible outrage and I have come with Mr. Evans to protest against any of your men going into town tonight, for if they do go, I fear the people cannot be controlled and I will not answer for their lives."

Voshelle later testified that it was Evans, not Dr. Combe, who had warned Major Penrose that his men would be shot down in the streets if no arrest were made that night. Whatever the exact wording of the warning and regardless of who made it, the situation clearly imposed on Major Penrose the duty to exercise "special vigilance"—not to protect the townspeople from his men, as charged, but to protect his men from the townspeople.

When trouble broke out a few hours later, the Major naturally assumed the shots were being fired by angry civilians. He took defensive measures to protect his men and his garrison. He ordered the alarm sounded, the companies formed, and the armed men deployed inside the reservation wall, facing the town.

"I gave them most positive instructions as to firing," he said. "They were not to fire under any circumstances unless it was in preservation of life, and under no circumstances were they to fire unless under order of their captain; and I might add, which I have not stated before, that my instructions to the company commanders when they went out on the firing line they were not to fire unless they received an order from me to do so; that my station would be at the central gate there."

Major Penrose was stationed at the central gate an hour or so after the shooting ended when Captain Lyon's patrol returned with the two Combe brothers and the astonishing news that on the other side of the garrison wall, where an armed mob had formed, it had been taken for granted that men of his command had terrorized the town and left young Frank Natus lying dead in the rear courtyard of the Ruby Saloon and Joe Dominguez nursing a shattered right arm.

"Major," Dr. Combe remembered saying, "your men have shot up the town; have killed one citizen, badly wounded the lieutenant of police, killed his horse, and shot into quite a number of houses."

The Mayor had no doubt of the soldiers' guilt even though he personally had not seen a single black man fire a single shot. He had heard the shooting, seen a bloodstain and a dead horse, and on entering Joe Crixell's saloon had heard a group of men call out to him, "Mr. Mayor, the Negroes are shooting on the town." Not one of these men, it developed later, had seen any soldiers do any shooting.

"Dr. Combe," the Mayor quoted Major Penrose as replying to his accusation, "I can't believe that; it has been reported to me that the citizens have fired on the post."

At the time of their conversation near the main gate in the early-morning darkness, neither Major Penrose nor Mayor Combe had been confronted with any Springfield-rifle shells or clips picked up along the route of the raiders.

"I had no faith at all in the doctor's report that my men had done the shooting," Major Penrose testified, "but to satisfy myself beyond any reasonable doubt I gave the orders to have these rifles locked up and to be inspected as soon as they could see in the daylight."

As a hunter, the Major had learned that a night inspection of a gun could not be relied on to disclose whether it had been recently fired.

"I arrived at this conclusion from my experience with shot-guns," he said. "I always clean them myself after I come home at night, and with a shotgun dismantled, so that I can hold the barrels right to the light—a Rochester—it frequently occurs that when I think I have them polished until they look like a mirror the next morning they look like they have not been cleaned."

Two captains at Fort Sam Houston—John F. Preston and H. M. Dichmann—verified Major Penrose's conclusion in an experiment with four marked rifles which had been thoroughly cleaned beforehand. One gun was fired twice, another eight times, and a third fifteen times. The fourth gun used in the experiment was not fired.

That night, after a rag and a brush had been run through the rifles twice (the work of a minute), it proved to be impossible for the two officers to tell that any of the rifles had been fired that day. The rifle that had been fired eight times, when inspected under bright electric light, came out more brilliant than the unfired rifle. Next morning, by daylight it was a different story, Captain Preston said.

"The three that had been fired showed powder stains in them, and even the rifle which had been brilliant last night was dim this morning."

At the end of the twelve-hour period between the Mayor's afternoon warning of trouble brewing in town and the early-morning inspection of the men's rifles, Major Penrose had no clues except the shells and clips Captain Macklin had found at the mouth of the Cowen alley. Mayor Combe brought some additional shells, then returned later in the day with Captain Kelly, who spoke for the newly formed Citizen's Committee in laying the blame for the raid on the soldiers. Grudgingly, Major Penrose had agreed.

"Were it not for the damaging evidence of the empty shells and used clips," he had then reported to his superiors in San Antonio, "I should be of the firm belief that none of my men was in any way connected with the crime."

Nearly eight months later, when he testified before the Senate Military Affairs Committee, he had changed his mind.

"I was of the belief that some of my men were implicated in this matter," he said, "but since that time, having heard the testimony adduced before my court and having read very carefully the testimony that has been brought out before this committee, there is a strong, a very strong, belief in my mind that my men had nothing whatever to do with it."

The Army officers sitting in judgment on him at Fort Sam Houston disagreed. When they announced their verdict, they achieved the politically desirable effect of satisfying the White House and the War Department by rewriting one of the specifications in such a manner as to declare the black soldiers guilty, their white commanding officer innocent.

Jesse Wheeler's *Daily Herald* was disappointed by Major Penrose's acquittal, but not surprised because it had been "evident from the beginning that the intention of those in charge of the matter was to 'whitewash' the accused officer." * The trial was a "farce," the paper snorted, and called on the Texas courts to take a hand in bringing the perjurers to justice. In the editor's opinion, "the blackest perjurer of them all" was the post scavenger who had sworn in San Antonio and later in Washington that the raid began on the town side of the garrison wall. When he got back to Texas after testifying before the Senate Military Affairs Committee, Tamayo decided to go no farther south than San Antonio.

"I am afraid that if I ever go to Brownsville they will get me in trouble," he wrote Senator Foraker, and asked if he or the committee could compel Mr. Wheeler to "publish my testimony so the citizens of Brownsville may read it."

Mr. Wheeler had no time or space for testimony that tended to clear the soldiers and incriminate his subscribers. He was preoccupied just then with defending Brownsville against the defamatory evidence given the Senate committee by Captain Dana W. Kilburn, who had been stationed at Fort Brown just before the black troops arrived.

"The majority of the people down there were of a very low order of intelligence," Captain Kilburn testified, and estimated that only about a dozen families "had some refinement about their homes."

"By people who had some refinement, do you mean people that had a piano in the house?" a Missouri senator asked.

"Not necessarily, no sir."

"People that had a common-school education—that would be some refinement?"

"I mean people that were ladies and gentlemen."

Captain Kilburn had heard John Tillman threaten to have the Negro soldiers driven out of town in three weeks. The townspeople were prejudiced against all soldiers, regardless of race, the Captain explained, and cited the case of two white men of his company who had been barred from a local skating rink simply because they were in uniform.

---

* Major Penrose got in his licks just before leaving the stand. Asked if he had kept in touch with local affairs by reading the daily paper, he replied, "I did not consider it worth taking."

"This was a skating rink where ladies and children congregated?" a southern senator asked.

"Well, everybody went there, Mexicans and everybody else. Of course the poorer class of Mexicans were kept out, like they would be in any place."

Although it was unwilling to soil its columns with any documentation of the Captain's "depravity," the *Daily Herald* reported that "the vileness of Kilburn's record would disgrace a decent paper." Editorial sympathy was expressed for the popular Los Angeles girl he had married in Brownsville.

No Brownsville witnesses were called back to San Antonio in mid-April when Captain Macklin's court-martial got under way in Fort Sam Houston's hop room. Proof of the soldiers' participation in the raid was not relevant to the one specific charge leveled against the defendant. He was accused of having failed "to perform the duties enjoined upon an officer of the day in case of alarm, retiring to his quarters, from which it was found impossible to arouse him or bring him forth during the continuance of a considerable amount of small-arms fire at or in the vicinity of Fort Brown, Texas."

"He is a hard sleeper," Major Penrose said on the opening day of the trial, and a succession of witnesses took the stand to bear him out.

"A very sound sleeper," Lieutenant Lawrason testified, and, asked to give an example, he told of an incident at Fort Reno, when Macklin was post exchange officer. "I went to town one day and brought some money out for him—some change—and when I came to give it to him he was asleep in an easy-chair in his front room. I shook him by the shoulder and spoke to him several times and told him that I had the money, and he nodded his head and said, 'All right,' and I was about to put it down and leave when Mrs. Macklin came in and laughed and said he was still asleep. She shook him and spoke to him and woke him up, and he thanked me for bringing the money, and verified it—counted it."

"Have you ever seen any other person who was as difficult to awaken as Captain Macklin?" Lawrason was asked, and he replied: "I do not believe I ever have, sir."

Dr. Ira C. Brown, a former brigade surgeon who had shared a double set of quarters with the Macklins at Fort Niobrara, considered the Captain an "unusually" sound sleeper, as he could attest from his own experience in Nebraska. The Browns and the Macklins had been separated by a lath and plaster partition in their one-story adobe quarters. The two families used to signal one another by knocking on the wall. The system worked for Macklin only when he was awake.

"I have pounded on the wall on my side," Dr. Brown recalled, "and Captain Macklin was asleep on a divan right on the other side of it, and I could not awaken him."

Corporal Ray Burdett, who finally succeeded in prodding Macklin from his bed about an hour after the shooting ended, was not available as a witness at the Captain's trial. Three other men who tried to awaken him that night did show up, however. There was some question as to whether all three of them had reached the right door, but two swore they'd heard him sing out, "All right," and the third said he'd left after getting no reply.

"I was very much tired out; very tired, indeed," Macklin explained to the officers of the court.

He had been up late the night before and, after twelve humid hours as officer of the day, he was exhausted when he dropped into bed about ten minutes to twelve. Before retiring he had left orders with the trumpeter of the guard to call him for reveille. This was the first thought that came to him when he was awakened around an hour later.

"I thought I heard a knock downstairs, and I called out, 'All right.' I got up and looked at the clock, and I said, 'Why, I must have been dreaming.' The impression was that that call was a call for reveille—that is, the knock was the orderly trumpeter calling me for reveille—and I lay down again and went to sleep."

Apparently it was Private Hairston, the sentinel guarding the officers' quarters, who awakened the officer of the day at five minutes to one. As Hairston told it, he knocked three times, calling the Captain by name each time, and the Captain called back, "All right," but never put in an appearance.

"About that time," Hairston said, "Corporal Burdett met me in about forty or fifty feet of the house and asked me if I could get Captain Macklin up. I told him no; and he said, 'Come; I will get him up.' So he went and rapped on the door and he told . . . Captain Macklin to get up; they were shooting on the quarters; they wanted him at once. So he gotten up and he come out of the house immediately; I guess a minute after he told him."

As Captain Macklin ran across the parade ground, he encountered only one person, Captain Lyon.

"I asked him where he had been," Lyon testified, "and he said he had been asleep, he hadn't waked up, and I told him he had better go and report at once to Major Penrose."

"What did you say to Captain Macklin?" Major Penrose was asked, and he replied, "Well, I think I said, 'My God, Ed, I am glad to see you.'"

On the first day of Macklin's trial, the court asked Major Penrose if, in view of the unusual circumstances, he felt that the accused had performed the duties required of an officer of the day.

"I think that he did," the Major answered. "He did not retire until after the prescribed period for him to retire, and that he slept through I don't think we can count against Captain Macklin."

The court agreed. Macklin was acquitted "fully and honorably." The Brownsville *Daily Herald* managed to work an indignant editorial into its front-page headline:

SECOND MILITARY WHITEWASH
PERPETRATED AT SAM HOUSTON

" 'Fully and honorably acquitted' is a most unusual verdict," Major Penrose wrote Senator Foraker from Fort Reno, "but he deserves it all, and the court is to be congratulated on their fearlessness. I should have had the same verdict."

Although Penrose had been found not guilty on both specific charges filed against him, the court had decided in his case that men of his command "did assemble, armed with rifles, and did proceed to the town of Brownsville, Texas, and did then and there shoot and wound and kill certain citizens thereof." However, as far as the defendant was concerned, the court had attached "no criminality thereto on his part."

The Penrose verdict represented a triumph of military and

legal cant over logic and justice. The white commanding officer, who bore the ultimate responsibility for his men's discipline, was free to resume his chosen career. The black noncommissioned officers and enlisted men, who had not been put on trial, were dishonored and debarred from military service, although not one of them had ever been given a chance to stand in a public place, confront his accusers, and, with the assistance of counsel, defend himself against specific charges of criminal conduct.

20

"The box was bursted."

No LAWYERS REPRESENTING the discharged soldiers were admitted to the Senate hearing room when the Military Affairs Committee began its investigation of what it called the Brownsville affray.* Some senators kept referring to the proceedings as a "trial" and had to be reminded that it was a "hearing." A score of ex-soldiers collected in the corridor, but only a few were admitted to the committee room where Senator Foraker was waiting to argue their case.

"Now, Sergeant," the Ohio senator asked the committee's first witness, Israel Harris, "you heard this firing. You have been eleven years in the Army. I suppose that you can tell from the firing what kind of arms are being fired—from the report?"

"Well, from the report of the rifles that night, and from what I heard, they were mixed—different kinds."

"Did you hear the report of any Springfield rifle, such as you were carrying?"

"I could not hear the report of any Springfield rifle."

"What kind of rifles did they seem to be?"

* "The word 'affray' naturally implies a disturbance in which two sides take part, a brawl, or a riot. In the Brownsville affair there was distinctly only one party taking part, and that was the attacking one. In other words, it was a raid, pure and simple."—Brownsville *Daily Herald,* January 28, 1907.

"It sounded like they were Winchesters and six-shooters, or something like that, from the firing."

"I believe the people in Brownsville did it," said the second witness, D Company's First Sergeant Jacob Frazier, who was described for Washington *Post* readers as "straight as an arrow, black as the ace of spades, standing six feet three and a half inches in his stockings, and conducting himself with a decidedly military bearing."

"Your first impression was that the people of Brownsville had attacked the post?" echoed Senator Foster of Louisiana.

"Yes, sir," Frazier said, and went on to explain that when he discovered the town had been shot up with Springfield bullets, he had begun to think that "some of the soldiers must have undoubtedly done it." But by the time he was given his discharge papers at Fort Reno, he had come back to the belief that the attack had been staged by townspeople to rid the garrison of black troops.

"Because I could not hear any soldiers make any remarks whatever, anything about it," he testified when asked why he had changed his mind again. As a first sergeant, he said, it was clear to him that "if any of the men did it, they would be very careful about talking it before me; that is, if I went just boldly up and tried to find out if any of the men did the shooting that they would not say anything; but if I stood around and talked, what you might say in favor, as if I did not think it of much importance—as if when you want to find out anything you talk in favor of it, you don't mean it, but talk in favor, to get them to say something about it—well, I did that to several men."

When no one in any of the three companies appeared to have any guilty knowledge of the raid, Frazier was persuaded of the battalion's innocence. "I have been with the Army a considerable while now," he said, "I have been with a great many men since I have been in the Army, and I know just about how a soldier will do. He may do something and keep very close for a day or two, will not say anything about it at all, but after he thinks everything is over he will come out and make his brags about it, what he did, and how well he got off with it, and all like that, and that is why I believe that if a soldier did it, I would have found it out."

"Have you at any time withheld any knowledge of which you were possessed either from General Garlington or Major Blocksom?" Sergeant Frazier was asked.

"No, sir," he replied. "I was only questioned by Major Blocksom. I never seen General Garlington."

"You never saw General Garlington?"

"No, sir."

"Didn't he call upon you when he went to El Reno?"

"No, sir."

"The soldiers are daily swearing to their own innocence and endeavoring to fasten the foul crime which they committed upon the innocent and outraged people of Brownsville," the *Daily Herald* declared at the close of the second week of the Senate hearings.

Along Elizabeth Street, in the better saloons and gambling establishments, it was generally agreed that the town was the victim of a plot to suppress the truth. It was common gossip that Captain Macklin not only knew the names of the raiders, but had been their leader. Indeed, as the *Daily Herald* pointed out, Macklin had gone into Joe Crixell's saloon some eight hours before the raid and, after listening to some remarks by a dairyman named Billingsley, had predicted the attack by the soldiers.

Crixell's affidavit to this effect had been deleted from the Purdy-Blocksom report because of the effect its publication might have had on the forthcoming trials of Major Penrose and Captain Macklin. When Captain Charles E. Hay, Jr., judge advocate at the Penrose court-martial, failed to call Crixell to the stand, Elizabeth Street commentators figured the prosecutor was hesitant to push the case against a major who might someday be the colonel of his regiment. Not until late May did Crixell and Billingsley get a chance to tell their stories in a public forum.

"Absolutely false," Major Penrose wired Senator Foraker after reading their Senate testimony, and in a follow-up letter the same day, May 28, he added, "Of all the perjured testimony given by the Brownsville witnesses, these two men have stooped to the lowest, and I hope Captain Macklin will be given an opportunity to contradict their statements before your committee, and have his statement supported by Captain Lyon and Lieutenant Lawrason."

Macklin, Lyon, and Lawrason came into his saloon Monday afternoon eight or ten hours before the shooting, when the town was buzzing with the story of the attack on Lon Evans' wife, Joe Crixell testified before the Senate committee, as he had stated in a grand-jury affidavit in mid-September. The three officers ordered a round of gin fizzes, the saloonkeeper continued, and while he was making the drinks, Macklin struck up a conversation.

"Joe," the Captain was quoted as saying, "have you ever heard anything about a nigger being hit over the head with a six-shooter around here lately?"

"Yes, I heard a little about it," Crixell said he replied, and then went on to say that, as he understood it, Fred Tate had hit a nigger over the head with a six-shooter when he'd refused to yield the sidewalk to some ladies.

"Yes," Macklin was then supposed to have said, "that is what they claim, but Major Penrose and myself have investigated this thing thoroughly, and we have found out that these Negro soldiers have been imposed on by the citizens and Federal officers of this town, and this thing has got to be stopped. Now, Joe, suppose these niggers would jump that barracks fence and shoot this damn town up any one of these nights. We could not prevent it."

It was just about this time, Crixell went on, that Albert W. Billingsley dropped by for a drink. Billingsley was a loud-talking, quick-tempered dairyman (after the raid Mayor Combe threatened to put him under arrest if he didn't calm down). He corroborated Crixell's testimony about the presence of the three officers in the saloon that Monday afternoon.

As Billingsley told it, "I walked to the end of the counter— we very often shake dice down there for the drinks—and I said to Crixell, 'I will shake the first dice out of the box for the drinks.'

Seeing these men in there was why I went in. I went in for a little information. Crixell came up to me and brought the dice box and threw the dice out on the counter, and I began talking to him, and I said, 'Have you heard anything more about the Evans affair?' He says, 'Nothing, particular.' I says, 'What do these officers say about it?' We were talking in a very low tone, not intending to be heard. He says, 'Nothing.' I says, 'Have they done anything, or do they act like they are going to do anything in regard to this matter?' He says, 'I don't think they will do anything,' and I says, 'Well, there ought to be something done, some way.' I says, 'At the rate these fellows are carrying on here, I don't think that the soldiers or the officers either ought to be allowed in town if they don't do something to help or assist us or to stop these men from conducting themselves the way they are acting in the city.' Then I turned around and walked out. That is all I said to him."

Billingsley's parting words, as Crixell remembered them, were more provocative and were spoken in a voice loud enough for the three officers to hear. "It is a shame," he heard Billingsley say. "We ought not to allow even these white officers to come in town. They are just as bad as the Negroes." When Billingsley left, Crixell continued, he rejoined the officers. Macklin looked at Lyon and made some inaudible comment, then remarked to Crixell, "Yes, these niggers will surprise this fellow yet."

"No, sir," Macklin said when asked if he had made such a statement. "A remark of that kind in my position would be suicidal. I never made such a remark as that."

Lyon and Lawrason testified they had heard no such remark by Macklin. All three officers agreed they had repaired to Crixell's place for a gin fizz on the day of the raid, but it was in the morning, around ten o'clock, not in the afternoon, as both Crixell and Billingsley had testified. Captain Lyon was precise in establishing the time as midmorning.

"On that morning I had been on a practice march of twelve miles with my company. I left the post at five-thirty o'clock. The rate of marching is about three miles an hour. I made twelve miles. That consumed about four hours. I got back to the post at about half past nine. I had a certain inspection regarding the condition of the men's feet after this march, which we were required to make, and as soon as that was completed Mr. Lawrason and I went down to Crixell's saloon to get something cold to drink. On the way down we met Captain Macklin and he went with us, so that it must have been somewhere in the neighborhood of ten o'clock."

While Lyon and Lawrason were out on the practice march, Macklin drilled C Company until nine o'clock; then he returned to his quarters, changed clothes, and walked uptown to the *Daily Herald* printing office to check on some work he'd ordered for his company. As he left the office, he said, he ran into Lyon and Lawrason heading back to the garrison with their two companies.

"I told Captain Lyon that his printing which he had ordered there at the office was finished, and asked him if he wanted me to get it, and he said yes," Macklin testified. "I stayed in that printing office for about ten or fifteen minutes. When Captain Lyon and Mr. Lawrason returned to the town, which was a very short distance from the post, we all three went to Crixell's saloon, and we ordered three gin fizzes, one apiece."

"And this was about what hour of the day?"

"About ten o'clock in the morning, sir."

In an unguarded moment toward the close of his testimony, Crixell mentioned a visit Mayor Combe had paid his saloon on the afternoon of the raid. "He said, 'Joe, do you hear many of these people around here talking about this Evans affair?' I said, 'No, not many.' He said, 'If you hear anybody say anything about it, you tell them that I have just come from a conference with Major Penrose, have had a long talk with him, and not to say anything, but let the thing go, and that he will find the guilty one.'"

Crixell put the time of the Mayor's visit at "about two or three o'clock," roughly the same time he said the three officers had come in to slake their thirst. Dr. Combe could hardly have referred to his conference with Major Penrose two or three hours before it took place. Nor could Captain Macklin have discussed the Evans affair either that morning at ten o'clock or that afternoon between two and four. Not until that evening, sometime after five-thirty, when Major Penrose advised him of his decision to establish an eight-o'clock curfew as a result of his meeting with the Mayor and Mr. Evans, did Macklin first learn of the reported attack on Mrs. Evans.

"It was in the paper that morning," Crixell sputtered when this discrepancy was brought to his attention, but the Brownsville *Daily Herald* was not a morning paper. It hit the streets sometime between four and five o'clock in the afternoon.*

The Crixell brothers' bar was Lieutenant Leckie's favorite drinking place in Brownsville.

"Come out here, and I will show you how near they come to getting us," Teofilo Crixell said one day, and showed the Lieutenant a bullet hole in a two-by-four upright supporting a wooden awning above the sidewalk directly across the street from the Ruby Saloon, where the raid had ended in murder. "That is one of the shots fired that night."

"You are mistaken about that," Leckie said. "That is about a .44 or .45."

"No," Crixell insisted, and when a group of local barflies backed him up, Leckie suggested cutting the bullet out of the post. He dug into the soft pine with his penknife, then the job was finished with a brace and bit. The Lieutenant was so sure of what he would find that he not only put his professional standing in jeopardy, he also bet a round of drinks that the hole had not been made by a steel-jacketed Springfield-rifle bullet. He won. It turned out to have been made by a lead bullet.

"It was all lead?" Senator Foraker asked.

"It was all lead," the Lieutenant replied.

"And no pieces of steel around about the bullet?"

"No, sir."

An attempt was made by senators hostile to the soldiers to

* After giving his Senate testimony, Joe Crixell returned home in triumph and Mayor Combe appointed him chief of police. On an August night just six years after the Brownsville Raid, he was gunned down on Elizabeth Street near his old saloon. The *Daily Herald* named his assailant in a front-page story, but the man was never brought to trial. "Just one of those election squabbles," explains a local antiquarian.

show that the lead bullet could have been one of the reduced-range cartridges used for guard duty, but Senator Foraker called in expert witnesses to prove that its proportion of tin and antimony did not correspond with the composition of the guard ammunition made for the Army by the Union Metallic Cartridge Company.

At Fort Brown, only C Company had been issued these lead bullets. The other two companies had steel-jacketed ball ammunition. If soldiers had conspired to attack the town, Foraker pointed out, it was most improbable they would have used reduced-range cartridges containing only about one-third as much powder as the ammunition assigned B and D Companies. The men had such little confidence in the lead bullets that in the early-morning hours following the raid, when C Company was being deployed to defend the garrison, Artificer Rudy called on his quartermaster sergeant to unlock the storeroom and bring out ball ammunition.

During the shooting spree, witnesses on both sides of the garrison wall heard from a hundred and fifty to three hundred shots, but afterward only about forty exploded shells came into the hands of the military authorities, and nobody could explain why so much gunplay had produced so few spent cartridges, none of which had been recovered inside the military reservation.

At daybreak, when Captain Macklin found six or seven empty shells at the mouth of the Cowen alley, he also picked up six clips, enough to accommodate thirty cartridges. Neither he nor Major Penrose seems to have speculated on the whereabouts of the missing shells, nor did Macklin remark on an even more significant detail which struck him later. He had found the shells lying in a circular area not more than ten inches in diameter. If they had been ejected by the action of a Springfield rifle, they would have been scattered over an area not ten inches in diameter but closer to ten feet.

"I picked up two of them in my hand," Major Penrose testified," and saw that they were Frankford arsenal shells."

The bullets recovered from the three houses in the immediate vicinity (Cowen, Yturria, Garza) were of a different composition. They had been manufactured by the Union Metallic Cartridge Company. Thus, the raiders had fired one kind of .30-caliber shell, Captain Macklin had found another.

The Macklin shells disappeared before they could be placed in evidence, but thirty-three other shells, or "cartridge cases," as the Army's ordnance experts preferred to call them, were retrieved from the streets of Brownsville and sent to the Springfield Arsenal for microscopic study. They were compared with cartridge cases fired from each of the rifles in the possession of the three companies at Fort Brown. The thirty-three exploded shells proved to have been fired from four Springfield rifles, all of which belonged to B Company.

Three of the rifles had been assigned to Privates Ernest English, Thomas Taylor, and Joseph L. Wilson. All three men swore they had been asleep in B Company's barracks when the shooting began. They had jumped up, grabbed a gun (presumably their own), answered roll call, formed a line of skirmishers along the garrison wall, and, when dismissed, had turned in their weapons. The rifles had remained locked up until daylight, when they had been removed from the gunracks, inspected by the company commander, and found to bear no signs of having been recently fired.

Even if a trio of soldiers had somehow managed to shoot up the town with the English-Taylor-Wilson rifles and had then contrived to clean them before inspection, it was impossible to link the raiders with the shells fired from the fourth gun. Rifle No. 45683 belonged to William Blaney, B Company's former quartermaster sergeant. Blaney was on furlough during July and August. He never set foot in Brownsville and none of the raiders, whether soldiers or civilians, could have fired his rifle in the town that night.

On June 8, six weeks before the three companies set out for Texas, Sergeant Blaney had got in some target practice at Fort Niobrara (he was a crack shot), then cleaned his rifle and locked it in the company's storeroom. That evening, before going on furlough, he had turned the storeroom keys over to Walker McCurdy, who had been picked to replace him as quartermaster sergeant.

Blaney was so attached to his rifle that his successor took care to see that it didn't get issued to someone else by mistake during the Sergeant's absence. McCurdy wrote Blaney's name on a slip of paper and tucked it in the chamber of No. 45683. It was still there three months later when Blaney rejoined his company at Fort Reno. Meanwhile, the rifle had traveled to Brownsville in one of B Company's arm chests.

On the night of the raid it was in the company storeroom, still in the same chest, the lid fastened by ten screws. Some iron bunks were piled on top of the chest and the storeroom door was secured by two locks requiring separate keys, both of which were in McCurdy's possession.

Sometime around three or four o'clock in the morning, after the garrison had calmed down and the men of his company had gone back to bed, Lieutenant Lawrason finished counting the rifles in the gunracks on the second floor of B Company's barracks. He went downstairs and, without explaining why, ordered Sergeant McCurdy to unlock the storeroom. He wanted to finish counting the seventy rifles assigned to his company.

"What did you do when you got in there?" McCurdy was asked.

"I got in there and I had a lot of bunks on top of the arm chest. I taken them off, taken my screw-driver, and opened the boxes."

"What then? Did you find the guns in there or not?"

"Yes, sir; found the guns just like I packed them at Niobrara."

Lieutenant Lawrason corroborated every essential detail of the Sergeant's testimony. The arm chests had been buried under iron quartermaster bunks and T-shaped iron uprights designed to hold mosquito bars, he said. They had not been tampered with since the day he watched them being unloaded from wagons at Fort Brown and carried into the storeroom. He counted the rifles. None was missing.

"When you looked at them was there any indication that they had been disturbed in any way whatever since they had been boxed up at Fort Niobrara?"

"No, sir; there was not."

When Administration apologists found themselves staring down the barrel of the fourth gun, they made a frantic effort to cast doubt on Walker McCurdy's integrity. They got no support from any of the officers who knew him. A sixteen-year veteran with overseas duty in Cuba and the Philippines, McCurdy had left a lasting impression on one of the regiment's former commanding officers.

"McCurdy is a good man and a trustworthy man," said General Burt. "I would believe him absolutely. I recall an incident about McCurdy which occurred at Fort Missoula, that when he was charged with a grave offense, and he had come up under examination, on his own testimony he was relieved, because when I said, 'Sergeant McCurdy, is that true as you state to me?' he said, 'It is, Colonel,' and he was relieved from the offense. I do not recall exactly what it was, but I remember his being before me at the time."

"And you had that confidence in him?" Senator Foraker asked.

"Yes, sir."

To the War Department's chagrin, its ordnance experts came up with still more evidence that the exploded shells found in Brownsville after the raid had not been fired in Brownsville during the raid. Some of the shells showed they had been inserted in a rifle two or more times before they had been fired; some had double indentations on the cap, indicating that the first attempt to fire them had failed but the second had succeeded. The battalion's officers and men had no trouble clearing up the mystery.

As for the shells which had been put in a rifle, removed, and reinserted, it was obvious to any Army man that soldiers on a target range often find themselves with ball ammunition in their rifles when given the order to cease firing. They are required to remove the cartridges and then put them back in the chamber when firing is resumed.

The double indentation could be traced back to the spring of 1906, when the three companies had turned in their old Krags at Fort Niobrara and received their new Springfields. The rifles had been so heavily oiled with cosmoline that, in spite of heroic efforts to clean them, the men had often found that when they got out on the target range the firing pin failed to strike the primer with sufficient force the first time to explode the cartridge. Once the chamber had been worked over again with coal oil, the second try would usually prove successful.

"After you got that cosmoline out and got the spring to working properly and got the mechanism all oiled up, it was a sure shot every time, was it not, according to your experience?" Senator Foraker asked Lieutenant Lawrason.

"Yes, sir," he replied. "The mainspring was an unusually strong one, and unless a primer was defective there would never be a case of misfire."

"If these shells were fired out of the different guns belonging to the Twenty-fifth Infantry described here, with this double indentation, where would you think they had been fired, at what place?"

"I should think on the target range at Fort Niobrara."

"At Niobrara?"

"That was the only place it could be."

The two different marks on the cartridges indicated that they had been inserted in two different rifles, Lawrason continued. "On the target range," he explained, "two men always fire at the same firing point, first the one on the right and then the one on the left, and frequently, when we were having this trouble with the springs, if a cartridge failed to fire in one gun it was passed over to the other man and tried in his rifle."

It was most unlikely, Lawrason believed, that the cartridges with the double indentations had been fired by trained men on a midnight raid.

"If a cartridge failed to fire," he said, "I should think that the man would snatch his bolt open—and that would extract the cartridge and throw it some distance—and put in a new one."

When the bolt of a Springfield rifle is pulled back, laymen in the Senate were told by experts, the ejector throws the cartridge a distance of some eight to ten feet. Men shooting up an unfriendly town in the middle of the night would hardly have taken the trouble to root around an unlighted alley for a shell that had misfired.

If the exploded shells found in Brownsville after the raid were fired from four B Company rifles at Fort Niobrara weeks before the raid, as the evidence indicated, the next question to be settled was how they got from Nebraska to Texas. B Company's quartermaster sergeant, Walker McCurdy, had the answer.

After target practice, he explained, the men were supposed to decap and clean the spent shells before leaving the rifle range. The shells were then packed and sent back to the arsenal. In Nebraska, due to a fouled-up requisition, B Company had been forced to make do with a decapper designed for a Krag and filed down to fit the new Springfield cartridge cases. The decapper broke, and the company accumulated from fifteen hundred to sixteen hundred exploded shells, none of which had been worked on. They were in the same condition as when first picked up at the range.

These exploded shells were carried to Fort Brown in a venerable footlocker that didn't survive the trip intact. "The box was bursted," said McCurdy, and Sergeant Sanders supported his testimony. For several days, while the company storeroom was being put in order, the open box sat on B Company's back porch, where the cartridge cases were within view and within reach of the town's brown-eyed, quick-fingered young scavengers.

"There was nobody watching," McCurdy said. "They could have taken them, sir."

"Where there clips in that box?" he was asked.

"Oh, yes," he replied; "those clips, with the shells, go in. They were there."

"You think there were clips in there?"

"I don't think anything about it; I know there were."

The Verdict

———◆◆◆◆———

21

"They ask no favors because they are Negroes, but only for justice because they are men."

THE EXPLODED SHELLS, which had been generally accepted as the most damaging evidence against the soldiers, turned out to be the most persuasive argument in their favor, but when the Senate Military Affairs Committee wound up its hearings on March 10, 1908, a majority of its members rested their decision less on the evidence than on partisan politics and personal prejudice. Four Republicans, supporting a Republican Administration in a presidential campaign year, sided with the committee's five Democrats who, in Foraker's words, "were against the Negroes before a word of testimony was heard." *

These nine senators signed a majority report affirming the soldiers' guilt. In effect, the five southern Democrats found them guilty of being black, the four Republicans of having embarrassed the President and the man most likely to succeed him by refusing to confess to a crime no loyal party member cared to think they might not have committed.

The committee's vote against the soldiers "carries not the slightest convincing moral or judicial weight," Professor Kelly Miller of Howard University wrote Foraker the next day. The southerners would have voted against the Negroes "five minutes after the account of the outbreak as certainly as after hearing the evidence. No judge in Christendom would regard them as competent jurors in the case. And yet the President relies upon this vote to substantiate his charge and to justify his action."

Proof of the men's guilt was "abundant and conclusive," the majority reported, and Roosevelt agreed that they had come to "the only conclusion that can justly be reached in the matter." Having put Brownsville behind him, he hoped, the President set out to bring disaffected black Republicans back into Abraham's bosom, for 1908 was an election year.

On March 11, the same day the Military Affairs Committee submitted its reports, the Senate received a message from the White House taking note of the expiration of the time limit during which the dismissed soldiers had been given a chance to qualify for re-enlistment. Many of them had filed applications; none had met the President's conditions. He proposed giving them another year to meet the same requirements. They would have to convince him that they were not "within the class whose discharge was deemed necessary in order to maintain the discipline and morale of the Army."

The nine senators who signed the majority report split on party lines. The four Republicans agreed to file a supplementary

---

* The four Republicans: Chairman Warren (Wyoming), Lodge (Massachusetts), Warner (Missouri), Du Pont (Delaware); the five Democrats: Taliaferro (Florida), Foster (Louisiana), Overman (North Carolina), Frazier (Tennessee), McCreary (Kentucky).

report endorsing the proposal to permit reinstatement of any soldier who could establish to the President's satisfaction that he had not participated in the affray and had "no guilty knowledge" of it. The five Democrats on the committee refused to go along with this unabashed effort to hold black Republican voters in line.

The Administration plan was such a patent swindle that even some Republican senators who agreed that the town had been shot up by a few soldiers balked at subjecting the rest of the men to this political fraud. After a year and a half (for which no back pay was to be provided), innocent men who had served their country well were to be permitted to resume their military careers only if they could do what none of them had thus far succeeded in doing, prove their innocence of "guilty knowledge."

"How are these men going to prove their innocence?" asked Oregon's Republican senator, Charles W. Fulton. "What evidence are they to bring to show that they are innocent? How can a man prove a negative?"

Three Republicans on the Military Affairs Committee joined Senator Foraker in dissenting from the majority report, but they too were divided and ended up filing two minority reports. Senators Bulkeley (Connecticut), Hemenway (Indiana), and Scott (West Virginia) agreed with Foraker that the testimony was too contradictory and unreliable to sustain the charge against the soldiers. In short, they returned the ancient Scottish verdict, "Not proven." Two dissenters—Foraker and Bulkeley—went one step further. They flatly declared that "the weight of the testimony shows that none of the soldiers of the Twenty-fifth U.S. Infantry participated in the shooting affray."

Undoubtedly, all four members of the minority concluded, some of the soldiers were innocent men who had "by their long and faithful service acquired valuable rights of which they are deprived by a discharge without honor." The minority recommended their reinstatement, the correction of their service records, and the restoration of their rights. No mention was made of the President's unattainable terms, the necessity of proving an unprovable innocence of "guilty knowledge."

Essentially, the New York *Times* observed, the difference between the four Republicans who signed the majority report and the four who dissented from it "is that the former would reinstate the soldiers who can satisfy the authorities that they are innocent, while the latter would reinstate those who are not shown to be guilty." A grave wrong had been done, the editorial continued, but instead of facing and correcting it, Roosevelt and his friends were making an undignified effort to save face.

"They have not the courage to confess their original error; the endeavor to escape its consequences leaves them distinctly ridiculous."

When Missouri's Senator Warner introduced the Administration's bill, he added a humane touch to Roosevelt's original proposal—back pay and allowances were to be granted—but S. 6206 would not clear the records of soldiers who had been dismissed without honor and without cause, nor would it restore the stripes of the battalion's noncommissioned officers, some of whom had shared with the President the horror, though not the headlines, of the assault on Santiago de Cuba.

The soldiers, under Roosevelt's proposal, would be treated like innocent bystanders who had been clubbed and crippled for life when a blundering constabulary found them at the scene of a crime. The President had no intention of binding up their wounds; it was enough to spare them further punishment. As Foraker saw it, the soldiers were citizens of a civilized country, men presumed to be innocent until proof of their guilt had been established by constitutionally acceptable procedures.

Under Foraker's bill (S. 5729), a soldier would be able to re-enlist, have his service record cleared, pick up his back pay, and regain his former rank once he had taken an oath attesting his innocence. Roosevelt was outraged by this "proposal to condone murder and perjury in the past and put a premium upon perjury in the future by permitting any murderer or perjurer, who will again perjure himself, to be restored to the United States Army."

The President ignored Section 2 of the Foraker bill, which specifically stated that any soldier making such an oath would still be liable to prosecution and punishment if it should later develop that he had taken part in the raid or had guilty knowledge of it. As head of the constabulary that had roughed up the innocent bystanders, Roosevelt took the position that the soldiers must prove their innocence. As a lawyer, Foraker argued that it was up to the Government to prove their guilt.

A month after the Military Affairs Committee reached its split decision, Senator Foraker let it be known that on April 14 he would take the Senate floor to speak again on the Brownsville matter. Black men and women crowded outside the public galleries four hours before the doors were opened. It was, they sensed, to be a historic address. They were not disappointed.

"He seemed inspired by his subject," the New York *Times* reported the next morning, "and spoke with all his oldtime fire and vigor."

"Libel," he trumpeted at the outset, flourishing a newspaper clipping which had spread the rumor that he intended to speak for three days and deliver a bitter attack on the President and his Secretary of War.

"I have at no time had any purpose to attack the President or Secretary Taft in connection with this matter or in connection with any other matter. I have had no vengeance to seek and no occasion to seek any, I hope. In this whole matter I have simply sought to present to the Senate, in so far as I might be able to do so, the facts in regard to this unfortunate affair."

Step by step, he led a spellbound audience across the murky ground, from the one-sided investigations of Blocksom, Purdy, and Garlington to the testimony given by some sixty soldiers who had answered the Senate committee's questions with "straightforward frankness" and "manifest truthfulness."

They had awakened to the sound of gunfire on the town side of the garrison wall, they said, and the physical evidence tended to bear them out. No exploded shells or clips had been found anywhere inside the fort. They swore they had no knowledge of the crime, and both their white commissioned officers and their black NCOs had come to believe them. It was difficult to believe otherwise when a year and a half of relentless probing had failed to turn up a single clue incriminating a single soldier.

The senators on the Military Affairs Committee had listened, asked questions, and, for reasons of their own, a majority of them had chosen to write off the men as perjurers and to accept as "incontestable evidence" of their guilt the contradictory testimony of some fifteen townspeople who swore they had seen what no human eyes could possibly have distinguished in the dark streets and alleys of Brownsville on the moonless night of August 13.

"In all the immediate neighborhood of the points where, according to all the witnesses, the first shots were fired, whether inside or outside the reservation, it was as dark as a very dark night could make it," Senator Foraker reminded his colleagues. "These witnesses testified that hearing the firing they went to their windows, looked out into this darkness, and at a distance ranging all the way from thirty up to one hundred and fifty feet saw the firing party and recognized them as soldiers from the garrison by the color of their faces, by the uniforms they wore, and the guns they carried."

Major Penrose, on the other hand, had been unable to distinguish one of his white officers from a black enlisted man at a distance of ten feet. Other officers had also testified to their inability to make such an identification at distances of from five to ten feet. Their testimony had been backed up by tests conducted at Fort McIntosh by officers of the Twenty-sixth Infantry.

"Almost every night as I pass along the streets," Foraker continued, "I find myself experimenting in this way, looking to see at a distance if I can recognize whether a man whom I see moving is a white man or a colored man or how he is dressed. I ask every senator here to experiment in that way. It is no trouble. It is rather interesting, and when you have thus experimented for yourself you will be able to set aside all this so-called testimony of 'eyewitnesses,' for there is not one of them who was in a situation where he could tell anything at all that was reliable."

Aside from the unreliable testimony of the townspeople, the case against the soldiers rested on untenable physical evidence. Not only had a disproportionate number of clips been found with the exploded shells dropped by the raiders, but also some of the bullets had been fired from a rifle they could not possibly have got their hands on and others, showing the marks of ejection and reinsertion, could have been fired in Brownsville only if desperate men had retrieved them in a dark, muddy alley after their shots had already sounded the alarm in a heavily armed community.

Furthermore, no credible motive had been established for the soldiers to do violence to a town where they had run into surprisingly little difficulty. Again the circumstantial evidence favored the soldiers. The few minor clashes between the blacks and the townspeople had all involved men of C Company, which happened to be the only one of the three companies that had been issued lead bullets used for guard duty instead of steel-jacketed ball ammunition. The seven bullets recovered from houses hit by the raiders had all been steel-jacketed. The lead bullet Lieutenant Leckie recovered from the post in front of Crixell brothers' saloon seemed to have been fired from a .45 Colt revolver.

Ten revolvers for each company had been issued to the battalion at Fort Niobrara. None of these revolvers had ever been removed from the chests in which they had been delivered, except one that was in the possession of a commissioned officer. No evidence had been brought forth to suggest that any other revolvers or pistols had been available to the soldiers on the night of the raid, but Major Penrose and Mayor Combe, along with several other knowledgeable witnesses, were convinced that the first shots fired by the raiders had been pistol shots.

"In view of this testimony, it cannot well be doubted that the firing was commenced that night by somebody other than the soldiers," Foraker said.

The President, he continued, had no precedent for his outrageous demand that the condemned men must prove their innocence of "guilty knowledge" to the same judge who, after pronouncing their guilt and fixing their punishment, had declared that there were "very few, if any" of the soldiers dismissed who could have been ignorant of what occurred.

"The vilest horse thief, the most dangerous burglar, or the bloodiest murderer would not be required either to prove his innocence or to submit to a trial before a judge who had in even the most casual way expressed the opinion that the defendant was guilty," Foraker argued in closing his defense of the black battalion.

"Such a performance would be justly denounced as a denial of one of the most sacred rights of citizenship and a lasting disgrace to the judge who perpetrated it.

"Who are these men that it should be even suggested that they should be treated worse than common criminals?

"They are at once both citizens and soldiers of the Republic. Aside from these charges, which they deny, their behavior, both in the Army and out of it, has justly excited the highest commendation. Their record is without spot or blemish.

"They are typical representatives of a race that has ever been loyal to America and American institutions; a race that has never raised a hostile hand against our country's flag; a race that has contributed to the nation tens of thousands of brave defenders, not one of whom has ever turned traitor or faltered in his fidelity.

"In every war in which we have permitted them to participate they have distinguished themselves for efficiency and valor. They have shed their blood and laid down their lives in the fierce shock of battle, side by side with their white comrades. . . .

"Faithfully, uncomplainingly, with pride and devotion, they have performed all their duties and kept all their obligations.

"They ask no favors because they are Negroes, but only for justice because they are men."

So great was the hubbub when Foraker's peroration ended that the Senate reading clerk found it impossible to make himself heard. A presidential request for four new battleships was drowned out by cheering blacks who hooted the Vice President's threat to clear the galleries. Downstairs on the Senate floor, Foraker's friends crowded around to shake his hand, clap him on the back. The reading clerk managed to get through Roosevelt's message by reading the first and last lines of each page, skipping the rest.

"After reading your speech," Cornell President J. G. Schurman wrote Foraker, "I am absolutely convinced, as I had previously been led to believe, that the President has made a terrible mistake." Dr. Schurman praised the "spirit" of the address. It reminded him of "a scientific investigation or a judicial inquiry, where the sole object is to discover the truth on the basis of the facts of the case."

"In the whole matter," Foraker replied at once, "I have at no time had any thought of personal advantage, political or otherwise. The case interested me, in the first place, because of the great, broad question of constitutional power, on the one hand, and of constitutional rights of citizenship, on the other. Does a soldier when he enlists cease to be a citizen, and can he be dealt with in a time of peace, where crime is involved, in the arbitrary, dictatorial, and tyrannical manner in which these soldiers were dealt with. That they were Negroes cut no figure whatever. I thought of them only as American citizens."

Roosevelt summoned young William E. Borah of Idaho to the White House and asked him to rebut Foraker. On April 20, when the freshman senator from Boise took the floor, it was in the attentive presence of Senate veterans who had remained in the chamber to hear only one other maiden speech, their own. Men whose togas had been earned in the service of Roosevelt's "malefactors of great wealth" were curious about this back-country lawyer. His unwholesome interest in workmen's compensation and employers' liability had aroused misgivings which began to fade as he summed up the Administration's case against the black soldiers and concluded his hour-and-a-half presentation by expounding on a timeless theme.

"This is a government of law and order," Borah declared, and pleased both sides of the aisle by delivering a glancing blow at malcontents and labor agitators. "If the disturbers and raiders and dynamiters throughout this country think that the American people as a whole will connive at the violation of law, they misunderstand the instinct and the inspiration of the Anglo-Saxon race."

After paying tribute to the American Negro ("No man would take from the colored race of this country one iota of praise or honor for the heroic climb which it has made from slavery to its respectable position in the civilization of the world"), Borah looked the black Republican voter square in the eye and warned him that "the party which gave the colored man his freedom will also teach him that this Government can only be preserved by observing the law and observing the rights of citizens in their homes."

At this, according to the *Congressional Record,* there were "manifestations of applause in the galleries." Georgia's scholarly Senator Augustus Octavius Bacon, a classicist and a Confederate veteran, crossed over from the Democratic side of the chamber to congratulate Borah. "I don't know whether you are a statesman or not," Bacon told him, "but you are a lawyer."

The Senate hearings, Roosevelt wrote Michigan's Republican senator, William Alden Smith, had "proved beyond all possible doubt, beyond all intelligent and honest opposition" that from ten to twenty Negro soldiers had shot up the town and a large number of others had concealed their "guilty knowledge" of the crime.

"There is no more question about it than there is that Czolgosz shot McKinley, or that Guiteau shot Garfield, and the move on behalf of these murderers is as essentially vicious as a move on behalf of Guiteau or Czolgosz would have been. Mr. Foraker's proposal is simply to replace murderers in the public armed forces of the United States on the sole condition that to the crime of murder in the past they add the crime of perjury in the future."

As far as Roosevelt was concerned, Foraker's bill was "a purely academic measure," because even if it were passed over his veto—a prospect the President considered impossible—"it would be clearly unconstitutional and I should pay not the slightest heed to it." Roosevelt, and Roosevelt alone, was to determine whether any of the men he had dismissed without honor could convince him they had no guilty knowledge of the affair. To the New York *World,* it was incredible that the President would take on such a duty, much less seek it.

"If he insists that the men whom he has already accused and punished shall again be tried by him," the *World* declared, "he will confess that he is governed by vindictiveness, not by a sense of justice."

22

"Both parties impress me as competent, earnest men . . ."

WITH THE REPUBLICAN national convention only two months away, Secretary Taft was eager to dispose of the Brownsville issue. He drafted a twenty-five-thousand-word reply to Senator Foraker's eloquent defense of the black battalion, but Cabot Lodge talked him out of delivering it. Senator Lodge, unfortunately, was not around when Taft's secretary brought him a letter which was to embroil the Roosevelt Administration in its last ludicrous attempt to prove what had so often been proved "conclusively."

"I spent three weeks in Brownsville last April–May, and became thoroughly satisfied that, following a conspiracy, fourteen or more soldiers of Company B shot up the town," wrote Herbert J. Browne, former editor of the Roanoke (Virginia) *Times* on April 13, 1908, and Taft sent for him immediately.

He showed up with William G. Baldwin, head of a Roanoke detective agency. The two men made such a favorable impression that Taft offered them a five-thousand-dollar contract to look into the Brownsville affair with a view to identifying the guilty soldiers and uncovering the facts connected with the battalion's conspiracy of silence. Browne and Baldwin were to submit their final report no later than June 15, the day before the Republican national convention was to open in Chicago. Nothing in the War Department's arrangement with the two investigators contemplated any line of inquiry that might tend to clear the soldiers of the crime for which they had been punished (or "disciplined," as the Administration preferred to call it).

In a confidential letter to the President accompanying the proposed contract, Taft tactfully suggested that the Senate hearings had established "beyond any reasonable doubt" the correctness of Roosevelt's conclusions, but that if Congress passed the Administration's bill providing for reinstatement of innocent soldiers, the Browne-Baldwin investigation would help him carry out his obligation "to identify the men who did the shooting and to establish the innocence of as many as are innocent among those discharged."

Meanwhile, Taft was checking on Baldwin's professional reputation. He would not sign the contract until he was satisfied as to the man's integrity and reliability, he assured the President. There was no need to be concerned about Browne, Taft felt. He identified the man as "a journalist of considerable experience," who had already made an investigation of the Brownsville affray "under circumstances not necessary to repeat."

The circumstances of Browne's earlier work on the case might strike Secretary Taft as "not necessary to repeat," but they were not without interest and, if word of the new investigation had leaked out, the circumstances would have made front-page headlines. Browne's previous trip to Brownsville had been subsidized by Senator Foraker.

One Saturday night in early April 1907, just a year before Taft received his letter from Browne, the man had come to Foraker's home with a tip on the Brownsville Raid. Seven civilians had shot up the town, Browne had learned on "good authority." Three of the raiders had fled to Mexico, he said, but the other four were now willing to talk, if they could be assured of immunity from prosecution.

Browne had no particular interest in pursuing the matter himself, he told the Senator, but if he could get his affairs in order, he would be happy to go to Texas, round up the four men, and arrange to make their testimony available to the Senate Military Affairs Committee. Monday afternoon Browne was back, ready to light out for Brownsville if Senator Foraker would provide expense money and agreed to pay him a reasonable fee should his mission prove successful. The Senator wrote out a check for five hundred dollars.

"Have been going over the Government's evidence," Browne reported from Galveston on April 19. "A flimsier lot of fabrications never was put together. I not only intend to get the direct evidence, but to destroy the Government's case on its own presentation."

After stopping off in San Antonio to see Major Penrose ("He cleared up several minor difficulties and gave me a number of valuable hints"), Browne reached Austin on Saturday morning, April 20. He had "a very interesting confidential talk" with the new governor, who was afraid at first that his caller had simply picked up some "irresponsible gossip, but finally became convinced that I was posted and meant business."

Because of the "wretched" train service south of San Antonio, Browne was unable to get to Brownsville before Wednesday, April 24. The next day, writing from the Leahy Hotel, he assured Senator Foraker that he was well on his way to wrapping up the case.

"Mrs. Leahy, with whom I am stopping, is the most important witness here. She is the widow of an ex-soldier, is half French, half Irish, about 36, smart as chain lightning, was born just across the Rio Grande, has lived here all her life, knows all the ins and outs of Army post life, and knows a lot. I am working with great care, of necessity, as the slightest suspicion of my errand would mean a calamity. On everything else Brownsville is 'safe and sane,' but the slightest suggestion of this affair sets them frothing at the mouth. When I have thoroughly absorbed Mrs. Leahy's story I can tell whether it is advisable to have her subpoenaed. The citizens' committee do not want her in Washington. She says the Negroes were treated outrageously, insulted and imposed upon in every imaginable way. It is evident that Brownsville doesn't want her to talk, especially as she has a tongue like a razor, Irish wit and French elan, has a host of friends, and is highly respected by both Mexicans and Americans."

After spending the weekend at the Widow Leahy's establishment and discovering that Louis Cowen was "the head devil in this business," Browne advised Foraker on Monday, April 29:

"My Dear Senator: I am going out hunting ocelots (Mexican wildcats) with Louis Cowen and his gang. I think every one of the prospective party was mixed up in the affray. I'll see their rifles and come back with the whole story. I'm protected. My 'toughs' are as 'tough' as his. . . . Expect to close up and get away the latter part of the week. The crude way in which the Government handled this whole business is farcical."

By Friday, May 10, holed up at the New St. Charles in New Orleans, Browne was happy to report that he had "cleaned up the Brownsville situation."

"The Negro troops shot up the town. I can name four of them.

"The town gang headed by Cowen had made plans to do them up, but the soldiers got started too quickly.

"There is a tacit understanding between the leading men of Brownsville and the officers to minimize and cover up certain phases of the affair. . . ."

Senator Foraker realized he had been bilked of five hundred dollars. His money had bought nothing more than an imaginative digest of published testimony, newspaper theorizing, and Elizabeth Street gossip. He broke off his relationship with Herbert J. Browne.

Such were the circumstances the Secretary of War found it unnecessary to repeat when he intimated to the President that Browne and his Roanoke associate might accomplish in two months what the Army's Inspector General, the Department of Justice, the Secret Service, and the United States Senate had failed to do in twenty months—prove a single black soldier guilty of taking part in the Brownsville Raid.

"Both parties impress me as competent, earnest men, from whose work results of importance may be confidently expected," the Judge Advocate General reported on April 20, 1908, when Browne and Baldwin went to work for the War Department.

Posing as a sympathetic newspaperman eager to write "the true story of Brownsville," Browne called on Napoleon B. Marshall, a black Washington lawyer who had been working on the case with Foraker and knew many of the soldiers. Marshall gave Browne some of the men's home addresses, and eight Baldwin operatives fanned out over the country to run them down.

"We have located 118 members of the three companies," Browne reported May 24, "and are making good progress."

Throughout May and June, Baldwin agents turned in reports on such ex-soldiers as Temple Thornton ("He says he has never been able to tell who really did the shooting; that the majority of the soldiers believe it was done by the town people or the Mexicans"), J. Reeves ("He knew nothing and did not want to be bothered"), A. Franklin (". . . am thoroughly convinced that he does not know who did the shooting"), and Joseph Howard, whose name was incorrectly given as James (". . . got him full of whisky, and am satisfied now that he knows absolutely nothing about the shooting").

Sergeant George Jackson, the man in charge of B Company's gun racks on the night of the shooting, was one of "the head devils in the whole business," Browne assumed from the start, but the Baldwin operative who finally ran him down in Louisville, Kentucky, found Jackson a disappointing deponent.

"He does not believe that any of the soldiers did the shooting, but that it was done by town people," the operative reported on May 12, and three days later he was ready to call it quits. "I was with Jackson for some time last night and talked very freely over the shooting and the way the soldiers had been treated by the white people at Brownsville. He says he knows absolutely nothing about the matter."

Browne and Baldwin missed their June 15 deadline. The next day Republican worthies crowded into Chicago's ancient coliseum for the quadrennial rites attending the selection of a candidate for President of the United States. Mrs. Taft, following the proceedings by phone in her husband's office next door to the White House, had a few uneasy minutes when demonstrations for Roosevelt seemed to be getting out of hand, but finally, when a vote was taken, the delegates did what was expected of them. They nominated Taft. A few days later the candidate got reassuring word on the Brownsville investigation.

"I am expecting important additional information early next week," Browne reported.

The important additional information was filtering in from Monroe, Georgia, where William Lawson, an illiterate black employee of the Baldwin agency, was piecing together what purported to be a confession wrung from young Boyd Conyers, a former member of B Company. On July 10 Browne had glad tidings for the War Department.

"Ex Private Boyd Conyers has confessed to our representative at Monroe, Georgia, in the presence of a disinterested witness, that he [Conyers], John Hollomon, of Company B, John Brown, of Company B, and a fourth man, believed by me to be either Carolina De Saussure of Company B, or R. C. Collier of Company C, shot Lieutenant Dominguez and Frank Natus."

An exceedingly happy Judge Advocate General had the pleasure of passing the word on to Roosevelt's secretary. "I am sure that the President will be glad to hear that his judgment as to the complicity of certain men of the regiment was entirely correct," General Davis wrote on July 15, not knowing that still more good news was on its way from Browne and Baldwin.

They had secured a statement from James Powell, an Atlanta Negro, naming Conyers, Hollomon, and Brown as raiders. Powell said he had been honorably discharged from the Tenth Cavalry in August 1906, and had left San Francisco immediately. He had reached Brownsville a few days before the raid, he said, and on the afternoon of August 13, while he was in the new Negro saloon with the three B Company conspirators, he had heard them talking about the attack to be made on the town that night.

"Sir," Browne wrote General Davis on July 30, "I have the honor to report that we now have sufficient evidence, circumstantial and direct, to indict, convict, and hang, under the laws of Texas, four ex-soldiers of the Twenty-fifth Infantry, for the murder of Frank Natus."

Conyers, Hollomon, and Brown, who had been named by James Powell, were to be joined on the Texas scaffold by David Powell, a former D Company corporal who, as noncommissioned officer in charge of quarters on the night of the raid, had been responsible for the keys to the gun racks in his barracks.

"The report of the investigating officers is very full and is also satisfactory," Acting Secretary of War Robert Shaw Oliver reported to the President on September 1 in a confidential message which recommended that a new agreement be drawn up to continue the investigation. The agreement was signed that same day. Brown and Baldwin were to get another five thousand dollars, and their work was to be finished by October 10.

On September 10 the two investigators collected an initial payment of two thousand dollars under their new contract. The next day disaster set in. They discovered that the James Powell statement incriminating Brown, Conyers, and Hollomon was a complete fabrication. The Atlanta Negro had never been near Brownsville. This left the two investigators nothing to go on except an oral confession Boyd Conyers was supposed to have made to William Lawson in Monroe, Georgia. Lawson was the same illiterate Baldwin operative who had dug up the James Powell confession.

On October 16, confident that they were about to close the case, Browne and Baldwin brought William Lawson to Washington to mark his X at the bottom of an affidavit attesting to the details of the "confession" purportedly made by Boyd Conyers.

"All the material evidence obtained is conclusive to my mind," Browne declared, "that not six men in the three companies were without knowledge more or less intimate of the fact that B Company men shot up Brownsville. We are still working."

They worked throughout the presidential campaign, and on December 5 submitted a report based on the Lawson affidavit. Four days later Browne signed a sworn statement elaborating on Lawson's version of what Conyers had told him ("I personally obtained from Conyers further information . . .")

"Captain Baldwin and I," Browne wrote President-elect Taft's successor in the War Department, "would like to continue our work."

It had taken Senator Foraker only a few weeks and one five-hundred-dollar check to take the measure of Herbert J. Browne. President Roosevelt, after nearly eight months and the payment of ten thousand dollars, still took the man seriously. On December 11, with the President's blessing, the Judge Advocate General signed a contract with Browne, agreeing to pay him another five thousand dollars to keep up his good work.* Three days later the Browne-Baldwin report was submitted to the Senate.

"This report," the President declared with a straight face, "enables us to fix with tolerable definiteness at least some of the criminals who took the lead in the murderous shooting of private citizens at Brownsville. It establishes clearly the fact that the colored soldiers did the shooting; but upon this point further record was unnecessary, as the fact that the colored soldiers did the shooting has already been established beyond all possibility of doubt. The investigation has not gone far enough to enable us to determine all the facts, and we will proceed with it."

Browne and Baldwin, the President conceded, had collected "some statements that are obviously worthless," but their report had made it clear to him that "only by carrying on the investigation as the War Department has actually carried it on is there the slightest chance of bringing the offenders to justice or of separating not the innocent, for there were doubtless hardly any innocent, but the less guilty from those whose guilt was heinous."

Proof of this heinous guilt, as Browne and Baldwin had reconstructed the crime, rested primarily on William Lawson's affidavit containing the substance of what the investigators proclaimed to be a confession by Boyd Conyers.

"I have every reason to believe that his confession is genuine and gives for the first time the true secret history of the Brownsville raid," Browne declared in the report the President had read, approved, and passed along to the Senate.

Roosevelt had no idea that Foraker was waiting on the Senate floor with a pocketful of letters Boyd Conyers had written to him throughout the summer and fall, detailing the crude, bumbling, comic efforts first of Lawson, then of Browne and Baldwin, to piece together this bizarre work of fiction.

* "Mr. Baldwin's name is not mentioned in this contract, although I have been told he is still engaged in this important service," Foraker wryly noted some weeks later. Baldwin's name may have been dropped because the law under which the President was paying the two investigators from military contingency funds specifically prohibited expenditures for detective agencies. Browne, as a journalist, was not covered by the statute.

23

". . . I would be willing to go to Texas . . ."

BOYD CONYERS had paid little attention to Esther Crew's new boarder when the man turned up in Monroe, Georgia, on June 5, 1908. Conyers was busy cleaning National Guard equipment for a ten-day encampment to be held the following month at Chickamauga Park. His day's work done, he hurried home to nurse a sick wife.

"I love my wife and try to do all I possibly can to show appreciations," he explained.

On June 6, after spending a rainy day at the armory cleaning rifles, Conyers dropped by a local hangout and was introduced to the new Negro in town. The man's name was Will Lawson, and Conyers was given to understand that he worked for a hat drummer. It was a brief, casual encounter, Conyers recalled, and nothing was said about the Brownsville Raid. He had no other conversation with Lawson, he swore, until they met at the sheriff's office the morning after his return from Chickamauga.

During Conyers' absence with the National Guard outfit, a boarder at Esther Crew's named Parker had quarreled with Lawson, stolen a suit of clothes, and skipped town. Before leaving, he had sent a warning to Mrs. Conyers to get word to her husband that Lawson was a detective working on the Brownsville case. The man's secret had come out because of his inability to read and write. He had prevailed on Parker to prepare his reports. In this way, Parker had learned of the confession Lawson claimed Conyers had given him.

"Who told you, Conyers, that this man had made a claim that you had made a confession to him?" Conyers was later asked.

"My mother-in-law," he said. "After I returned from Chickamauga, she was at the train, my wife's mother, and she said,

'Buddy'—they always called me 'Buddy'—she says, 'you know that old black nigger that has been hanging around here?' I said, 'Which one?' She says, 'They call him Lawson.' I said, 'Yes, I seen him,' and she said, 'They say he's a detective here after you about that Brownsville matter,' and I said, 'I don't care what he is after.'"

But the next morning, when he spotted Lawson on the opposite side of the street, Conyers asked Sheriff Arnold to find out what the man was up to.

"All right, I have been wanting to investigate him anyway," the Sheriff recalled answering, and went on to describe the incident.

"So I stepped across the street to Lawson and told him I wanted to see him over to my office a few minutes. He came over with me, and I carried him in the office and I asked him, I says, 'What is your name and what is your business here?' He says, 'Have you a right to know?' I says, 'Yes.' He says, 'Who are you?' I says, 'You know who I am.' 'Well,' he says, 'if you have a right to know, I can show you.' I says, 'All right; I would like to know because you have been here a month, and I see you hanging around here and not doing anything.' He says, 'I have got to step down to my boardinghouse.' I says, 'All right.' So he went over to his boardinghouse, Esther Crew's; and he came back shortly, and with him he brought a paper or letter sufficient to show me that he was working with the Baldwin Detective Agency.

"About that time this boy, 'Buddy' Conyers, stepped in my office and he says to Lawson, 'Have you ever had any talk with me around here?' Lawson says, 'Yes.' Conyers says to him, 'Lawson, you know that's a lie. I ain't had no talk with you.' Lawson says, 'Yes, I had a talk with you.' He says, 'When?' He says, 'When we took a drink together under the steps across the street,' designating to my mind the steps up by the side of Mr. Felker's building. Conyers says to him, he says, 'You are a liar.'"

"I am just as innocent of taking any part in that trouble that night as God is on high," Conyers wrote Senator Foraker later that day; "and the fact is I don't know any more than I have told you about it."

Conyers had testified before the Senate committee on February 20, 1907. By chance, Foraker had been presiding that morning and had administered the oath to the personable young Georgia recruit. He had never forgotten "his frank, open, manly face and manner" as he told how he had been on guard duty the night of the shooting. He had just been relieved and gone to sleep in a guardhouse bunk when, he said, "I was awakened by several voices hollering outside: 'Guard,' and I got up and fell in line with the other guard."

"You were ordered to fall in, and then what occurred?" Senator Foraker asked.

"Well, the shooting were going on in town at the time, and when I was standing in the ranks there there were bullets came overhead between the guardhouse and the post exchange, which we call the canteen, and while I was in the ranks I said: 'If this shooting keeps on I will soon wake up.' I had just waked up and felt a little drowsy, and I hadn't opened my eyes good. I said: 'I will soon wake up if they keep up that.'"

"Did you have a beat there, or were you simply stationary, standing in one place?"

"Yes, sir; I was standing there and the shooting kept on in town, and I asked the commander of the guard would he permit me to lie down there at the corner . . ."

"What did you want to lie down there for?"

"Because I was liable to get shot."

"You heard some bullets go over?"

"Yes, sir; I heard some bullets come over, and a stray bullet could hurt me just as good as an intentional one, you know."

On September 1, 1908, while Browne and Baldwin were in Washington signing their second five-thousand-dollar contract, Conyers was getting off his second letter to Senator Foraker. The Negro detective had left town, he was happy to report, and "the man he said was coming for me has never come."

A week later, however, a white man going by the name of Wallace L. Gray showed up in Monroe on the evening train. The name was familiar to Conyers. Mr. Gray had written him from Roanoke, Virginia, some months before, offering him a job at sixty to seventy-five dollars a month. Conyers had declined ("I couldn't accept the position then, as my wife was so sick and I couldn't leave her"). Wallace L. Gray, it now developed, was the man Will Lawson worked for. His real name was W. G. Baldwin.

"I goes up to the sheriff's office that night and talked with him in the presence of the sheriff," Conyers wrote the Senator in his next letter. "The first question he asked me was I in Brownsville, Tex., Monday night, August 13, 1906. I told him I was, and he asked me what had taken place there. I told him shooting occurred that night, between 11 and 12 o'clock, I suppose. Then he said, 'Who did the shooting?' I told him I did not know. He asked me where was I at when the shooting taken place. I told him: 'On guard and don't know who did the shooting, sir; I wasn't on post. I was asleep when the shooting occurred. . . .'

"Then Mr. Baldwin said, 'That tale is all right, but I want to ask you a question, Do you know an ex-soldier by the name of Powell?' 'No, sir; I do not know him.' 'He says he knows you, and says he heard you, John Brown, John Hollomon, and ex-soldier Allison, who ran the saloon, make a plot that day before the shooting had taken place to shoot up the town that night,' and I told Mr. Baldwin that couldn't be true because I was on guard and wasn't allowed to speak to anybody, let alone being in Allison's saloon that day. . . .'

"He said that part is all right, too, but don't you know that men of B Company did the shooting that night, 'No, sir; I do not know and furthermore I don't believe the soldiers did it'; he said, 'Oh! there ain't no story about that; we know they did it and know the most of them that did it'; I said, 'I am glad you all have been able to find the guilty party'; he said, 'Now what about the Negro Lawson I sent down here; what did you tell him?' I said, 'Sir, I didn't even have any private talk with Lawson at all.' And he said, 'Why, Lawson said you did, and taken a drink with him.' And I said, 'I can prove I didn't talk with him while he was here. . . .'"

A few weeks later another white stranger came to Monroe and introduced himself to Conyers as Mr. Browne. In the interval between Baldwin's visit in September and Browne's in October, Baldwin had gone to Atlanta, talked to James Powell, and discovered he had never been within three thousand miles of Allison's saloon, where he was supposed to have overheard John Brown and John Hollomon plotting the raid with Boyd Conyers. This should have sufficed to put Conyers in the clear and send the investigators scurrying off in a more promising direction, but with no real leads to follow they kept sniffing at the only scent they had, even though they knew it to be false.

Sheriff Arnold was present when Mr. Browne first questioned him, Conyers reported to Senator Foraker.

"He said: 'Do you know an ex-soldier Powell?' I said: 'No, sir; I don't know him.' He said: 'Well, he knows you, and said you, John Hollomon and John Brown said you all were going to shoot up that town.' I said: 'I haven't seen that Negro; haven't told him anything. . . .'

"He said: 'We have been able to prove that B Company men did the shooting, and what I want you to tell me is just the men that did the shooting; I know you can if you will; we already know three men that did it, but we want the whole gang. The three are you, John Hollomon, and John Brown.'

"He said: 'Now, suppose you dream over it tonight and come in the morning and tell me and Mr. Arnold about it; we will see that nobody don't hurt you if you were in it.' And I said: 'Mr. Browne, what do you want me to do—tell a lie? Pick out this man and that man and say they were in it? It is impossible for me to do that.'"

Mr. Browne left town next morning, Conyers continued, but on October 11 he was back and, again in the presence of Sheriff Arnold, he went on with his interrogation.

"He said: 'I want to ask you a few more questions. I want to know, and I want you to tell the truth. Tell me who talked with you in Washington before you went on the stand.' I told him no one. 'Now,' he said, 'isn't it true that Mr. Foraker told you all how to swear before you went in the committee room?' I said: 'No, sir. I saw him passing, and some one said, "There goes

Senator Foraker." ' He said: 'Who met you at the train when you went to Washington?' I told him no one. Then he wanted to know if I had any letters from Mr. Foraker. I said: 'Sir, I have only one letter from him.' Then he asked me if I had it with me. I said: 'No, sir; but I can get it as quick as you ever saw anybody get anything if you think it will do you any good.' He said: 'I will be glad for you to go and get it. I would like to see some of the Senator's writing.' I came home and got the letter and showed it to him." *

After reading the Foraker letter and, according to Conyers, shrugging it off with the remark "There is nothing there to hurt anyone," Browne became curious about B Company's baseball team and asked Conyers if he happened to have a group photograph of the players.

"I told him I did," Conyers wrote. "He told me he would like to see it; for me to go and get it, if it wasn't too much trouble. I told him it wouldn't be any trouble, so I got it and showed it to him. Then he took their names down, right to left, like they were in the picture. Then he began to point out some of the men in the picture to Mr. Arnold that he thought was implicated in the matter; then he wanted to know if I had any of the rest of the soldiers' pictures; if so, he wanted to see them. I showed him all I had. He kept trying to persuade me to tell him who did the shooting, which was impossible for me to tell him; he also repeats, 'There is a lot of them talking now'; said 'John Brown has acknowledged that he was in the shooting.' † I said, 'Mr. Browne, if John has been man enough to tell you he was in the shooting, it looks funny he didn't tell you who else was in it.' He said, 'That's all right; it's all coming out.'

"Then he began to ask me about my family; said it would be bad for me to have to leave a young family and be turned over

---

* It acknowledged Conyers' first letter, asked for additional information, and closed with the comment, "I remember you very well as a witness before the committee, and I am sure you did not there testify to anything except only the truth." The letter was "extremely obstructive," Browne subsequently stated under oath, because Conyers had apparently taken it as "a mandate to adhere to the false story told by him before the Senate Committee on Military Affairs."

† John Brown had made no such acknowledgment.

to the State of Texas. I told him, 'Before I would be willing to swear a lie on anybody, I would be willing to go to Texas or anywhere else, because the truth stands in its place.' He said, 'You know if you go to Texas nobody knows the results you will get there. You may never return here any more.' I said, 'God's will must be done; and if it is His will for me to go, I suffer His will may be done.' "

Browne and Baldwin, with the full weight of the White House and the War Department behind them, had done everything they could to trick, tempt, and terrorize a young Negro preoccupied with his work and his ailing wife. They had offered him money, confronted him with what they knew to be perjured testimony, promised him protection, and tried to frighten him with the prospect of a Texas noose.

"Oh," Foraker cried out after reading Boyd Conyers' letters aloud to his colleagues, "shame upon a Government that will employ all its power, every power that it commands, not for the purpose of the protection of men in their right to be presumed innocent until they are proven guilty, but to prove men, who claim they are innocent, to be guilty of a heinous crime, and to do it behind the door and in the dark."

Foraker proposed, and on December 16 the Senate agreed, that the Secretary of War be directed to provide a complete report on his Department's arrangements with Browne and Baldwin. The report was waiting when the senators resumed work after the Christmas holidays. Foraker, by that time, had become a lame-duck senator.

24

"He brought Foraker a message from the President."

SENATOR FORAKER'S DEFENSE OF the black soldiers had aroused what his wife called the "virulent hostility" of President Roosevelt. Throughout the Brownsville debate the Senator's Sixteenth Street mansion was under surveillance. Callers who used to drop by during the day began to show up only after dark. Mail was tampered with, guests were scrutinized by Secret Service sentries.

"Washington became a haunted house," Julia Foraker recalled years later. "We lived for months under this strain. Men with a furtive slant to their eyes were on hand when the postman came in the mornings; relays were still hanging around when my daughters went to balls at night."

At afternoon receptions Mrs. Foraker found herself shadowed by a gate-crashing detective, "an American journalist, afterwards in the World War in German pay." Cornelia Fairbanks, the Vice President's wife, would draw her off to a corner and the two old school friends would talk in whispers.

"Poor Mrs. Fairbanks!" Julia sighed. "She must have been quite worn out by Brownsville. She was, of course, very often at the White House, and constantly meeting the President at Cabinet dinners, where her place was on his right. The President couldn't keep off the subject of Foraker and his wicked interest in the black battalion. He would pound the table at a point. The glasses shivered."

Foraker was no longer invited to the White House, not even on such formal occasions as the President's dinner for the diplomatic corps, and the Senator's patronage recommendations were ignored. Foraker learned from newspaper reports that Roosevelt, with the advice and consent of Booker T. Washington, was thinking of appointing Ralph W. Tyler to the position of surveyor of the port of Cincinnati. Tyler, a black journalist, was secretary to the owner of two Columbus, Ohio, newspapers hostile to Foraker.*

When a newspaperman asked him about the rumored appointment, the Senator sarcastically suggested that he consult "the third Senator from Ohio—Booker Washington." A few weeks later, a discharged D Company corporal named Winter Washington was to appear before the Senate Military Affairs Committee. A senator jokingly asked if the witness were the Tuskegee principal.

"No," Foraker snapped, "Booker Washington is too busy attending to his senatorial duties to come here."

Foraker's old friends in the Senate, buckling under pressure from the White House, began to renege on their promises of support for measures he was pushing. They turned away in embarrassment when they ran into him in the cloakroom.

"In the end, officially," Mrs. Foraker always remembered with pride, "Foraker came to press his fight for justice almost alone, to lead the forlornest of hopes. There was something gallant in this that touched the imagination."

His lonely fight impressed a former President, the only Democrat to occupy the White House in the postwar years.

"Whatever may be the whole truth about the Brownsville case," Grover Cleveland told an English magazine writer, "it has been a display of genuine courage for a Republican Senator to take the position assumed by Mr. Foraker. It is due to him that there has been a real discussion of the President's action in all its bearings."

The President and the Ohio senator had stumbled into what Mrs. Foraker called "a monstrous labyrinth," and neither man could find his way out. Roosevelt was not one to dine in public on crow; Foraker was incapable of surrendering a strong position on solid constitutional ground.

---

* Roosevelt later reconsidered and put Tyler to work as a Navy Department auditor. Some said the President changed his mind because his son-in-law feared the appointment might cost him his seat in the House; others said it was done to hold the Ohio delegation in line for Taft at the forthcoming Republican national convention.

"The thing was too much for Foraker's sense of justice," his wife declared, "too much for his legal sense."

Roosevelt was not a lawyer and, in Taft's view, "was impatient at the delays in the administration of justice." In his handling of the Brownsville affair, which had so outraged the legal sensibilities of Senator Foraker, the President had rendered what he liked to think of as "substantial justice."

"How do you know that substantial justice was done?" Roosevelt was later asked in another connection.

"Because I did it," he said; "because I was doing my best."

"You mean to say that when you do a thing, thereby substantial justice is done?"

"I do. When I do a thing, I do it so as to do substantial justice. I mean just that."

Never in his pronouncements from the throne or in his private correspondence did Roosevelt appear to doubt that on the Brownsville question he was right and Foraker wrong, but when a white flag was tentatively hoisted, it was raised by the President, not the Senator. Mrs. Foraker revealed the truce terms in her sprightly reminiscences, when she told of the night Senator Boies Penrose paid an unexpected call.

"He brought Foraker a message from the President. It was this: If Senator Foraker would drop the Brownsville fight Mr. Roosevelt was prepared to offer him any distinguished post which he might desire. An ambassadorship, perhaps. If so, which embassy would the Senator prefer?"

The Senator preferred to keep his seat in the United States Senate.

Arrangements for Foraker's re-election were made by order of Rhode Island's Nelson W. Aldrich, who owned most of the state he had come to the Senate to represent, and by Eugene Hale of Maine, who spent much of his time in the Senate shouting down the radical notions Bob La Follette had brought with him from Wisconsin. The Senate's wealthy right-wing cabalists were delighted at the prospect of retaining an influential senator of their own stripe and, at the same time, indirectly rebuking a President they preferred not to attack directly.

On September 10, his re-election seemingly assured, Senator Foraker dropped by Taft's Cincinnati headquarters for a friendly talk. Foraker "can be useful with the colored vote and with the Grand Army vote," Taft had written the Kansas City *Star's* publisher a few days before the visit. When the two candidates parted, it was with the announcement that they would meet in a public display of party harmony at a Republican gathering scheduled to be held at the Music Hall on Tuesday, September 22.

"All that talk about a peace pact is unfounded," Taft beamed, "because there has been nothing but peace."

Suddenly, on the night of September 17, Foraker was knifed from behind, not by the hand of Roosevelt or Taft, but by William Randolph Hearst, who had come to Columbus to make a political speech. To illustrate his point that "the Republican party has been for a long time the beneficiary of trust corruption," Hearst read some letters written to Senator Foraker from 1900 to 1903 by John D. Archbold, vice president of the Standard Oil Company.

The Senator parried the attack in the afternoon papers of September 18, but that same night, in St. Louis, Hearst came back with an artfully juxtaposed series of letters which made it appear that Foraker had received fifty thousand dollars from Standard Oil for opposing a certain piece of antitrust legislation. Actually, the Senator explained, the money had been advanced to help a newspaper friend buy the *Ohio State Journal*. The deal had fallen through and the fifty thousand dollars had been returned.

It was too late for a factual rebuttal, however. Emotionally, Hearst had carried the day by exposing the Senator's friendly relations with a politically unpopular outfit he had once served as counsel. Foraker found himself fighting for his political life. Much depended on what Taft decided to do about the Republican meeting at the Music Hall Tuesday night. His presence on the platform with Foraker would be interpreted as an endorsement, his absence as repudiation.

"My Dear Judge," Foraker wrote on Saturday, September 19: "Having read in the newspapers that some of your friends and

possibly you, are in doubt as to the propriety of my speaking
with you at Music Hall next Tuesday night, I have concluded not
to attend the meeting. I take this action not because I deem the
answers I made to Mr. Hearst's charges insufficient, nor because
of any lack of loyalty to your cause, but only because I do not
wish to do anything that might injure the cause or embarrass you
personally."

The letter was delivered to Taft by two of Foraker's senatorial
colleagues, Charles Dick of Ohio and W. Murray Crane of
Massachusetts, who happened to be in Cincinnati at the time.
The candidate, they reported on their return from his headquarters, was very much "disturbed and embarrassed." Apparently he had been in touch with Roosevelt by phone. If
he were running for President, Roosevelt later advised in a
confidential telegram, he would "decline to appear upon the
platform with Foraker." This was what he had already made up
his mind to do, Taft announced, and the President issued a
statement praising the candidate's latest display of a "fearless
and aggressive honesty."

"I was both surprised and mortified by Mr. Taft's action,"
Foraker recalled in his memoirs.

To Mrs. Foraker it was an unforgivable act of moral coward-
ice, something of which her husband would have been incapable.
Taft, for his part, was proud of having refused to heed panicky
advisers who had urged him to wash his hands of the Senator in
public by taking the initiative in canceling arrangements to appear with him at the Republican meeting.

"If it would win me every vote in the United States, I cannot hit a man when he is down," Taft was quoted as saying, but
his squeamishness did not extend to offering a helping hand to
a man who was down, even though it was the same man who, in
1887, had first put him on the bench in Ohio.

"These revelations about Foraker are very ugly," Roosevelt
exulted in a letter to Cabot Lodge on the same Saturday Taft
was weaseling away from the Senator's side. "They of course
show, what everyone on the inside knew, that Foraker was
not really influenced in the least by any feeling for the Negro,
but that he acted as the agent of the corporations."

"At a funeral," Alice Roosevelt Longworth once quipped, "father always wants to be the corpse, and at a wedding he always wants to be the bride."

In the presidential campaign of 1908, neither corpse nor bride, Roosevelt kept bobbing up with advice for the candidate. Taft should give up golf for the duration ("I have received literally hundreds of letters from the West protesting about it . . . It is just like my tennis . . ."), and he should try to appear to be enjoying himself on the hustings ("Let the audience see you smile . . .")

"I have decided to put a little vim in the campaign," the President wrote Nick Longworth, and, on September 21, issued a long statement calculated not only to liven things up but also help eliminate Joseph Benson Foraker from public life.

Roosevelt attacked the Senator's opposition to his "great policies of internal reform" and dismissed the Brownsville agitation as "merely one phase of the effort by the representatives of certain law-defying corporations to bring discredit upon the Administration because it was seeking to cut out the evils connected not only with the corrupt use of wealth, but especially with the corrupt alliance between certain business men of large fortune and certain politicians of great influence."

"The President's sneering suspicion that the Senator opposed his Brownsville policy to please the Standard Oil Company is so far-fetched as to seem absurd," declared *Harper's Weekly*. "Nobody in any degree familiar with his protracted struggle on behalf of the colored soldiers would question the sincerity of his motives for an instant. The character of the man also deserves consideration, and it is a significant and telling fact that no one of the many who know him well believes Senator Foraker capable of a consciously dishonorable act. He is a whole-souled, big-hearted, courageous man of great ability, who has given exceptionally valuable service to his country." *

But, in the words of the Cincinnati *Enquirer*, the Senator's

---

* "Foraker is a brilliant man; he was a gallant soldier," Roosevelt conceded in a letter to Cabot Lodge, September 25, 1908. "I lament the fact that he was also a corrupt man and as this was so I am glad that he was exposed."

"political epitaph has been written." On January 2, 1909, Ohio Republicans caucused and chose a Cleveland congressman, Theodore E. Burton, to succeed Foraker. The election was held ten days later when, by coincidence, the Senator had taken the floor to deliver what proved to be his farewell address. It was, the New York *Times* reported, "a vigorous, vitriolic valedictory."

25

". . . *atrocious, disreputable, and disgraceful* . . ."

ON THE AFTERNOON OF January 12, 1909, impassive black faces stared down from the Senate galleries at the commanding figure of the old Civil War officer who had marched through Georgia before many of them were born. At the top of his form, the Senator began to dissect the War Department's red-faced report on its dealings with Browne and Baldwin. The two investigators had been hired by the Roosevelt Administration, explained Secretary of War Luke E. Wright, because "the ordinary agencies at the disposal of the Executive . . . had not been completely successful, especially in determining what particular individuals, *if any,** had been engaged in the affair as participants . . ."

In other words, Foraker snorted, Government departments had brought their resources to bear on Brownsville and "had failed to identify any man in that battalion as a participator in that shooting affray; they had failed to identify any man in the battalion as guilty of this newly described crime—a conspiracy of silence. . . . So they resorted to the employment of these detectives."

The two investigators had been paid from a military contingency fund which, by statute, was not to be used for such a purpose, Foraker charged, and in the strongest language he had yet used against the President, he accused Roosevelt not only of having defied the Constitution and the Congress, but also of

* Foraker bore down heavily on this slip of the bureaucratic tongue.

having flaunted "all the restraints of law, decency and propriety in his mad pursuit of these helpless victims of his ill-considered action."

The Administration's two hired hands had not hesitated to use "fraudulent impersonation, misrepresentation, lying, deceit, treachery, liquor, and intoxication, coupled with promises of immunity and the excitement of hope and fear and the offer of employment and remunerative wages," Foraker declared, and produced a letter he had recently received from George W. Gray, a former member of C Company who had been approached by Baldwin and offered sixty dollars a month if he would go around the country spying on other ex-soldiers.

"I told him I would," wrote Gray, "as I was innocent and ignorant, and if the guilt could be found that easy, I would try. So there was nothing I found, and he tried very hard to get me to say something false; and after he found out he could not handle me, he failed to come up to his promise in regards to the pay. Then I came back, and since then he sends me $25 and asked me if I would make a statement that the shooting came from B Company."

To document this point, Foraker then read Baldwin's letter to Gray, dated October 8, 1908; "Could you make a statement that from the sounds of the guns and flashes that you are satisfied that the shooting came from B barrack, and that you are satisfied that no shots were fired by either C or D?"

As a Baldwin agent, George Gray had gone to Monroe, talked to Boyd Conyers, and learned nothing.

"George asked for me when he came," Conyers had written Foraker, "and a little boy showed him where I live. He came to my home, and I prepared dinner for him and treated him nice, and also taken near half a day off from work to carry him around and introduce him to my friends and people and good white friends."

Browne and Baldwin, having failed to get anything out of Conyers, had proceeded to concoct their own version of what they had wanted him to say and had then palmed their work off on the President, the press, and the public as a "confession."

"In all the history of crime and its detection nothing more atrocious, disreputable, and disgraceful has ever been recorded," Senator Foraker declared, and added that such "wicked fabrications," running contrary to "the elementary principles of common-law justice," would never be admissible as evidence in a judicial proceeding. He cited a recent Supreme Court decision which had stated the general rule that "a confession must be free and voluntary—that is, not produced by inducements engendering either hope or fear . . ." °

Aside from being inadmissible as evidence in a court of law, the so-called Conyers confession had been ruled out of any serious discussion of the Brownsville case because, as Foraker was pleased to point out, it had been proved a fraud in the public prints. An Associated Press reporter had interviewed Sheriff E. C. Arnold of Monroe, the man Conyers said was present during his two talks with Browne. The Sheriff had corroborated the statements Conyers had made in reporting the interviews to Senator Foraker.

"I have known Mr. Arnold for fifteen or twenty years," said Senator Clay of Georgia when the Sheriff's name was tossed into play. "He is a most excellent man in every respect."

"I do not think Mr. Arnold needs a certificate of character," Senator Foraker replied, and added sarcastically, "except only to those who imagine that every man who does not agree to what is put out from certain places is dishonest or actuated by some unworthy purpose or motive. I venture to say he would compare favorably either with Herbert J. Browne or William Lawson."

Spread out on a table in front of him, available to any senator who cared to examine them, were the originals of a series of affidavits Foraker proceeded to read into the *Congressional Record*. They refuted Lawson's sworn statement regarding the Conyers "confession" point by point.

° If this has a familiar ring, consider the statement Senator Lodge made on the Senate floor on December 16, 1908: "The pendulum has swung to the other extreme. Before the era of reform there was little or no public sympathy with the criminal. Today we seem almost to have reached the point where the sympathy is so strictly confined to the criminal that there is none left for the victim of the crime."

Lawson: *"On the morning of June 8, between eight and nine o'clock, I met Conyers about halfway between the station house and Main Street. We talked some twenty or twenty-five minutes. I broached the Brownsville case and mentioned the fact that the soldiers had shown their good sense by keeping their mouths while at Washington. I then asked him what the motive was for the shooting. He told me that the 'crackers' at Brownsville had made threats that they would have no Negro soldiers at Brownsville, and the soldiers had made it up in their minds that if they bothered them that they would go in and clean up the ground."*

Conyers could not have talked to Lawson on the morning of June 8 between eight and nine o'clock because he was helping grade a National Guard target range some three miles from town, stated G. Wes Giles, a fellow worker who rode out to the job with him that morning. "We left town about six o'clock, or sunup," Giles said, and was corroborated by the contractor, W. J. Mayfield, who recalled that "we began work about six o'clock, or sunup, in the morning and worked until sundown in the afternoon." In addition to his memory, Mayfield added, "my time book kept by me bears me out."

Lawson: *"I was with Conyers nearly every day, and went to Gainesville, Ga., on an excursion with him on the 15th of June."*

Giles was in charge of the refreshment car on the Gainesville outing. "I tried to get Conyers to go on the excursion," he declared, "but he told me that he had a family to keep up and would have to work." According to the sworn statement of O. J. Adams, the postmaster's clerk, Conyers worked at the post office, cleaning up and washing windows, until eleven or twelve o'clock on the day of the excursion. The train had left town about seven o'clock that morning.

Once it had begun to become apparent to Browne and Baldwin that their man was in error about the excursion, they tried to play down its importance. Conyers, they insisted, had made his piecemeal confession to Lawson on two other dates—on June 8, when Conyers had two witnesses and a time-book to prove that he was three miles from the scene of the alleged conversation, and on June 29.

Lawson: *"On this date June 29 I met him at Joe Blassingame's,*

and had a pint bottle of liquor, offered him a drink—he would
not drink in the house, but we went up the street and we stopped
under a storehouse porch, near Main Street. We took a drink or
two, and I started the Brownsville case again. . . . In this con-
versation Conyers told me that John Brown, J. H. Hollomon, and
a man named Powell, and several others came down where he
was on guard, and that they went downtown and just gave them
hell, and after they shot out all of their cartridges they ran back
to the barracks."

Blassingame (his real name was John, not Joe) remembered
the incident and swore that no offer of liquor was made. Even if
Conyers had agreed to share an illegal pint of whiskey with the
black detective, Sheriff Arnold doubted that Buddie would have
picked "a storehouse porch near Main Street." The only porch
Lawson could have been referring to happened to be "in the
business heart of the city, in full view of the courthouse, of the
public square, the city hall, and other public buildings." In the
Sheriff's opinion, "it would have been impossible for them to
have taken a drink at that place without being seen and cases
made against them in the police court."

Just a week before they filed their December 5, 1908, report on
"the true secret history of the Brownsville raid," Browne and
Baldwin had made another desperate stab at shoring up its
underpinnings with some credible evidence to support Lawson's
story. W. G. Baldwin's brother, A. H. Baldwin, had gone to
Monroe. The failure of his mission was chronicled in the affidavit
of a local notary public. Senator Foraker read it aloud with
obvious relish.

"On the night of November 28, 1908, and immediately after
supper," Fred D. McGarrity, white, deposed, "a gentleman who
registered at the hotel where I boarded introduced himself to me
as A. H. Baldwin, having previously learned that I was a notary
public, and requested me to go with him to the house of one
Lewis Anderson, colored, for the purpose of attesting an affidavit.
I went with him, as it was only a few hundred yards, not knowing the nature of the business.

"When we reached the place, we found there Lewis Anderson

and one William Lawson, a Negro detective, who then requested Anderson to repeat what he had told him that Boyd (Buddie) Conyers had told him about the Brownsville raid. Anderson, who is an old man, vehemently denied having told Lawson anything about Conyers; said that Conyer's name had never been mentioned between them but one time, and that was on one occasion when Conyers passed by and Lawson asked him if that was Conyers, and he told him yes. Anderson further stated that he had had no talk with Conyers; that he had only spoken to him one time, and then only to say 'howdy'; that he had nothing to do with 'these young niggers.'

"Lawson insisted on Anderson making an affidavit that Conyers had admitted to him that he knew a great deal more about the shooting at Brownsville than he had told. Lawson insisted that Anderson had told him these things while out fishing. Anderson strongly denied having told Lawson any such thing, and got his Bible and placed his hands on it and denied that he had ever made any such statements to Lawson, or that he had ever had any conversation with Conyers about the matter in any way, at the same time calling up, or stating that God would strike him dead if he was telling a lie."

When the elderly Negro made it quite clear that he had no intention of signing the affidavit, Baldwin asked McGarrity to accompany him to Boyd Conyers' home. McGarrity's version of this encounter was substantially the same as the report Senator Foraker had received from Conyers in the last of his letters. Baldwin told Conyers he had in his pocket the sworn statement of a man who had seen him with Lawson on the Gainesville excursion. The affiant's name, misspelled by both McGarrity and Conyers, was Alonzo Hinton of Winder, Georgia.

"I told him I didn't care what he had," Conyers wrote Foraker; "I could prove by every person on that train that I didn't go; and I have proved it. The excursion was run on the 15th day of June, and the people he asked that were on the train told him, 'No; I didn't go'; but his Negro he had here went. I went by the depot that morning to see if my mother-in-law went off, and was talking to a lot of the boys and girls. I was in my work clothes and had my dinner with me to go to work. That is what all the people told the detective."

Of all the men, women, and children who took off for Gainesville that Sunday morning, only Alonzo Hinton seemed to recall having seen Conyers on the train. Later, after he had signed the white detective's paper telling about the excursion, Hinton realized he'd made a mistake. He hadn't seen Bud Conyers that day; he'd seen Bud (Charlie) Cowan.

Lawson, by his own admission, had talked to Conyers only three times. Thus his story of the confession derived from their meetings on June 8, when Conyers was at work three miles away; June 15, when Lawson went to Gainesville and Conyers stayed home to pick up another day's pay; and June 29, when Conyers was supposed to have sneaked a few drinks in what the Sheriff of Walton County described as "one of the most conspicuous places in the city."

Once he had disposed of William Lawson, Senator Foraker turned his attention to Herbert J. Browne, who had claimed in a sworn statement that Boyd Conyers had given him "further information," which included the names of the ten other members of B Company who had gone out with him to shoot up the town.

"I found Boyd Conyers in a disturbed frame of mind," Browne had stated. "No claim is made that his original declarations to William Lawson were other than those of a criminal boasting to one of his own race of his crime and of his success in escaping discovery. His subsequent declarations to me were given partly during moments of contrition and in a desire to unload his conscience by a confession and partly as a result of careful and persistent questioning."

This "careful and persistent questioning" had been done in Sheriff Arnold's presence on two occasions, October 6 and 11, 1908. The Sheriff read Boyd Conyers' version, as reported in his letters to Senator Foraker, and, under oath, praised its "remarkable accuracy." The Sheriff also read Browne's sworn account of the same two interviews and, still under oath, pronounced it "the most absolutely false, the most willful misrepresentation of the truth, and the most shameful perversion of what really did take place between them that I have ever seen over the signature of any person."

The first of the two sessions was held in the Sheriff's office after supper, Arnold recalled. He had not only listened to Browne's careful, persistent questioning, he had also pitched in and helped.

"I fastened the doors," he stated, "so no one could interrupt us, and then we put him through the most rigid examination I have ever seen any person subjected to in all of my long experience in dealing with criminals. I had always believed that some of the soldiers 'shot up Brownsville,' and for this reason I was glad of an opportunity to aid in getting at the bottom of it, finding out the guilty ones, so that they might be properly punished. . . .* We kept Conyers under a most severe cross-examination until about 11 o'clock that night, but without getting any information, he positively denying all the time that he knew anything to tell, as he was asleep at the time of the shooting."

Browne left town the following day, but returned at noon on October 11, and Conyers was subjected to another "most rigid examination" by both men. It was during this session that the inquisitors tainted whatever confession Conyers might have made by offering "inducements engendering either hope or fear." Their inducements were intended to engender the hope of living to old age in Walton County, Georgia, and the fear of dying prematurely in Cameron County, Texas.

"Conyers had known me all his life," the Sheriff stated, "and had absolute confidence in my ability to carry out any promise I made him. I told him that if he would just tell the whole thing —just own up and tell it—no matter how guilty he might be, I had it in my power to see that he was pardoned and would not be punished, but if he did not tell it and it had to be proved on him, then he would be severely punished. We made all sorts of promises to him; then we told him what the consequences would

* He was also interested in collecting the reward, which he offered to split with Conyers.

be if he did not tell it, but he still denied knowing anything or who did the shooting."

Describing this second interrogation in a letter to Senator Foraker, Conyers had mentioned Browne's desire to see his group photograph of B Company's baseball team. Conyers had run home, fetched the picture, and helped him record the name of each player. Some weeks later, when Browne submitted his report to the War Department, he listed the ten names he said Conyers had identified as fellow raiders. Five of them were B Company ballplayers.

Sheriff Arnold described this phase of the investigation: "When we had utterly failed to get a confession or any information out of Conyers as to who did the shooting, then Mr. Browne asked him to give the names of some of the baseball players and also the names of some of the most reckless and turbulent members of his company. This Conyers did, giving several names, and these same names, so given by Conyers in my presence, Mr. Browne, in his report, says were furnished him by Conyers as the ones participating in the shooting. I point this out as a fair example as to how Mr. Browne has perverted the truth and the real facts in the case in his report."

The few soldiers who conscientiously tried to help their white officers investigate the shooting "were called 'dog robbers,' and made to feel the displeasure of their fellows," Browne and Baldwin reported, and attributed this intelligence to the evidence given them by Private Elmer Brown of Company B.[*]

Elmer Brown, serving his sixth hitch, was a reliable soldier who took care of Major Penrose's horses—"a man that I placed a great deal of dependence in," the Major said. On the night of August 13 Browne bedded down in the corral as usual, sleeping within reach of the horses. Private Alfred Williams ran in from the quartermaster's stable and woke him up.

"What did he tell you?" Senator Foraker asked when Brown appeared before the Senate committee.

* Not to be confused with Private John Brown of the same company who figured in the Conyers "confession."

"He said, 'Get up, Brown; did you hear all this noise?' I said, 'No; what is it?' 'Well, they are playing fire call or to arms over there,' he said; 'I think it is to arms.' And I said, 'If you don't know what it is, I ain't going to get up,' and I just dozed right off to sleep again, as I had orders from the commanding officer to stay with his horses."

Two years after the shooting Brown was living in Washington, D.C., working at the Bureau of Engraving and Printing cleaning the steam presses. One day, sometime in July 1908, a white man came to see him and said he wanted to talk about the Brownsville matter. Brown asked if he was an Army officer, and the man said no, but that he was connected with the Army and that he had been sent by the Judge Advocate General. Later, Brown checked with General Davis' office and found that the man, a Mr. Browne, did represent the War Department.

He was trying to get information that would enable the President to restore the men to the Army, Mr. Browne said, and he wanted Elmer Brown to tell him who did the shooting, and all he knew about it. Brown said he had no knowledge on the subject, and that his previous testimony had been complete and truthful.

"Mr. Browne thereupon told him that if he would tell who did the shooting and all about it, he would take the affiant's name to the President, and the President would reinstate him in the Army," Brown stated in his affidavit, and then recalled that later, about the first week in August, he received another visit from Mr. Browne.

"At this time he had with him a group photograph of the baseball club belonging to Company B. He asked affiant the names of all these men shown in the group, and put the names down, as affiant gave them, on a piece of paper. He had with him, also, the roll of the company, and called off each man's name in turn and asked affiant about it. Affiant answered his questions as well as he could."

According to the Browne-Baldwin report, Elmer Brown furnished a list of eight "suspects," seven of whom had been named in the Conyers "confession." The additional name was that of Joseph L. Wilson, whose "gun was one in which shells picked up in the alley were found to fit." Wilson, a B Company ballplayer, testified he was asleep in his barracks when the shooting broke out and, a few minutes later, he answered his name at roll call.

The Browne-Baldwin list of eight suspects attributed to him was "a falsehood," Elmer Brown stated under oath. He denied that he had "ever named any such list, or ever named anyone mentioned in the list as suspected by him of having anything to do with the shooting, or as having knowledge of the shooting."

At no time during the two hours Senator Foraker held the floor did his black admirers break in on his performance to applaud, not even when he paused dramatically in midsentence to charge Browne and Baldwin with perjury or when he sarcastically exclaimed, "Oh, such plotting, such planning, simply to save somebody's face—I need not say whose."

"There was a solemnity about the affair that precluded any attempt at interruption," the *Times* man wrote, and observed that although the Senate galleries were packed, "the seats assigned the President were empty."

The Face-Saving

———◀•••▶———

26

"Mr. Herbert J. Browne, he sent me for the picture."

As HIS SENATE TERM drew to a close, Foraker pushed frantically
for the creation of a tribunal which would enable the soldiers to
confront their accusers and answer specific charges. As men presumed to be innocent, Foraker argued, they should be permitted
to re-enlist unless the Government could establish their guilt as
either principals or accessories.

Senator Aldrich, On January 29, presented a substitute measure less likely to embarrass the President or his successor. A
court of inquiry composed of high-ranking Army officers would
be called on to decide whether any of the men "qualified for re-

enlistment." The men, in short, were to be presumed guilty, then compelled to prove their innocence.

"Jedwood justice," snorted Ben Tillman, drawing on a Scottish-border phrase to give the departing President one last jab of his pitchfork. "When the lords of the marches caught some man who might have been suspected of stealing cattle or committing some other offense, they would hang him first and then try him afterwards. These Negroes have been 'hanged,' so far as the President could do it, and now the Senate proposes to give them a trial and a tardy justice to those who may be able to prove their innocence, although I doubt if any can prove it."

Lacking the votes to put across his own bill, Foraker had to choose between the Administration's tribunal or none at all. Reluctantly, he decided to back the Aldrich proposal. At least it would give the soldiers a forum in the coming months when, after his departure, there would be no one in Congress to plead their case. The Aldrich bill passed the Senate on February 23 and the House a few days later. Roosevelt signed it on March 2.

"You've got your commission," a prophetic Army officer remarked to Senator Foraker after reading the names of the retired generals who were to sit on the court of inquiry,* "but it's packed. The verdict will be one that will save the President's face. You'll see."

A few weeks after Taft moved into the White House, eight of the Brownsville soldiers, including First Sergeants Sanders and Frazier, filed a request with the War Department to have Captain Lyon represent them before the court of inquiry.

"The President does not think there is any obligation on your part to arrange for his employment to defend these men," Taft's secretary advised the department on April 17.

The older men of the battalion then turned to Brigadier General Aaron S. Daggett, who had commanded the Twenty-fifth in Cuba. "The court is packed against them," the General declared in a letter to Foraker, but he agreed to appear on the men's behalf. First, however, he gave them to understand that he

---

* Lieutenant General Samuel B. M. Young, Major General Joseph P. Sanger, Brigadier General John M. Wilson, Brigadier General Theodore Schwan, Brigadier General Butler D. Price.

looked on the Brownsville Raid as an "atrocious crime" and thought that its perpetrators should be hanged.

"I also said that, should I engage in this case, I would be as zealous in bringing out evidence to show who did that crime, whether they be white or black, as I would be in bringing about justice and a restoration to the Army of the innocent," he later explained.

For General Daggett, the court of inquiry might offer an opportunity to get at the truth, no matter where the search should lead, but the Secretary of War in the new Taft Administration had no intention of creating a review board that would place five retired generals in the position of sitting in judgment on an action taken by a former commander in chief. The soldiers were to be on trial, not Theodore Roosevelt.

The War Department's stance came to light when some naïve underling was asked to prepare a letter of instructions to guide the generals in their inquiry. In the draft submitted to the Secretary's office for approval, the court was directed to "determine whether there was probably such guilt as principals or accessories before or after the fact as to warrant the action taken under the power conferred by the Fourth Article of War."

The words were hastily deleted before they could give rise to what the Secretary's office called "annoying and unwarranted criticism by the press." In the final text, which instructed the court to "determine and report upon the disciplinary aspects of their case," the Department achieved a bureaucratic murkiness sufficient to keep the press at a respectful distance.

As senior counsel for the soldiers, General Daggett explained to former Senator Foraker, he intended to see to it that each man who took the witness stand was presumed innocent until proven guilty.

"I shall present his record," the General wrote, "and say there is absolutely nothing against him and request that his re-enlistment be authorized. If the court requires him to *prove* his innocence, I shall say that they require an impossibility, a requirement never before made by a civilized country."

Should the court persist in following such an uncivilized

procedure, the General thought he might protest by withdrawing as the men's chief apologist.

"What would be the effect of this action on the public?" he asked, and Foraker advised him to "make as strong, earnest and vigorous a protest as possible, but not retire from the case."

After spending six months poring over the official records of the affair, the court of inquiry decided in the fall of 1909 that it was ready to have a look at Brownsville.

"The court does not expect to take any testimony there unless there is some new evidence," the presiding general explained. "It does not expect to repeat any evidence that has already been given."

The generals debarked from the noon train on Friday, November 26, and were met by Captain Charles R. Howland, who, as the court's recorder, would present the Government's case. Captain Howland had spent the past week going over the ground the generals would cover and lining up witnesses they would hear. He escorted them to the Miller Hotel, where rooms had been booked for them and for the court reporter, whose young wife was the only woman in the party, a circumstance she found to her liking. Her husband had refused to leave Washington without her.

Mayor Combe, Judge Bartlett, Commissioner Creager, and other local dignitaries called on the generals that evening. They were received in the large second-floor room at the rear of the Miller Hotel where the Odin family had bedded down on the night of the raid. The bullet holes were still visible.

The next morning, when the court settled down to work in the courtroom of the Federal Building, Captain Howland got things off to a helpful start by introducing an accurate map of the fort and the town. The Penrose-Macklin courts-martial and the Senate Military Affairs Committee hearings had been confused at times by misleading maps. As Howland now explained, Elizabeth Street and the parallel streets named for presidents (Washington, Adams, Jefferson, Madison, Monroe) did not run true north from the fort. The senators, for convenience, had referred to Washington Street as being east of Elizabeth. In reality, it was northeast.

Monday morning, with General Daggett on hand to speak for the soldiers (he had arrived the night before), Captain Howland brought out the first bit of new evidence. The three barracks occupied by the black soldiers had burned to the ground a few weeks earlier. Several townspeople, including the Mayor and Captain Kelly, testified they had heard cartridges exploding in the flames.

No troops had occupied the barracks since the departure of Major Penrose's command more than three years earlier, Captain Howland pointed out. The implication that the men had left live shells scattered around their quarters was clearly intended to suggest to the court that ball ammunition had been available to them on the night of the shooting.

"Has the reservation been open to the public all of the time since the troops left?" General Daggett asked.

"Yes, sir," he was told, and he let it go at that.

The generals were taken on a tour of the town, which included walking the length of the garrison wall, peering at what had once been the Allison-Hollomon beer joint, and listening to such star witnesses as Katie Leahy, Louis Cowen, and George W. Rendall. Captain Howland put Teofilo Crixell under oath to tell how much beer he had supplied Allison and Hollomon. Enough to fill about three thousand bottles, Crixell thought. He had also slipped them two or three cases of whiskey, he said, although they had been licensed to handle only malt liquor.

The court didn't question any other saloonkeeper, not even Mr. Weller, who, for some reason, had never been officially interrogated about the raid despite the threats he and his customers had been heard making against the black soldiers. Like Blocksom and Purdy before them, the generals mingled only with townspeople of the better sort. They avoided the Mexican mescal dives where they might have got a somewhat different slant on "the nigger raid."

The generals spent what amounted to a long weekend in Brownsville, from Friday noon to the following Tuesday afternoon, when they left on the 3:50 train. Back in Washington, shivering in their drafty, makeshift accommodations on New York Avenue, they began taking the testimony of the soldiers.

The men were questioned first by Captain Howland and then by defense counsel—General Daggett and Napoleon B. Marshall, the Negro lawyer who had worked on the case with Senator Foraker. Early in the proceedings, when Boyd Conyers took the stand on the morning of December 14, it became apparent that Captain Howland's credulity had not been strained by the Browne-Baldwin report. He began to build his case against the soldiers on what had been palmed off on Roosevelt and Taft as the "Conyers confession."

"Yes, sir, I went up there, after they opened up, two or three times," Conyers said when Captain Howland asked if he had patronized the Allison-Hollomon saloon, where he was supposed to have planned the raid with John Hollomon and John Brown.

"Were you up there on the 13th of August?"

"No, sir; I couldn't be up there on the 13th," Conyers explained, "because I was on guard duty. I immediately was put on guard duty after we came off the practice march."

"Were you up there on the 12th, the day before?"

"Sunday?"

Captain Howland nodded, then got an unexpected answer from the young man he was trying to expose as a cold-blooded assassin.

"No, sir," Conyers said. "That was my busiest day, on Sundays. I always taken a great interest in myself trying to make a little money, and I run a bootblack stand there. I had thirty-eight or forty customers, and I was shining shoes all the time when I wasn't on duty. I got one dollar a month every month, and I made thirty-eight or forty dollars a month shining shoes."

Undaunted, Captain Howland tried to bring out the black youth's hatred of the white people he had supposedly conspired to terrorize and slaughter.

"How did the white people treat you down there at Brownsville?"

"I was treated just as nice in Brownsville as I was at Monroe," Conyers testified. "They are both southern states, you know, and about on the same plan, you know, the two states, and I never had any trouble all the while I was in Brownsville."

Before he left the stand that afternoon, Conyers was asked if there were any one person, above all others, that he would like the court to summon in his defense.

"Mr. Herbert J. Browne," Conyers said. "I would like to have him."

Before Browne took the stand, Sheriff Arnold came up from Monroe to testify. He had been present during both of Browne's interviews with Conyers, on October 6 and 11, 1908, and was willing to swear that no "confession" of any sort had been made at either of the two sessions. Browne was not at all disturbed by this development.

Conyers did not come out with his "full confession" in the presence of the Sheriff, Browne explained, and favored the court with a new version of when and where he had obtained the "confession." On two occasions, neither of which had ever been mentioned before, Conyers had sought him out for a private talk, Browne testified, and it was during their second conversation that he was told in detail how the raid was pulled off by the soldiers.

Around eleven o'clock on the night of October 6, Browne said, he was returning to his hotel after spending four hours questioning Conyers in the Sheriff's office. Suddenly, as Browne reached the door, Conyers stepped from the shadow of a tree or the hotel awning and told him, "Mr. Browne, there is a good deal more in this case than what you know anything about. The Negroes will kill me if I say anything."

"I did not feel as though I wanted a confession from him under those circumstances," Browne continued, "or under any circumstances that would rest on my unsupported statement. If he had anything of that sort to say, I felt he should say it in the presence of the Sheriff."

But instead of pursuing the matter the next day when he was scheduled to continue questioning Conyers in the Sheriff's office, Browne abruptly canceled the interview and left town. When he talked to Arnold before his departure, he said nothing about his meeting with Conyers the night before, even though this hitherto-unmentioned conversation had brought out fresh details, including information on how "we got the cartridges."

Browne returned to Monroe on Sunday, October 11, and spent the afternoon with Sheriff Arnold and Conyers. It was during this interview that Conyers trotted home to get the picture of B Company's baseball team. Once the questioning had ended, Conyers left and, Browne said, he walked back to his hotel with the Sheriff, got his luggage, and took a buggy to the depot. Again, Conyers materialized and waited while Browne paid the driver and gave him money to settle his hotel bill.

"He drove away," Browne testified, "and then Buddy stood there and talked with me, and then and there is where Buddy Conyers told the rest."

When Marshall cross-examined the witness, a black man confronting what he intended to unmask as a white perjurer, the lawyer was correct and contemptuous. Why, he asked Browne, had he neglected to mention the time and place of the Conyers confession when he first reported it in the sworn statement he submitted to the War Department?

"Because," Browne said, "having had some experience with Negro criminals, I had concluded it was inadvisable to give them too much opportunity to perfect fraudulent alibis, and my wisdom in that respect I think is borne out, in my judgment."

"I will first ask you what experience have you had with Negro criminals?"

"I was for three years the editor of the Roanoke *Times,* and during my experience in that town we had to clean out about the worst nest of Negro criminals that ever infested a civilized community. And in that way I was thrown somewhat intimately in contact with their maneuvers and methods of handling crime and escaping punishment."

"Some lynching occurred at that time?"

"Yes; some very regrettable lynchings occurred during that time."

"Now, the fact that Sheriff Arnold denied absolutely that Conyers had made any confession in his presence had nothing to do with the fixing of the time and place of the confession on your part?"

"None whatever."

Boyd Conyers, still under oath, was brought back to the stand to answer questions about the two conversations Browne had revealed for the first time. Neither of them took place, Conyers swore, and witnesses backed him up. Sheriff Arnold had walked to the hotel with Browne on the night of October 6. He had not seen Boyd Conyers lurking in the shadow of what Browne had described as either a tree or the hotel awning. There was no tree in front of the Walton Hotel, and it had no awning.

As for October 11, when he was supposed to have delivered the major part of his confession while Browne waited for the 5:55 P.M. train, Conyers said he had left the Sheriff's office that evening and hurried over to Mr. Lancaster's to look after his horses. He was more than an hour late.

"Mr. Lancaster, he asked me, 'Boyd, where have you been?' I says, 'I have been to Mr. Arnold's office.' He says, 'Do you know what time it is?' I says, 'No, sir; it's after five.' He says, 'These horses should have been fed here at four o'clock. I have gotten mighty tired of these detectives interfering with my work.'"

According to Browne, when his buggy drove up to the depot that evening, Conyers was waiting for him. "I thought I would have barely time to catch my train," Browne testified, "but the train was apparently late or something. At any rate I had fifteen or twenty minutes at the train."

"It left on time," said the station agent when asked if the 5:55 P.M. train had been late that Sunday, and he brought out the depot records to prove it.

"After you reached the station that evening," the driver of Browne's buggy, James M. Baker, was asked, "how many minutes elapsed before the train departed?"

"About a minute," he stated under oath, and was supported by William M. Cook, a livery man who had seen Browne get in the buggy. "Baker was returning from a trip to the train when he met Sheriff Arnold and Browne going toward the station, just

beyond the hotel. The Sheriff called out to him to get this man
to the station quick, as he wanted to catch the train, and Baker
turned and Browne got in the buggy. I remember looking to see
how much time they had and it was three minutes."

The Sheriff, Browne, and Conyers all agreed that it was during the Sunday-afternoon session in Arnold's office on October 11
that the group photograph of B Company's baseball team was
brought into play. Again, Browne told one story, the Sheriff and
Conyers quite another.

"'Supposing,'" Browne testified he asked Conyers, "'the soldiers did the shooting; do you think that they would stand almost under the eaves of the barracks, fifty yards or so away, for
an interval of several minutes, knowing that the men inside were
apprehensive of a raid, in which case they would be liable to be
shot down like so many rabbits, unless the men on the inside
knew who it was that was doing the shooting?'

"Well, he went somewhat in the air on that and had no answer. I pressed that point, and he weakened. He got nervous,
and he wrestled in his chair, and grabbed hold of the arms of it;
and he was smoking a cigarette at the time, and it fell out of
his mouth, and then I pressed on my point, and I said, 'Boyd,
three witnesses saw a man, one of the soldiers, with a jammed
gun, where the Cowen alley crosses the street by the Leahy
Hotel, and saw another man take the gun from him and fix it,'
and when I threw that shot at him, he pretty nearly fell out of
his chair; his jaw dropped and his face look to be about a foot
long, and he turned as near ashy as he could for his color, and just
then the Sheriff intervened.

"He said, 'Buddy, haven't you got some pictures of these
men?' and Buddy gasped and got his breath and said he had. I
think the interval saved Buddy Conyers, because the Sheriff said,
'How long will it take you to get them?' and he said about ten
minutes, and he went to his house and got a photograph of the
baseball team and two or three other members of the baseball
team. All right; that golden opportunity was sent glimmering by
the Sheriff."

"Did you regard this Sheriff's presence as obstructive?"

Browne was asked, and he said, "When the Sheriff saved him, after the question had been put to him about the jamming of the gun in the Cowen alley. Then it seemed to me very plain that the Sheriff was protecting him." *

"During the interview between yourself, Browne, and Conyers on October 11, 1908," Sheriff Arnold was asked, "did Conyers at any time wrestle in his chair or grab hold of the arms of it, and was he smoking a cigarette, which he let fall from his mouth?"

"He did not," the Sheriff replied, "nor did he show any signs of fear during our conversation. He did smoke occasionally."

"When Browne told Conyers in the above interview that one of the soldiers got his gun jammed in Cowen alley, did he [Conyers] nearly fall out of his chair, and did you notice his jaw drop?"

"He did not, nor was there a change in his expression."

"When Browne told Conyers about a soldier's gun getting jammed, as aforesaid, did you at that time intervene and say, 'Buddy, haven't you got some pictures of these men?' "

"I did not; the request for the pictures came from Browne."

Boyd Conyers was recalled to the stand and asked who had sent him home to get the picture, the Sheriff or Herbert J. Browne.

"Mr. Herbert J. Browne, he sent me for the picture."

"Mr. Browne," the Sheriff testified, "took the picture and began to point with his pencil, and he says, 'Now, do you know these men?' and Conyers says, 'Yes, sir,' and he started over and named the whole crowd on there—Conyers called the names of every one. He says, 'Now, Boyd,' he says, 'you know the tough, turbulent fellows on this group. Who are the most tough and turbulent of this crowd here?' Well, he pointed out—Boyd Conyers says, 'John Hollomon . . .' He [Browne] says, 'John is a pretty bad egg, isn't he?' and he [Conyers] says, 'Yes, sir,' and he named over several more there, and some Conyers said were pretty rough, to use his words, pretty rough; and another he says,

---

* Nevertheless, in their December 5 report Browne and Baldwin stated that "Boyd Conyers is the man whose gun jammed at the exit of the alley by the Cowen house."

'Well, I never known him to be a sort of bad fellow.' He would
go on and name the whole group over that way on the baseball
picture."

It was from Boyd Conyers, Browne testified, that he first
learned of Hollomon's money-lending activities. He said Conyers
described Hollomon as a "hard man" who "always got every
dollar that was coming to him." To make sure that no debt went
unpaid, Hollomon was reported to have organized a gang of
thugs and terrorists, "the dirty dozen." Most of these debt col-
lectors, it seems, had been recruited from B Company's baseball
team. Its captain was the flashy outfielder, John Hollomon.

"That was the key of it; that he was captain of the baseball
team," Browne told the court of inquiry, "and if any man had
trouble with John Hollomon, there would be occasion taken later
on to beat him up, and that was the way John Hollmon got his
money. He [Conyers] was telling this to explain his statement
that John Hollomon was a bad man, and that the bad men of the
battalion were his men, under his control."

In his testimony before the court of inquiry, Browne swore
he first learned of Hollomon's money-lending activities when he
talked to Boyd Conyers in October 1908, but five months before
that meeting, in a report to Secretary Taft, Browne had referred
to "John Hollomon, the Shylock of Company B."

27

"You took from the rich and left the poor alone?"

JOHN HOLLOMON, the eighteen-dollar-a-month buck private who
occasionally lent his thirty-four-dollar-a-month first sergeant cigar
money, was identified in the Browne-Baldwin report as "the chief
conspirator and organizer of the raid." But for some reason he
had never testified about the affair before Will Lawson, the Baldwin agency's black detective, reported finding him in Macon,
Georgia, in early September 1908.

"He is known to very few, even among his own color," Browne and Baldwin reported on the basis of Lawson's information. "He keeps very much to himself. He lives with a woman who passes as his wife and runs a small grocery store in a Negro suburb."

After his dismissal from the Army, John Hollomon and ex-Sergeant James R. Reid had traveled through Texas and Louisiana with a moving-picture show. In June 1907 Hollomon had sold his interest, parted company with Reid, and headed for Missouri. At the time Will Lawson was supposed to have interviewed him in Macon, Georgia, Hollomon was living in St. Louis. He had not been near Macon for five years.

"Why were you called the financial man of that battalion?" Hollomon was asked when he made his debut as a witness before the court of inquiry.

"Well," he explained, "in the Army it has been a custom since I went there—I found it when I went there—that the money lenders would lend the soldiers money at twenty-five per cent for any fractional part of a month; if a man borrowed one dollar three days before payday, he would pay a dollar twenty-five for it on payday. I saw in that a good way to make money; other soldiers were doing it and I began." *

At Fort Niobrara he had established a stage line to haul the men four miles into the town of Valentine. Once they got there, they could buy drinks or food or almost anything else they wanted, and charge it to Hollomon. His fee for credit as well as for cash was twenty-five per cent.

"Being a money lender," he testified, "sometimes the rush on me would be so great I wouldn't have the cash money and I would fall short. I couldn't accommodate all the men; and I went down to the town there, and made a deposit—I can't remember just how much it was—with a saloonkeeper and asked him if he would recognize orders I sent in to the amount of the deposit and when that ran out to notify me, and I would come in and make another deposit. I went over to the drugstore and established an

---

* "It's a common occurrence," First Sergeant Mingo Sanders said when asked why he had permitted such a usurious practice. "I met the Army that way in 1881, and I left it that way."

account there. He did not require me to make a deposit. I also went to the general merchandise store and did the same thing; and whenever the men came up and wanted anything from town, I could give them an order for it, whether it was whiskey, shoes, or meals at the restaurant, or something from the drugstore."

A month after he opened up a line of credit for his fellow soldiers in Nebraska, Hollomon increased his take on their thirst by shifting his business to a saloon where he had been offered a ten per cent discount. The deal proved to be so mutually advantageous that the discount was raised to thirty-five per cent. Thus, by getting thirty-five per cent from the saloonkeeper and twenty-five per cent from the men, Hollomon was taking in a monthly profit of sixty per cent on the battalion's drinking by the time the three companies were ordered to Brownsville.

"They will give you a warm reception down there," Hollomon remembered the Nebraska townspeople saying when they heard the soldiers were to be sent to Texas. The men replied with such remarks as, "Well, we can give them as good as they send" or "If they don't want us down there, let them send us away."

"Are you able to tell the members of the court whether or not the men were angry because of the discrimination in drinking in saloons in Brownsville between blacks and whites?" Hollomon was asked.

"I am able to say that they didn't like it," he replied. "They would say such things as, 'If we can't drink as any other man can, our money is just as good as theirs, we don't drink any place at all.'"

Even before he left Nebraska, Hollomon said, he had planned to open a saloon in Brownsville. The same idea had occurred to Private Ernest Allison, who was to be discharged on August 12. Hollomon suggested they go into business together, and Allison agreed. He was short of cash and needed a backer. They got part of their money from their beer distributors, the Crixell brothers, but Hollomon had an extra five hundred to six hundred dollars to kick in, if the need arose.

The Allison-Hollomon saloon opened its doors on Friday, August 10, the day before payday. It was an immediate success. Monday afternoon Hollomon went to a local bank and deposited a hundred dollars, then settled his accounts with the Crixell brothers for the beer, cigars, and soda pop they had delivered. Business attended to, Hollomon set about making some domestic arrangements.

He paid three dollars rent for a house across from his saloon, hired a retired black soldier to pick up the household goods he'd shipped from Nebraska, and bought some dining-room chairs. Everything was to be in readiness for the arrival of his six-year-old son and his "housekeeper." Mrs. Hollomon, still legally his spouse, was in Macon, Georgia, scraping along on the three-fifty to four dollars a week she earned as a laundress. She got no help from John Hollomon.

Like most other saloonkeepers in Brownsville, Hollomon gave his customers a chance to test their skill and luck at dice and cards.

"How much of a rake-off did you get?" he was asked.

"That would depend upon what was on the table," he said. "Occasionally I would go round and look, and if a man had a pile of money on the table in front of him, two or three hundred dollars, I would take three or four, or, maybe, five dollars. If he had six or eight dollars, I didn't take anything."

"You took from the rich and left the poor alone?"

"Yes, sir; that is it; and if a man lost all he had, I would give him two or three dollars to start up again."

Before the eight-o'clock curfew emptied the place Monday night, August 13, between twenty-five and thirty soldiers were drinking beer, Hollomon testified, and an indeterminate number were in the adjoining shed gambling. Business was so brisk that three men had to be called in to help Allison tend bar.

"Was there considerable irritation about being ordered in at eight o'clock by the men who were drinking; did they want to stay out?"

"There didn't appear to be any unusual irritation about it more than any other order that soldiers get and don't like," Hollomon said.

"How much did the men show the effect of liquor on the night of the 13th in the saloon?"

"Well, I don't think any more than they did on any other night. I'm quite sure they didn't."

Hollomon left the saloon around 7:30 or 7:45, he said, and walked back to B Company's barracks. He hung around the card tables, watching (he'd given up gambling), and at nine o'clock, when the lights went out and the poker games ended, he drifted into the reading room and spent about an hour and a half looking at the newspapers.

"I then went up to the second floor to my bunk and went to bed. Later—I did not know at that time just what time it was— I was awakened by the firing of shots. I rolled out of my bunk, sat on the floor, put on my shoes, and then felt for my trousers. They were not on the bedpost where I had lain them that night, and I went around to my locker and got a pair, put them on as quickly as possible, put my ammunition belt around my waist, went to the gun rack for my rifle, got that, went downstairs, and fell in line . . ."

"When you got down to your company," General Daggett asked, "was there any firing going on?"

"Yes, sir," Hollomon said, and on this detail he had been corroborated by First Sergeant Mingo Sanders in his Senate testimony.

The firing was still going on when he reached B Company's barracks, grabbed a lantern from Sergeant Jackson, and ordered his men to fall in, Sergeant Sanders had told the senators. Some of his men ("I suppose three or four, four or five") were kneeling or lying down to avoid what they took to be the line of fire.

"Stand up!" Sanders shouted, and when Private Hollomon said, "You have got that light there, and you will be the cause of us all getting killed," the First Sergeant snapped back, "If you get killed, you will get killed as a soldier." Sanders also made some other remarks at the time, but he preferred not to repeat them in the presence of United States senators.

"I am positive I did not get down nor make any attempt to get down on my knees," Hollomon insisted, but he did admit to the five retired generals sitting in judgment on him that he'd spoken to Sanders about the lantern. "I said, 'Put out the lights, Sergeant, they are firing this way; the light will draw fire.'"

"You told the first sergeant of your company to put the light out?"

"Yes, sir."

"Had you given the first sergeant orders before that?"

"No, sir."

"That is the only time you ever gave him an order?"

"I didn't think I was giving him an order at that time."

"You thought it was advice?"

"I asked him to do so."

"What did the first sergeant say?"

"He said, 'Damn the light; fall in.'"

According to the Will Lawson affidavit on which the Browne-Baldwin story of the raid was built, John Hollomon and John Brown helped shoot up the town, then scampered back to the garrison. They were late for roll call, Lawson deposed, so someone answered for them. According to Sergeant Sanders, John Hollomon was conspicuously present when he called the roll and John Brown was recorded as absent. He was asleep at the bakeshop, it turned out, and had heard no shooting.

"If I had any intention of committing a crime of that kind," Hollomon remarked to the generals in passing, "John Brown would have been one of the last men in the world that I would have selected to help carry out a deed of that kind."

"Why not?"

"That man put in about six years without learning to right shoulder arms. He was dumb and stupid. You couldn't learn him anything."

"Is John Brown too dumb to bake bread?"

"That is about all he could do in the Army."

"He was an assistant baker, wasn't he, on extra duty?"

"Yes, sir; I believe they kept him on extra duty because he couldn't do nothing else."

In picking John Hollomon as the chief architect of the raid, the "custodian and distributor of the cartridges," Browne and Baldwin had singled out the one man in the outfit who had benefited from the town's Jim Crow drinking arrangements. Segregation had given him a virtual monopoly on the thirst of a hundred and seventy men who had little to do with their spare time except drink beer, gamble, and fend off mosquitoes and Mexican whores.

"If I had had any previous knowledge of any crime contemplated by the soldiers," Hollomon testified, "I would have done everything in my power to prevent it."

"Why would you?"

"If for no other reason, to protect my financial interest."

If the soldiers were guilty of the crime and vengeance their motive, it would seem reasonable to look for the criminals in the ranks of Company C, which contained all the men who had been maltreated by townspeople. But circumstantial evidence tended to exonerate this particular company. It was the only one of the three companies at Fort Brown that had been issued reduced-range lead cartridges instead of steel-jacketed ball ammunition. Also, the delay in opening the gun racks suggested that the raiders' rifles had come from some place other than C Company's barracks.

Captain Lyon's D Company had been eliminated almost from the outset, not only because it was so well-disciplined but also because it had been formed and counted so quickly that it could hardly have sheltered any late-arriving raiders. Even if they had managed to sneak into ranks, they would still have had to clean their rifles in the dark, and clean them with sufficient skill to pass their company commander's unusually strict inspection at dawn.

Once C and D Companies appeared to be in the clear, suspicion fastened on B Company. It had no other place to lodge. Unfortunately for the defenders of the Administration's action, however, no one could come up with a motive for even a single member of B Company, much less ten or twenty, to put his life in jeopardy by shooting up the town. Certainly the one man in the battalion who would be most unlikely to risk either his skin or his stripes in such an attack was First Sergeant Mingo Sanders.

But in his closing address, Captain Howland argued that the evidence placed before the court of inquiry had established "absolutely" that men of B Company had "fired with murderous intent from the upper and lower back porches" of their barracks, and had then "entered the town of Brownsville as part of a raiding party and there participated in the brutal and disgraceful affray of August 13." Company records, Howland continued, "would indicate that the controlling hand in Company B was the hand of Mingo Sanders."

In seeking to link Sanders with the conspirators, Howland was out to impeach the First Sergeant's testimony on two points: (1) the roll call of Company B began while the raid was still in progress and John Hollomon was on his knees in fear and (2) exploded shells from four guns assigned to Sanders' company could easily have been plucked from an open box on the back porch of the barracks and planted in the path of the raiders.

The First Sergeant's evidence was incorrect, Howland maintained, and could not have been given "unintentionally." In a word, Sanders was lying. However, nowhere in the Captain's long-winded summation (it ran to more than a hundred and fifty printed pages) did he enlighten the generals as to what possible motive could have inspired a dedicated noncommissioned officer, at the peak of his career, to sacrifice his life's work and his pension to join a criminal assault on a town he hardly knew and had no reason to harm.

"The appearance of Sergeant Sanders before this court was dignified and convincing," General Daggett declared. "His bearing during the vigorous, violent examination was honest and frank, yet calm and self-contained. Such bearing was born only of truth. He entered the courtroom with a spotless record; he left it with that record illuminated."

During the twenty-six years, six months, and seven days of his service in the United States Army, Mingo Sanders had got into trouble only once. In February 1898, while on a tour of duty at Fort Missoula, Montana, he had been tried by a summary court-martial for some minor infraction and fined one dollar. He was within a couple of years of retirement on three-quarters pay when he was dismissed without honor for failing to do what he swore he was unable to do—identify the Brownsville raiders.

"An exceptionally good man," Major Penrose testified, and

expressed his satisfaction that Sanders had done everything in his power to track down the culprits, "but, being first sergeant, he was less likely to hear what they wanted to conceal, for the very reason that they knew he would disclose it."

"He is a strict disciplinarian and always maintained good order and discipline in the company," said Lieutenant Lawrason, his company commander. "I don't believe he ever overlooked the delinquencies of the men and I think his reputation in this respect would tend to make the guilty men very careful indeed about permitting any inkling of the truth to reach him."

A week after the raid, Lieutenant James A. Higgins took command of Company B. "The company was in excellent condition when I took it," he declared, "particularly as to the control exercised by Sergeant Mingo Sanders over the men. I considered him equal in ability to any sergeant I had ever seen."

Sanders' conduct at Fort Reno, when the Inspector General delivered the Roosevelt ultimatum, was enough to change the thinking of Lieutenant Grier, the post's acting adjutant, who, at first, had gone along with the official view of the soldiers' guilt.

"What fact was there that could possibly change your opinion, Lieutenant?" an antisoldier senator asked.

"When these men did not come up and give up anybody—the names of anybody implicated in that raid—when they knew if they did not there was not any joke about it, but they would all go out of the service, and I knew old men like Sergeant Sanders, that I have seen personally handle the meanest kind of a soldier, and handle him mighty well, I began to think there was considerable doubt about it."

Much the same thought had come to Boyd Conyers, as he explained to the court of inquiry when he asked permission to take the stand again for a brief final statement.

"After we moved to Fort Reno, Oklahoma, when the orders came on a Sunday—I forgot the date—when we was to be disarmed the soldiers fell about on their bunks, and it was one of the saddest things I ever seen in my life. The soldiers were crying, even Mingo Sanders was crying and his wife was screaming, when we was disarmed. I never experienced such sadness in my life. We were fatigued there every day, and I believe if any man had been implicated in that shooting he would have told something about it. I know I would."

From Oklahoma, Sanders and his wife had made their way east to Washington, where he had found work as a laborer, hired a lawyer, and done everything he could to meet the impossible requirements the President had set up for re-enlistment applicants.

"And now," he said in taking his leave of the court of inquiry, "I am on my last examination, I suppose, by this grand court and I am now passed half a century, and I am also pleading to this court for mercy for my sake, because when a man gets to my age there is nobody wants him, and I wish that this court would consider my case to the bottom of their heart . . ."

Long before he bowed out of the presence of the five generals appointed to consider his case, Mingo Sanders had been condemned by a higher authority. President Roosevelt, packing to leave the White House, had read Herbert J. Browne's final report and then got off a letter to the Secretary of War on February 7, 1909.

The report, he found, "shows clearly that First Sergeant Mingo Sanders, in spite of his reputation for personal courage, was as thoroly dangerous, unprincipled and unworthy a soldier as ever wore the United States uniform, and that under no conceivable circumstances should he ever be allowed again in the army."

Browne's report, which Roosevelt accepted so readily, was permeated with the vindictive statements of a B Company deserter, one Samuel F. Holman, who spun a colorful tale of terrorist activity in Sergeant Sanders' company. The men cowered under the brutal fists of John Hollomon's "secret society of thugs and desperadoes," Holman said, and received fifteen dollars from Browne for his sworn statement.

It wasn't enough. Holman thought a hundred dollars would be "a fair payment" for his services, with an additional twenty-five dollars for his stenographer. When Browne refused to settle with him, Holman started dunning the President. Browne quickly got word to the War Department that he'd found the man "to be irresponsibly incorrect and unreliable in his declarations."

But as far as Mingo Sanders was concerned, it no longer mattered that the only derogatory information against him in the files of the War Department was "irresponsibly incorrect and unreliable." The vengeful fictions of a deserter had sufficed to cause a twenty-six-year veteran of the Indian wars, Cuba, and the Philippines to be forever barred from further service by his commander in chief.

The case of Mingo Sanders had been closed even before the court of inquiry was convened.*

28

". . . a farce should lead up to a grotesque climax."

IN THE SPRING OF 1910, after the last Brownsville soldier had appeared before the court of inquiry to swear to his innocence of both the original crime and any subsequent "conspiracy of silence," the men's junior counsel, Napoleon B. Marshall, attacked the procedures the generals had followed. As a protest, the black lawyer announced, he was going to refrain from making a closing argument for the defense. He gave two reasons.

First, he said, the generals had never made it clear to him whether they were sitting as "a court of inquiry or as a court-martial," and Captain Howland had proceeded more as a prosecutor than as "an impartial investigating officer." Second, "the instructions of the Secretary of War to this court conflict so fundamentally and totally with my legal training as to make it impossible for me to build an argument which would attempt to prove a negative."

Captain Howland was distressed by Marshall's "error," which had arisen, he liked to think, "from ignorance rather than inten-

* In the spring of 1912, when President Taft was in political trouble back home, he found Mingo Sanders working for the Government as a day laborer (at a dollar and seventy-five cents a day) and arranged for him to be sent to Ohio to attend "ten or twelve colored meetings."

tion." Quite clearly, he said, the court had conducted itself as a court of inquiry, not a court-martial. "No one is being tried for an offense before this court," he argued, "and this court has no authority whatsoever to punish any man."

It was a specious argument. Obviously the men were on trial when they came before the court and tried to prove to its satisfaction that they had taken no part in the raid and had no guilty knowledge of it. The court could punish any one of the soldiers simply by striking his name from the list of those ruled eligible for re-enlistment. He would never be given another chance to clear his name, collect his back pay, and resume his military career.

Captain Howland and defense counsel agreed on at least one point. If soldiers had shot up the town, none of the men should be permitted to re-enlist; if they had not shot up the town, all of them should be declared eligible.

"If you find that ten are qualified for re-enlistment," Captain Howland pointed out to the court, "apparently that will classify the others as men who were guilty of shooting in Brownsville, and it will practically punish them in that their status will thereafter be that of suspects not arrested."

Captain Howland had no doubt of the soldiers' guilt. The raid was the product of a conspiracy, he said, "and conspiracy as broad as the garrison." To bolster his point, he called attention to the testimony of the three noncommissioned officers in charge of quarters, all of whom had "slept with their heads on the keys to the gun racks." To Howland, this constituted "good evidence of conspiracy which was being planned and carried out by some master mind." To the layman, it might suggest nothing more than that naked men sleeping under a mosquito net on a stifling summer night could think of no safer place to put the keys to the gun racks.

"Suppose," General Daggett asked the court, "some of the soldiers did the shooting, who were they? What individual is there against whom there is a spark of evidence? Of course the alleged Conyers confession is not taken seriously."

But Captain Howland had taken it seriously. It was, he declared, "a bona fide confession, given as stated, and the witness Lawson and the witness Browne are witnesses in good standing before this court. No attempt has been made to impeach the credibility of either."

The credibility of both men had been thoroughly impeached. Witness Lawson, for example, swore he had gone on an excursion trip to Gainsville, Georgia, with Boyd Conyers but was unable to produce any witnesses who saw them together. And witness Lawson had also spent a week interviewing John Hollomon in a town John Hollomon had not visited in five years.

The credibility of witness Browne had already suffered extensive erosion before he casually brushed aside his previous sworn testimony and favored the generals with an account of two hitherto-undisclosed private talks with Conyers. Reliable witnesses had followed him to the stand and proved that no such meetings could have occurred.

After taking the testimony of eighty-two soldiers, the court brought its proceedings to an end, slamming the door in the faces of more than seventy other men who had asked to be heard. During their year-long deliberations, the five generals had found time for any witness whose evidence, no matter how questionable, had tended to incriminate the soldiers, but had refused to follow any leads that might clear them of the crime.

A pride of retired generals, serving a southern Democrat Secretary of War appointed by the Republican President who had executed the dismissal order of his predecessor, could hardly have been expected to set about their business in such a way as to prove that a scattering of black enlisted men were innocent of any wrongdoing and that two presidents (along with an incalculable number of West Pointers) were guilty of a monstrous injustice.

"To be successful a farce should lead up to a grotesque climax," the New York *World* noted when the generals concluded their work. "The court of inquiry has done all that could possibly be asked of it to make this Brownsville burlesque upon justice a triumph of absurdity."

The decision the generals handed down on April 6, 1910, reflected their rank and their race. They agreed unanimously that men of Major Penrose's command had shot up the town. Four generals (Schwan dissented) were of the opinion that the trouble could have been prevented if the officers and men had performed their respective duties immediately before the raid. They also believed that some of the criminals could have been discovered if a prompt and rigid inspection had been made of each soldier's arms, equipment, and ammunition.

For reasons known only to themselves and possibly their Maker, three generals (Young and Sanger dissented) ruled that fourteen men were qualified for re-enlistment.* The decision was final and irrevocable. The War Department would no longer consider applications from any of the other one hundred and fifty-three men who might still be alive and interested in resuming their careers as soldiers. For the rest of their lives they would be, in Captain Howland's phrase, "suspects not arrested."

The list of fourteen men did not include a single sergeant. The generals had put an end to the military careers of such old-timers as Mingo Sanders, Jacob Frazier, and Walker McCurdy. Three corporals qualified for re-enlistment. None of them had appeared before the court of inquiry and nothing in their Senate testimony helps unravel the mystery of how they came to make the generals' list.

To the *World's* editorial writer "the logic of the verdict is as clear as day. As the report reads, nobody is guilty; therefore everybody is guilty; and everybody being guilty, nobody is innocent, unless it be presumably the fourteen men recommended for re-enlistment. How they could escape being guilty when the entire battalion is guilty, except they were in Alaska or the Philippines or some equally distant place at the time of the shooting, is one of the mysteries of the case."

Instead of being in Alaska or the Philippines on the night of the shooting, two of the three corporals (Coltrane and Daniels)

* Jones A. Coltrane, Edward L. Daniels, and Edward Warfield of B Company; Lewis J. Baker, Clifford I. Adair, Henry W. Arvin, Calvin Smith, and John Smith of C Company; Robert Williams, Winter Washington, Elias Gant, John A. Jackson, Samuel E. Scott, and William Van Hook of D Company.

had testified in the Senate hearings that they were asleep in B Company's barracks, where, according to Captain Howland's reading of the evidence, the raid had begun with shooting from both the upper and lower porches. The shooting originated on the town side of the garrison wall, both corporals had sworn, and they had agreed with their first sergeant that it had still been going on when Mingo Sanders called the roll of their company.

The third corporal, D Company's Winter Washington, had also sworn he was asleep in his barracks when the shots awakened him. He, too, had identified them as coming from the town and had refused to budge from his conviction that none of the soldiers did any shooting that night.

"Have you any idea about who was engaged in it?" one of the senators had asked him.

"My ideas about it are, there is a lot of Mexicans and greasers around there, and my idea about it—at first we had an investigation and nothing could be found out about it; and I thought some of those cowboys or something might have fired in on the soldiers; fired in on us. That is my idea about it."

"If this shooting was not done by the Negroes, it must have been done by white men, was it not?" Senator Lodge had asked Captain Kelly.

"Yes, sir, taking Mexicans as white men," the Brownsville banker had replied, and then dismissed the notion as not worth discussing. "The proposition that white men went out in the night and shot up their own town, shot into the houses where there were women and children, in order to get rid of a few Negroes, is not to be considered for a moment. There was no reason for getting rid of those Negroes in the first place."

John Garner, Brownsville's up-and-coming new congressman, agreed. It was "preposterous" to think that anyone other than the soldiers had done the shooting, he said, and ridiculed newspaper speculation that "a dive-keeper of the town became incensed because one of the soldiers financed an opposition 'joint,' and that a number of citizens came to him as armed volunteers to avenge his grievance."

The local "dive-keeper" hardest hit by the new Negro beer

joint was John Tillman, proprietor of the Ruby Saloon, where the raid ended with its one fatality. Even before the three black companies arrived at Fort Brown, an officer of the departing Twenty-sixth Infantry had heard Tillman remark in the presence of three or four customers, "We will run the Negro troops out of town in three weeks, and have the white troops back."

In those days Tillman had been operating a nondescript grocery store on Elizabeth Street. By the time the black infantrymen showed up he was running the Ruby. When the neighboring saloonkeepers, H. H. Weller and the Crixell brothers, refused to serve the Negroes, Tillman set up a Jim Crow bar in the rear of his establishment. He never had a moment's trouble with the men, he said.

"Invariably they would walk to the front bar, the first bar in the house and would probably order drinks—sometimes two or three in a bunch—and ask for drinks, and I would invite them back to the next counter and welcomed them to be served there. . . . Some of them would walk back and some would go out and would not say a word. One made a remark one night, saying, 'You are entitled to your rules. If your rules don't suit us, we can go elsewhere.'"

The segregated bar turned out to be a profitable accommodation until Saturday night, August 11, when the soldiers blew their pay in the new saloon at Sixteenth and Monroe financed by John Hollomon and operated by Ernest Allison. The Negroes' defection not only cut into the Ruby's profits, but also impaired the economic well-being of the Mexican beer joints, where the difference between solvency and ruin often depended on the soldiers' trade.

At nine o'clock the following night Mrs. Lon Evans claimed to have been attacked by one of the soldiers. The next day—the day of the raid—the men about town most likely to join a lynch mob were rumored to have met in an Elizabeth Street saloon, Crixell's or Tillman's. Joe Crixell, who cried "nigger" at the sound of the first shots, denied that any such meeting took place; John Tillman, who strolled down Thirteenth Street at the height of the shooting, was never officially asked about it.

Tillman was not among the townspeople who gave testimony

to the Citizens' Committee. He was not called to the stand at the courts-martial of Major Penrose or Captain Macklin, and gave no evidence at either the Senate hearings or the court of inquiry. Only once, in a three-page affidavit taken by Purdy and Blocksom nearly five months after the raid, did he make a sworn contribution to the Brownsville records, and no questions were put to him that might have cast suspicion on any local saloonkeepers.

He was in the backyard of the Ruby drinking beer with some customers, Tillman stated, when he heard six or eight shots. The shooting had ceased temporarily by the time he reached the front door and Policeman Padron asked him, "Have you got a gun you can loan me?" Without stopping to ask what had happened to the Colt revolver Padron should have been carrying while on duty, Tillman dug up a pistol for him and then headed down Elizabeth Street toward his home on Adams, across from the garrison.

After assuring his wife there was nothing to worry about, Tillman started back uptown and ran into his next-door neighbor, J. P. McDonnel, a carpenter who had been going around town denouncing the War Department for putting Negro soldiers across the road from him. Although essential details of his testimony varied with each recital, McDonnel was to become one of the town's most sought-after witnesses against the soldiers. He swore he'd had a good look at the raiders.

"Who were those men?" a southern senator asked, and McDonnel said, "They were men of dark color, in United States uniform—Negroes, Negroes, Negroes."

But moments after the raid ended, when he was walking uptown with John Tillman, he had made no such positive identification. Instead of saying he had *seen* Negro soldiers, Tillman recalled, McDonnel had simply remarked that he *thought* they'd done the shooting.

If, as rumor persisted, a group of hotbloods had assembled in some local drinking place on Monday afternoon to plan a mock raid designed to discredit the soldiers, the town's saloonkeepers could hardly have been blind to the scheme's advantages. It held hope of getting the new Negro beer joint closed, the black troops transferred, and white soldiers restored to the garrison. Whatever the raiders may have set out to do that night, this was what they accomplished.

The next morning, while outraged townspeople were mounting a campaign to remove the black soldiers, a Mexican policeman showed up at Allison's door and ordered him to comply with the Mayor's directive closing the town's saloons. Allison protested and then sent a note to his beer distributors, Joe and Teofilo Crixell. The two brothers took a carriage out to the Negro bar and found it deserted except for a lone Mexican beer drinker and the proprietor.

"As we got there," Joe Crixell recalled, "my brother asked him, he says, 'What's the matter, Allison?' He says, 'Well, a Mexican officer came up here and commanded me to close my place of business, and I will not close it, because I have paid my license.' He was mad about it. I says, 'But you ought to close up. We are all closed up. Mayor Combe gave us orders to close up today on account of the shooting, and he is afraid the people will drink liquor, and you had better close up.' He finally decided to agree to close up the place."

Joe Crixell asked Allison where he was when the shooting broke out, and Allison said he was just getting ready to lie down. "What did you do?" Crixell asked, and Allison said, "Nothing; I just laid down. I thought it was firecrackers." It struck Crixell as strange that a man with sixteen years of Army service hadn't been able to distinguish rifle shots from firecrackers,* but Allison explained that his door had been shut and, besides, he was not an expert in these matters.

"Allison seemed to you to be a rather decent, orderly kind of a man, didn't he?" Senator Foraker asked, and Joe Crixell said, "Yes."

Although records of the Brownsville affray are heavily sprinkled with references to the Negro saloon and the man who ran it, there is no direct testimony from Allison. In Jim Wells's papers, however, along with copies of affidavits prepared for the

* Captain Kelly had made the same mistake.

Cameron County grand jury, there is a sworn statment drawn up some weeks earlier (August 22) for Allison's signature. In it, he swore he knew nothing of the shooting until Tuesday morning when the policeman came to close his place.

Allison stayed closed for one day and then reopened, but on hot afternoons when his place should have overflowed with beer drinkers and poker players, it was empty. The customers were confined to the garrison. After three or four days Allison decided to give up and move along.

"He came to me," Joe Crixell said, "and told me that he was going to leave, that he had found out he could not do anything with that place; told me, moreover, that he had some money in the bank, that he wanted to pay me what he owed me. He went to the bank and got the money and came back to the saloon and paid me what he owed me."

But before he could get out of town he was clapped into jail by Texas Ranger Captain Bill McDonald on suspicion of having conspired with a dozen soldiers to bring about his own financial ruin. When no indictments were returned against the Captain's suspects, Allison was hauled back before the grand jury on assault charges growing out of a Sunday-evening altercation at his place of business. He was returned to his cell, his bond set at five hundred dollars.

He spent the fall and winter in the county jail, and was still there in March when Lieutenant Leckie checked into the Leahy Hotel to do some investigative work for the Penrose court-martial, which was then in progress.

"I asked him why he thought they had him in there," Leckie said when he appeared before the Senate Military Affairs Committee, "and he said he thought that it was because they wanted to keep him from testifying before any court, and to prevent him from using his liquor license."

Allison's arrest sprang from an incident that took place the Sunday following the raid. A black railroad brakeman, Dee Dewalt, dropped by for a beer and was mistaken for a Mexican policeman. In an affidavit prepared for the Cameron County grand jury, Dewalt explained that once his identity had been cleared up, Allison apologized.

"We shook hands," Dewalt stated, "and he said if I was an officer, he was fixing to kill me right then."

The misunderstanding (both men had been drinking) was translated into formal charges of "assault with intent to commit murder." Allison spent eighteen months in the county jail before the District Attorney, on February 10, 1908, finally got around to having the case dismissed "for want of sufficient evidence to convict."

Nearly two years later, in January 1910, when Daggett and Marshall sought to subpoena Allison as a witness before the court of inquiry, they found him back in the Army, but, by an unfortunate coincidence, he was not available just at that time. He was on his way to Fort Slocum under armed guard. His sanity, it seems, had come into question. He was again to be placed be-behind bars, this time for observation.

29

". . . my heart has been wrung with sympathy for them . . ."

IN THEIR EFFORTS to shift the blame for the shooting from soldiers to civilians, Daggett and Marshall wanted to subpoena Mack Hamilton, a retired black cavalryman who had spent the afternoon before the raid working for John Tillman in his segregated saloon on Elizabeth Street. The generals refused to call the witness before the court of inquiry, even though Marshall claimed that Hamilton had not only overheard civilian conspirators planning an attack on the garrison but had even been asked to serve as their guide.

"And," the soldiers' junior counsel added, "I will briefly state further that we offer to prove by Mack Hamilton the names of fifteen or sixteen people who formed this shooting party, the ringleader, a photographer who came from a ranch outside of Brownsville."

He had first heard about Hamilton during the Penrose trial, Marshall continued. The Major's defense counsel had referred to the ex-cavalryman as an important witness who, unfortunately, was afraid to tell what he knew. At Marshall's instigation, Hamilton had been summoned to Washington to appear before the Senate Military Affairs Committee, but had not been called on to testify.

"He seemed to be in a terror-stricken frame of mind," Marshall said, and went on to explain that "his family still resided in Brownsville, and he wanted transportation for them to some place out of what he considered the zone of danger."

Mack Hamilton, it would seem, was just the sort of witness the court of inquiry was seeking in its pursuit of fresh evidence about the Brownsville affair, but Captain Howland vehemently opposed the subpoena.

"There is no money to bring Mack Hamilton here," he protested, and wondered why the man's evidence had not been given to the world by the Senate committee.

"The chief reason was a matter of extreme humanity," Marshall explained. "It was represented to us that that had Mack Hamilton been put on the stand that his wife and children would have suffered violence at the hands of a lawless element in Brownsville."

"There is not one scintilla of evidence in this record which shows that any man is in danger of life or limb in Brownsville for telling the truth before any court or tribunal," Howland solemnly declared.

But Mack Hamilton had already had a taste of Brownsville's administration of justice. In the early-morning hours after the shooting, when Sheriff Garza was trotting around town trying to discover what was going on, a fellow Mexican had suggested, "If you want to find out anything about this affair, just ask Mack Hamilton." On the basis of this offhand remark, the Sheriff had thrown the Negro in the county jail. He was still there a week later when Captain Bill McDonald blew into town.

"I then went to the jail to see Mack Hamilton, an ex-soldier that had been seen skulking around with Negro soldiers on the night of the murder and was evidently showing the Negroes where parties lived that they wanted to kill," the Ranger Captain had reported to Austin. "I got some good information from him against Corporal Miller."

Willie H. Miller was the C Company corporal who picked up a twenty-four-hour pass at noon on Monday, August 13, and then lost track of time in exploring the enticements of Matamoros. When he got back to Brownsville, sometime around nine-thirty or ten o'clock that night, he dropped in on his cousin, Mack Hamilton.

"Did Mack Hamilton tell you that the citizens were going to do some shooting that night?" Marshall asked when Miller testified before the court of inquiry.

"He told me that the citizens had wanted him to join them and go to the post and take somebody out of there that they claimed had caught some lady there—I don't know what they did to her, pulled her hair or did something."

"Didn't he tell you that they were going to the post that night to get that man out, or those men out?" Marshall demanded.

"He said they wanted him to join them to help to go and take somebody out of the post, who they thought did it, that night."

Any suggestion that the raiders were white townspeople, not black soldiers, upset Captain Howland.

"Did Hamilton mention what hour they were going to the post?" he asked when he took the witness.

"No, sir," Miller answered; "he said he wasn't going, and told me that he wouldn't go, wouldn't join them."

"Why didn't you go into the post then and convey this information to some officer or the officer of the day, you being a soldier?"

"I thought very little of it. I didn't think that the citizens had that little sense to go there and try to take a soldier out of the post; that's just the way I looked at it. If it had been anything I thought serious of, I would have went and told them."

"Did Hamilton tell you why he was afraid to furnish you with the names?"

"He didn't tell me why, but I just supposed he was afraid that I might tell it, and the people might do something to him down there."

"You were afraid they might do something to you?"

"I supposed that was why he was afraid to tell me. After he said he was afraid to tell me I didn't ask him to tell me any more."

"If the Brownsville people did the shooting, isn't it remarkable that not a single building in Fort Brown was struck?" the judge advocate had commented in closing his case against Major Penrose, and the same question was raised nearly three years later by the general presiding over the court of inquiry.

"They must have been very poor marksmen," the General suggested.

"Mack Hamilton dwells upon that," Marshall replied. "He said it was the purpose—and used the Spanish phrase they use. It is an idiomatic phrase and I cannot recall it, but literally translated into English it means 'to shoot over the brick.' He said 'over the brick,' over the barracks, the object being not to shoot into them, the object being to draw the men out and draw their fire, so that it would appear that the men had done the shooting there in the city of Brownsville."

White or black, civilian or military, the raiders were either border ruffians reared with revolvers and hunting rifles or soldiers trained on Army target ranges. In either case, they could hardly have fired a couple of hundred rounds in a sleeping town and killed only one person unless they were doing their best not to hit anyone. Their lone fatality appears to have been an accident.

No one, in or out of uniform, had any discoverable reason to murder the Ruby's young bartender. Evidently it was his fatal misfortune to come suddenly face to face with a group of startled raiders in a public place. The raid's other casualty, Police Lieutenant Dominguez, may have lost his right arm because he, too, chanced to cross the path of the raiders. If they were soldiers, they had no known reason to do him harm, but if they were local hellraisers, they could have had some old accounts to settle with the lawman.

"There goes the son of a bitch!" the proprietor of the Miller Hotel heard a raider call out. "Get him!"

Similar shouts were recalled in the testimony two policemen gave the Citizens' Committee. "Give it to him," Macedonio Ramirez had heard someone remark, and Genaro Padron remembered that just before the lieutenant was shot, he had heard voices saying, "There he goes. Shoot him."

After a remarkably peaceful payday weekend, the soldiers spent Monday morning drilling and marching across the countryside, By nine o'clock that night, when the lights were put out, the men were ready to take their rest. The mood of the barracks was drowsy, good-natured, relaxed. On the opposite side of the garrison wall, white southerners had spent the summer day rehashing the story of an attack on a white woman by a black soldier. The angry, hard-drinking, pistol-packing southerners had a motive for violence; the soldiers had none.

"What motive do you suppose the colored soldiers had, or do you know of a motive, for shooting up the town?" George W. Rendall was asked when he testified at the Senate hearings.

"I do not know of any motive personally, as far as my own knowledge is concerned," he said. "I don't know anything about it, only what I have heard. Now, in this block in the lower end of Elizabeth Street (I own nearly all that block) in that corner house there is a man lives by the name of Cowen. I think he is about a three-quarter blood Mexican himself and he is married to a Mexican woman, very light complexioned, and he has a lot of small children, mostly girls; but they are boyish sort of things, and it is right close to the garrison wall, and they are always mixing around among the soldiers; they are rather brisk, you know, in their way of talking, and one of those little girls, I think she is about twelve years of age—now I heard this conversation myself, some of it—they were talking to a soldier, and I think the man was on guard; I don't know, but he was at the wall, and he asked her if she was a half-blood Mexican or a half-blood nigger, something of that kind, and she answered back something, and he said, 'Well, you look like it.' 'Well,' said she, 'you look like an ape.' That was the only thing that I know of why they shot those shots in that town, simply because this little girl called him an ape."

It was a measure of the town's madness on the subject of "the nigger raid" that a seventy-two-year-old property owner could seriously believe it was triggered by a child's rude remark. Actually, the girl's mother told the Senate committee, her children had never had the slightest trouble with the black soldiers. When her four little girls had gone fishing in the lagoon behind the officers' quarters, she said, the men used to offer to share their bait with them.

The kindness of a black sergeant was still vivid in the memory of her son, Harold, sixty-odd years after the raid when he got to talking with a customer at his newsstand across from the Brownsville post office.

"I admired a campaign hat one of the soldiers had," Cowen recalled. "I didn't ask him for it, but he could see I wanted it. He asked me what size I wore, and a day or two later, just before the shooting, I came home at dusk and found a brand-new hat on the front door. I never knew the man's name. He was a sergeant."

The eyewitness account of the raid, as the eighty-one-year-old man told it in Brownsville on a spring day in 1969, was at variance with the testimony he'd given in Washington when he was nineteen. He'd gone outside to close the alley gate, he had told the senators, and had just returned to the dining room when he heard the first shots. As he recalled the scene in his old age, he was standing at a rear bedroom window eating a bowl of stew.

"If I'd stayed at that window, I'd have been killed," he said. "I dropped to the floor and seven shots came through that window." *

No one in Brownsville could explain why the raiders had pumped so much lead into the Cowen house.

"What grudge did you think they had at your particular house?" a senator asked Mrs. Cowen, and she said, "None at all; none whatsoever."

Her husband was equally mystified. "I do not see why they should have shot into my house at all, sir," he told Senator Foraker.

* "Four of them," his mother testified, when a senator asked how many bullets passed through Harold's window.

The Cowen house may have drawn the raiders' fire for a reason so obvious that no one remarked it at the time. The lights were on.

"The kitchen was open, and that helped to throw a light out into the yard," Mrs. Cowen testified, and told how her Mexican servant girl had gone to the kitchen window and seen the raiders in the alley. "She saw them put a gun over the fence and blow out this lamp on the table." Their bullets also extinguished the student lamp on the dining-room table and the large Rochester lamp hanging in the center hallway, illuminating the three back rooms of the house.

"Without a doubt they meant murder while they were at it," Mrs. Cowen was convinced, because they had fired into those three back rooms, where the family was distributed, instead of into the front rooms.

The front rooms were dark.

Farther uptown the raiders fired into the second-floor room of the Miller Hotel occupied by Hale Odin and his family. The Odins had an oil lamp burning in the room. Less than a block away, on Washington Street near Thirteenth, Fred Starck was awakened by shooting he judged to be in the vicinity of the hotel.

"I think there is fire in the post," his wife said, and a moment later eight bullets ripped through their frame house.

"Were there any lights in your house at this time?" Starck was asked at the Penrose trial.

"Yes, sir; one in the children's bedroom."

Fred Starck lived next door to Fred Tate, a fellow officer in the customs service who had bloodied the head of a black soldier he accused of jostling some white ladies on Elizabeth Street. In their efforts, to establish a motive for the soldiers to shoot at them, townspeople hit on the theory that the raiders had mistaken Starck's two-story home for Tate's one-story house on the adjoining lot.

Not at all, Senator Foraker countered. Smugglers along the border had good reason to shoot at the home of Fred Starck. He'd made some six hundred arrests, including the brief detention of a smuggler named Avila who had once worked in the

Starck house and knew it well. Avila had skipped bail and was
a fugitive from justice at the time of the raid.*

There was never any need to strain credulity with theories
about soldiers getting even with Fred Tate or smugglers with
Fred Starck. The evidence indicated that, with one exception, all
the bullets fired at the Starck house went through the children's
bedroom. From this indisputable fact, it would be reasonable to
assume that the raiders, black or white, were shooting at the
one thing that made the room different from the others—the
night lamp.

The route of the raid could hardly have been more foolhardy
for soldiers or more favorable for civilian conspirators.

According to the townspeople, the attack began with shots
fired from the men's barracks. If true, the soldiers started things
off by arousing the garrison and then plunged into a hostile,
heavily armed community, still shooting. Within minutes, as even
the least gifted conspirator could have foreseen, an armed mob
was swarming across the center of town and armed soldiers were
deployed along the garrison wall, facing the town.

If the raiders were soldiers, they had to sneak back into ranks
without being detected and clean their rifles in the darkness before they were locked up to await inspection at daybreak. Afterward, dozens of men who had to know the raiders' identity kept
the secret despite all the investigations, the examinations and
cross-examinations, the punishments, the five-hundred-dollar reward, and the undercover use of whiskey, false confessions,
promises of immunity, and threats of death on a Texas gallows.

"No one hundred and sixty-seven men ever lived who could
have withstood successfully such efforts to unearth the truth
about such a crime if they had been the parties who had committed it, or had possession of knowledge with respect thereto
which they were attempting to withhold," Foraker wrote in the

* Ironically, it was Tate, not Starck, who eventually met his death at
the hands of smugglers. In its report of the Tate murder, the *Daily Herald*,
on September 2, 1918, recalled his connection with the Brownsville Raid.
"The house fired into by the Negroes was thought by them to be the one
occupied by Mr. Tate." What had begun as supposition had come to be
considered historical fact.

summer of 1915, and predicted that no evidence of the guilt of any soldier would ever be found.

"Neither do I doubt," he added, "if the Government had spent the one-tenth part to discover the men who shot up Brownsville that it did spend to convict its innocent soldiers of a crime they never committed, the truth would have been easily and long ago established."

According to the soldiers, the raid began with shots fired on the town side of the garrison wall. If what they said was true, civilians assembled in the hospitable darkness of Garrison Road and, after throwing a scare into the sleeping fort, retreated up the Cowen alley, frightening the town. By the time both soldiers and townspeople had been aroused, the civilian raiders were in the friendly environs of the midtown saloons, where they could meld with neighbors who had swarmed into the streets with revolvers, shotguns, and rifles.

The soldiers' rifles passed a rigid inspection, but no one ever checked the assorted firearms the townspeople were brandishing shortly after the raid when Captain Lyon, on orders from Major Penrose, marched D Company through the town and came across armed civilians who passed themselves off as "officers of the law."

"All of us were armed," A. Wayne Wood later recalled when a local antiquarian asked for his recollections of the raid, and went on to give a palpably inaccurate account of what had occurred. "There were probably fifty civilians there at the moment, and another fifty arrived within the next ten minutes. Three or four junior officers of the United States Army were trying to subdue and control twelve or fourteen Negro troopers on the south side of the block; that is, south of Weller's saloon."

Mr. Wood could not have seen "three or four junior officers," because there were only five officers at Fort Brown that morning, and none of them left the garrison after the shooting except Captain Lyon, a combat officer whose men were not likely to get out of control. In fact, as even Inspector General Garlington conceded, D Company was the battalion's best-disciplined outfit.

Another history-minded resident, William Alfred Neale, also left an eyewitness account of the same scene which is at odds with the facts: "One of the Negro soldiers saw that I had an old model Springfield 47-70, and he made an effort to come where I was, at the same time he was trying to get the company to 'muss up ranks.' Mingo Sanders, first sergeant of Company B, Twenty-fifth Infantry, saw the men leaving the ranks and butted them back, using his rifle against some of their heads and at the same time he gave orders to march, which order was obeyed, leaving Captain Samuel P. Lyons [sic] on the sidewalk having it out with Dr. Fred Combe. His company marched into Fort Brown unknown to him."

Aside from the fact that it was Company D, not B, and that its first sergeant was Jacob Frazier, not Mingo Sanders, the Neale version of the incident is in error in stating that Captain Lyon was "having it out" with the Mayor while his men returned to the fort without him. All the principals agree that the Mayor and his brother, at Lyon's courteous invitation, marched to the garrison with the Captain and his company.

Before the raid, the Mayor and his Mexican constabulary marveled at the black soldiers' exemplary behavior, particularly on payday, when the men set a local record for orderliness and sobriety. After the raid, the same soldiers were pictured as black beasts thirsting for the white man's blood and aflame with desire for his women.

With no evidence of any such violence in the men's service records or in the two arrest-free weeks they'd spent at Fort Brown, the townspeople fastened eagerly on the testimony of a white railroad conductor named Lunkenheimer who had accompanied the soldiers to Brownsville. His evidence was contradicted by the men and their officers, but it convinced men like Mr. Neale that the battalion was composed of "the wildest set of niggers."

"We were told that they shot at all advertising signs on the road," he wrote; "they addressed shamefully all ladies that happened to be at the stopping stations, using language unfit to utter, and, I am told, went so far that they would show the women folk their private parts."

No white woman was better acquainted with the black battalion than Captain Lyon's wife, a general's daughter who, after growing up around soldiers, had spent fourteen years of her married life with the Twenty-fifth Infantry.

"I feel a love for and pride in the Regiment that such a close association with it must bring," she wrote Foraker two days after his Senate career ended. "I was at Fort Brown during the trouble and at Fort Reno through the time afterward, and believing as I did in the innocence of the men, and feeling the wicked injustice of the punishment given them, my heart has been wrung with sympathy for them . . ."

She thanked Foraker for devoting his final weeks as a senator to pressing for the creation of a tribunal which, she hoped, would restore the men to duty, and signed herself "a proud member of our beloved Regiment." A year later, in the summer of 1910, after the court of inquiry had finished what Foraker called its "shameful work," Mrs. Lyon was back in another courtroom, watching the last shameful act of the Brownsville drama. Her husband was on trial.

Captain Howland, who had done such a satisfactory job for the War Department in prosecuting the soldiers, was picked to present the case against Captain Lyon, but this time he found himself in a different judicial environment.

"The court is not packed," General Daggett wrote Foraker July 4, 1910, "but is, or appears to be, an intelligent, fair-minded body of officers. . . . They have sized up Howland, and treat him accordingly. They have also sized up Lyon, and treat him accordingly: that is, in the kindest and most courteous manner. How different from the Brownsville Court!"

Captain Lyon was acquitted, served in the World War, and, in the spring of 1920, after thirty years of service, retired with the rank of lieutenant colonel. Some weeks later, in September, Colonel Penrose (he got his wings in 1913) died in Lancaster, Pennsylvania. Captain Macklin, the raid's heavy-sleeping officer of the day, retired in 1910 and died the following year at Alamogordo, New Mexico.

General Daggett outlived them all. He was a month shy of his hundred and first birthday when the end came in May 1938, nearly forty years after his black troops had made possible the highly publicized assault on San Juan Hill by capturing the mountain village of El Caney in a dawn-to-dusk fight none of the men ever forgot.

"Seldom have troops been called upon to face a severer fire, and never have they acquitted themselves better . . . " the men were pleased to hear Colonel Daggett say before they left Cuba. "You may well return to the United States proud of your accomplishments, and if anyone asks you what you have done, point him to El Caney."

The old soldier's death commanded a full column in the New York *Times*, but the obituary dealt with him as a Civil War hero and said nothing about the black soldiers he had commanded in Cuba and had subsequently defended in Washington before Roosevelt's face-saving court of inquiry. Another Roosevelt was whooping things up in the White House that spring, and Brownsville had been forgotten.

"There is no use in raking up the past now," the first Roosevelt wrote Foraker in the late spring of 1916 after reading the former senator's *Notes of a Busy Life*, "but there were some things told me against you, or in reference to you, which (when I consider what I know now of my informants) would have carried no weight with me at the time had I been as well informed as at present."

Roosevelt's autobiography had appeared earlier, in 1913, and, as subsequent biographers have noted with interest, the author chose not to mention Brownsville. There was another significant omission—Booker T. Washington. Indeed, the index does not include the word "Negroes."

The Coda

———◆◆◆———

30

"This is a white man's country and white men must govern it."

IN ENGLAND Booker T. Washington sipped tea with Queen Victoria at Windsor Castle, but when he traveled across the rolling countryside of his native Virginia, he rode in a separate and cynically unequal railroad car for which he paid full fare. The Tuskegeean took this humiliating swindle in stride, but not Dr. W. E. B. Du Bois (Ph.D., Harvard '95).

Du Bois denounced Jim Crow cars designed "to make us pay first-class fare for third-class accommodations, render us open to insults and discomfort, and to crucify wantonly our manhood, womanhood, and self-respect." He demanded equal justice, equal educational and economic opportunities, and equal treatment in places of public entertainment. But first of all he demanded the right to vote.

"With the right to vote goes everything: Freedom, manhood, the honor of your wives, the chastity of your daughters, the right to work, and the chance to rise," Du Bois proclaimed the week of the Brownsville Raid. "We want full manhood suffrage, and we want it now."

"The Negro agrees with you that it is necessary to the salvation of the South that restriction be put upon the ballot," Washington stated in a letter to the Louisiana state constitutional convention in the spring of 1898, but, he added, "I beg of you further that in the degree that you close the ballot box against the ignorant you open the school house." Eight years later, the year of Brownsville and the bloody Atlanta race riot, he told a visiting English journalist, "The remedy lies in education, ours—*and theirs.*"

For Washington, equality was a long-range goal, something the Negro must earn by hard work, clean living, and an abiding faith in his white friends. Meanwhile, he should stay in his place and seek to improve his material lot through the sort of vocational training white philanthropists had subsidized first in Virginia at Hampton Institute, where young Washington had worked his way through school, and then in Alabama at Tuskegee, where he had given other black youngsters a chance to emulate his example.

"We are trying to instill into the Negro mind that if education does not make the Negro humble, simple, and of service to the community, then it will not be encouraged," the Tuskegeean told a group of white educators in 1912.

Du Bois, on the other hand, argued that gifted black children should be educated to become leaders, not servants. They should be made acquainted with ideas and the arts, not simply with the hoe and the loom. These exceptional men and women, working as teachers, lawyers, ministers, politicians, scientists, and writers would uplift the black masses, he argued, sending a chill down white spines. It was one thing to train a young Negro to work in a field, a factory, or a kitchen, but quite another to provide the sort of education that would enable him to compete with the white man as an intellectual equal.

The Tuskegee approach to the education of black youngsters received a presidential blessing in the fall of 1905 when Theodore Roosevelt visited the Alabama campus and praised its principal for concentrating on the three fields—"agriculture, mechanics, and household duties"—in which "the Negro can at present do most for himself and be most helpful to his white neighbors."

"If you save money, secure homes, become taxpayers, and lead clean, decent, modest lives, you will win the respect of your neighbors of both races," Roosevelt told the students, and warned them that "the race cannot expect to get everything at once."

Roosevelt, in the words of a scholarly admirer, "had not dismissed the possibility that Negroes might be inherently inferior to whites." His racial attitudes had come to public notice in 1899 with the appearance of *The Rough Riders*, a first-person-singular account of the Spanish-American War which, Mr. Dooley thought, might more aptly have been titled *Alone in Cuba*.

Colonel Roosevelt described his Rough Riders as mostly southwesterners with "a strong color prejudice." They grew to accept what the Spaniards called "smoked Yankees" and, in their own phrase, were willing "to drink out of the same canteen." For his part, Roosevelt praised the black soldiers ("no troops could have behaved better"), but found them "peculiarly dependent upon their white officers."

"Occasionally," he wrote, "they produced noncommissioned officers who can take the initiative and accept responsibility precisely like the best class of whites; but this cannot be expected normally, nor is it fair to expect it." *

During the same summer week that the white press was denouncing the black soldiers reported to have loosed their homicidal fury on a sleeping Texas town, dissident Negroes were

---

* On their way to a new camp after distinguishing themselves at El Caney, the men of the Twenty-fifth Infantry were cheered by white soldiers of the Second Massachusetts. "They have a good feeling for us," a black sergeant remarked to his regiment's chaplain. "They think you are soldiers," the chaplain said. The sergeant shook his head. "They *know* we are soldiers."

making their way to Harpers Ferry for the second annual conference of the Niagara Movement. They assembled on ground hallowed by John Brown to advance the program Du Bois had charted in a black declaration of independence.

"We refuse to allow the impression to remain that the Negro-American assents to inferiority, is submissive under oppression and apologetic before insults," the Niagarans announced, and went on to attack the color-line: "Any discrimination based simply on race or color is barbarous, we care not how hallowed it may be by custom, expediency, or prejudice."

"They are the victims of a prejudice that has to be destroyed," H. G. Wells wrote in *Harper's Weekly* that fall after making a journalistic tour of the United States during which he not only met both Washington and Du Bois, but also a succession of white southerners who soberly assured him, "If you eat with them, you've got to marry them."

The white men's fears lay deeply buried in the consciousness of a common guilt. For centuries they had degraded the women of black men. No retaliation could be more appropriate and, hence, more to be dreaded than the degradation of white women by black men. The southerner's obsession with rape and miscegenation sprang from his fears and his folklore, notably his fear of the black man's legendary sexual prowess and the myth of his intellectual inferiority.

Any attempt to break down the barriers between the races was regarded as a threat to the flower of the South's womanhood. This combination of sex and social equality lay behind the trouble in Brownsville. Two weeks after the town's leading saloonkeepers refused to permit the newly arrived black soldiers to drink with their white customers, the local newspaper hit the streets with a front-page story of an alleged assault on a white woman by a black man in an Army uniform. A few hours later the shooting began.

Along with a white President and his military bureaucracy, two generations of white historians, biographers, and encyclopedists have accepted the townspeople's belief that the shots were fired by black men protesting segregated bars rather than by white men protesting a reported rape attempt. The victim was never called to testify. In the South it was the gracious custom to spare outraged womanhood the painful necessity of fluttering into a court of law and confronting a black suspect whose life might be taken from him simply on the basis of a few words sobbed out in the arms of an anguished husband, brother, or father.

"I have three daughters," trumpeted South Carolina's "Pitchfork Ben" Tillman during the Senate debate on Brownsville, "but, so help me God, I had rather find either one of them killed by a tiger or a bear and gather up her bones and bury them, conscious that she had died in the purity of her maidenhood, than have her crawl to me and tell me the horrid story that she had been robbed of the jewel of her womanhood by a black fiend. The wild beast would only obey the instinct of nature, and we would hunt him down and kill him just as soon as possible. What shall we do with a man who has outbruted the brute and committed an act which is more cruel than death? Try him? Drag the victim into court, for she alone can furnish legal evidence, and make her testify to the fearful ordeal through which she has passed, undergoing a second crucifixion?"

At the turn of the century no average week went by without one or two lynchings. In his first inaugural address, President McKinley declared that "lynchings must not be tolerated," but as should have been clear to any well-informed citizen in the spring of 1897, mob violence had become the southern white supremacist's method of keeping the Negro in subjection.

"Lynch law is all we have left," Tillman told a northern-Michigan audience at the height of the Brownsville furor.

"No man can take part in the torture of a human being without having his own moral nature permanently lowered," Roosevelt reported to Congress a month after his dismissal of the black battalion. "Let justice be both sure and swift, but let it be justice under the law," he declared, having just demonstrated his own impatience with the law's delays by decreeing what the New York *World* referred to as an "executive lynching."

At the time of transition from Roosevelt to Taft, the Afro-American had enjoyed forty-odd years of an anomalous freedom, neither slave nor citizen. Every ten years, when the Federal Government took a census, Southern states made sure it counted the black one-third of their population, thus increasing the number of Democrats they could send to the House of Representatives, but when these white lawmakers came before the electorate, black voters were kept away from the polls by taxes, trumped-up tests, and shotguns.

Republican protests against this ancient fraud had become a ritual chant to be recited every four years when the party's white leaders met to draw up another set of platform pieties. When a southern senator made use of the Brownsville issue to defend the disenfranchisement of "ignorant blacks" as a means of preserving the South's institutions, no Republican colleague arose to ask why the policy had not been extended to include the disenfranchisement of "ignorant whites."

It was Thomas M. Patterson of Colorado, one of the Senate's four northern Democrats, who spoke out against disenfranchisement. The white southerners, he said, were determined to return "ten million Negroes to practical bondage, to range them side by side with the horse and the cow upon the plantation, to treat them with kindness if they merit it, to pat them as you pat a swift and kindly horse, to give them food as you would feed your animals, and deprive them of all political rights under the Constitution of our country."

"I believe they are men, but some of them are so near akin to the monkey that scientists are yet looking for the missing link," Senator Tillman snorted, and reverted to the white southerner's recurring theme: "These Negroes move where they please. They have a little smattering of education. Some of them have white blood in their veins and taught that they are as good as the white man, they ask, Why not as good as a white woman? And when caste feeling and race pride and every instinct that influences and controls the white women makes them spurn the thought, rape follows. Murder and rape become a monomania. The Negro becomes a fiend in human form."

"The question," as Wisconsin's diminutive Senator Spooner pointed out, "is whether, wherever a man is charged with this fiendish crime, he has not a right, sacred as the ark of the covenant, to say in a court of justice, 'I did not do it.'" *

"It is idle to reason about it; it is idle to preach about it," Tillman cried out. "Our brains reel under the staggering blow and hot blood surges to the heart. Civilization peels off us, any and all of us who are men, and we revert to the original savage type whose impulses under any and all such circumstances has always been to 'kill! kill! kill!'"

Fed up with such oratorical outbursts, Senator Patterson cited some statistics just released in New Orleans. During the preceding year there had been seventy-three lynchings in the United States, and an actual rape had figured in only thirteen of them. One lynching had involved a stolen calf, another the theft of one dollar. Violence fed on violence, the Colorado Democrat declared, and suggested it would end in the South only when its white rulers came to have a higher respect for the law.

"I will say to the Senator," Tillman snapped, "that as long as the Negroes continue to ravish white women we will continue to lynch them."

Once Tillman had finished, it was impossible to pretend, as the Administration and senators on both sides of the chamber had persisted in doing, that the Brownsville debate had nothing to do with the race question. Quite the contrary, it had served to unite white supremacists of the South and West.

"The race prejudice which exists on the Pacific coast is only another form of the race question which is presented to us in the South," declared Texas Representative James L. Slayden after taking a close look at the Yellow Peril in San Francisco, where the local board of education had come up with a plan to put Asian children in segregated schools.

"We of the West sympathize with the South in the crisis through which she is passing," said Oregon's Democratic Senator John M. Gearin, who shuddered at the thought that "Japan can send from one to five million of her people into the United States and never miss them." The white man on the West Coast could not compete with such an influx of coolies, he said, and Cali-

---

* This is the senator whom President Roosevelt selected to defend the order that denied the Brownsville soldiers their "sacred" right to appear in a court of justice and affirm their innocence.

fornia's Republican Senator George Perkins broke in to say he had just learned from the Commissioner of Immigration that in the last fiscal year 14,243 Japanese immigrants had entered the country.

"We can never absorb them or take them into our social life," Gearin continued, after thanking the Californian for his information.

The Oregon Democrat had the sympathetic attention of his southern colleagues when he reminded the Senate of the growth of the country's black population. In one generation since Appomattox it had shot up from four million to ten million.

"The two races have never mixed and never will mix," Gearin said.

On the race issue, as Brownsville had demonstrated, California and Texas, Oregon and South Carolina all spoke with one voice.

"The white race will control and dominate the earth," said Oregon, staving off the yellow hordes, and back came the echo from South Carolina, defying the black rapist: "This is the white man's country and white men must govern it."

"Register and vote whenever and wherever you have a right," advised the Niagara Movement leaders at the start of the 1908 campaign. "Remember Brownsville and establish next November the principle of Negro independence in voting, not only for punishing enemies, but for rebuking false friends."

"I have the strongest faith in the President's honesty of intention, high mindedness of purpose, sincere unselfishness, and courage, but I regret for these reasons all the more that this thing has occurred," Booker T. Washington wrote Oswald Garrison Villard.

"I can well believe that the awakening to the instability of Mr. Roosevelt has been a trying one for the colored people," replied the liberal editor of the New York *Evening Post*. "He is as the shifting sands and they must realize it."

By an impulsive stroke of the pen, Roosevelt had brought about a confrontation between the country's two most famous black citizens. While Du Bois attacked the President for "swag-

gering roughshod over the helpless black regiment whose bravery
made him famous," Washington schemed to destroy the Niagara
Movement (one of the speakers at its 1906 conference was a
Tuskegee spy) and, at the same time, to keep the North's five
hundred thousand black voters from quitting the Republican
party in disgust over the dismissal of the Brownsville soldiers.

"I did my utmost to prevent his taking the action he did,"
Washington wrote a friend the day after the order was made
public, and braced himself for the indignant letters he knew it
would provoke. "The Negroes are depleting the dictionary of
adjectives in their denunciation of the President," wrote an Ohio
Negro, and from Chicago came word that "you cannot find a
Negro who is not denouncing the President in frightful terms of
abuse."

Pulpits thundered with righteous wrath. "It is hard to believe that the man with the big stick disarming and crushing the
colored soldiers is the same Theodore Roosevelt who three years
ago declared that as long as he was President every man should
have a 'square deal,'" lamented the Reverend Clayton Powell,
and black congregations throughout the country were urged to
seek vengeance at the polls in the next presidential campaign.

"We have two years to work," northern ministers reminded the
men of their flock.

Booker Washington also had two years to work, and his resources were formidable. He spoke for black Americans when the
President was dispensing patronage and when white philanthropists were making out checks for Negro causes. With such access
to power and to money, he was able to pressure a great many
black editors into soft-pedaling the Brownsville issue.

"The bulk of the the Negro people," Washington reported
on the eve of the 1908 campaign, "are more and more inclined
to reach the decision that even though the President did go
against their wishes in dismissing the soldiers at Brownsville, he
has favored them in nine cases out of ten and the intelligent portion of the race does not believe that it is fair or wise to condemn
such good friends as President Roosevelt and Secretary Taft
because they might have done what is considered a mistake in
one case, but in nine cases have done what they have considered

right. It is not the part of common sense to cherish ill will against one who has helped us in so many ways as the President has."

"Politics," warned the Cleveland *Gazette,* "will yet KILL the great Tuskegee school. *Mark our prediction!* When it does, Mr. Washington will have no one but himself to blame—Taft is too big a load for any person or thing to carry."

In forcing black voters to choose between Taft and Bryan (Gene Debs seemed to have little appeal *), the two parties offered them hypocrisy and neglect on one hand, hatred and oppression on the other. It became easier for many blacks to make up their minds to string along with the Republicans after a state convention of West Virginia Democrats adopted a resolution declaring it had been a constitutional mistake to extend suffrage to "a race inferior in intelligence."

Bryan defended the South's disenfranchisement of the Negro, refused to discuss Brownsville, and outraged black newspaper readers with his views on lynching: "The fact that a Negro is lynched by a mob because of an outrage upon a woman ought not to increase the race prejudice that exists. White men are lynched for the same crime." In his December 1906 message to Congress, Roosevelt had made a similar statement, "A great many white men are lynched."

"If between the two parties who stand on identically the same platform you can prefer the party who perpetrated Brownsville, well and good!" exclaimed Du Bois. "But I shall vote for Bryan."

Negroes owed nothing to the Republican party, Du Bois contended. It took their support for granted, excluded them from its highest councils, and, despite control of all three branches of the Federal Government, it permitted racism to flourish. The Democrats were racists, too, of course, but the party offered real improvement of the Negro's lot by plumping for better working conditions for all wage-earners, black and white.

The Tuskegee Machine, however, had swung into action. Washington arranged for Taft to speak at Hampton Institute.

---

* Debs's biographer, Ray Ginger, devotes twenty-three pages of *The Bending Cross* (Rutgers, 1949) to the 1908 campaign and fails to mention Brownsville.

Field representatives of the Negro Business League were spreading the Republican gospel, and black officeholders were shouting, "Amen." When black Baptists convened in the nation's capital, Tuskegee forces contrived to sidetrack a resolution condemning Roosevelt's treatment of the black battalion. As a compromise, the delegates agreed to voice praise for Senator Foraker.

"The *Bee* because of the accursed and relentless opposition of the Democratic party to the race must of necessity stand for the Republican party," the editor of the Washington *Bee* grudgingly announced some weeks before the Republican national convention, and by the time the delegates assembled in Chicago (Roosevelt had set a precedent for New York by having a black man selected as a delegate-at-large), Negroes were clambering aboard the Taft bandwagon.

"When one considers the record of the Democratic party," declared the Dallas *Express*, "he must admit that it is out of the question for the colored man to vote for Bryan. The 'Jim Crow' laws of every Democratic State, the exclusion from the jury of almost every southern court, the mockery of a fair trial before every southern tribunal, all stand as brazen reminders of the eternal enmity of the Democracy toward the Negro."

In her study of the political repercussions of the Brownsville episode, Emma Lou Thornbrough concluded that it "did not lead to a marked defection of Negroes from the Republican party," but, she was quick to add, "This does not mean, however, that the discharge of the colored soldiers had not created a real threat to the traditional loyalty of Negroes to the Republican party. There is abundant evidence that the members of the race were aroused over the treatment of the soldiers as they had not been aroused by the action of any other President."

There appeared to have been a significant switch among black voters in Pennsylvania, Ohio, Indiana, and Illinois, where Taft's margin of victory was smaller than Roosevelt's in 1904. Du Bois took satisfaction in reflecting that "more Negroes voted against Mr. Taft than had ever before voted against a Republican candidate." In time, the black intellectual predicted, the "impossible alliance" between northern liberals and southern conservatives would come apart, and when it did, the black voter would carry the balance of power in key northern states.

"The Negro," Du Bois once wrote, "is a sort of seventh-son, born with a veil, and gifted with second-sight in this American world—a world which yields him no true self-consciousness, but only lets him see himself through the revelation of the other world. It is a peculiar sensation, this double-consciousness, this sense of always looking at one's self through the eyes of others, of measuring one's soul by the tape of a world that looks on in amused contempt and pity. One ever feels his two-ness—an American, a Negro; two souls, two thoughts, two unreconciled strivings; two warring ideals in one dark body, whose dogged strength alone keeps it from being torn asunder.

"The history of the American Negro is the history of this strife—this longing to attain self-conscious manhood, to merge his double self into a better and truer self. In this merging he wishes neither of the older selves to be lost. He would not Africanize America, for America has too much to teach the world and Africa. He would not bleach his Negro soul in a flood of white Americanism, for he knows that Negro blood has a message for the world. He simply wishes to make it possible for a man to be both a Negro and an American, without being cursed and spit upon by his fellows, without having the doors of Opportunity closed roughly in his face."

President-elect Taft left no doubt in anyone's mind as to his position on closing doors of opportunity in black faces. He would continue Roosevelt's policy of conferring with Booker Washington on the selection of Negroes for Federal appointments, he announced, but he would not antagonize white southerners by choosing blacks for dignified desk jobs in the South, as his predecessor had done when he named a Negro collector of the port of Charleston, South Carolina.

"I am not going to put into places of such prominence in the South, where the race feeling is strong, Negroes whose appointment will only tend to increase that race feeling; but I shall look about and make appointments in the North and recognize the

Negro as often as I can," Taft said, and went on to point out that no one had a constitutional right to hold office. "The question is one of fitness," he explained. "A one-legged man would hardly be selected for a mail carrier."

To be born black, according to this newly enunciated Taft Doctrine, was to be permanently maimed at birth. The founding fathers of the Niagara Movement refused to accept their official status as crippled Americans. They continued to protest, but in the first year of the new administration the Tuskegee Machine finally succeeded in crushing the movement. It proved to be a dubious victory, however. Within a year, the leaders, the principles, and the spirit of Niagara had been incorporated into a new organization of thoughtful blacks and sympathetic whites, the National Association for the Advancement of Colored People.

"We believe in taking what we can get but we don't believe in being satisfied with it and in permitting anybody for a moment to imagine we're satisfied," the Niagarans declared at their first convention in 1905, and two years later, when Roosevelt and Taft were frantically trying to justify rather than correct the wrong they had done, the black rebels demanded "full exoneration and reinstatement of our shamefully libeled soldiers."

The soldiers were never exonerated, and by the time a handful were reinstated in 1910, Brownsville was of so little interest to white newspaper readers that most editors wasted no space on the story. Since then, two generations of youngsters, black and white, have been reared in ignorance of this massive assault by two Presidents on the civil rights of one hundred and sixty-seven black Americans. They lived and died in the black man's limbo. Alive, they were denied the equity of the white man's justice and, dead, the vindication of his Jim Crow history.

THE DOCUMENTATION

Chronology

1906

JULY 23 Companies B, C, and D, Twenty-fifth Infantry (Colored) leave Fort Niobrara, Nebraska, for Fort Brown, Texas.

25 Soldiers reach Fort Brown.

AUGUST 5 Tate-Newton incident.

11 Quiet payday; Hollomon and Allison open a bar for soldiers.

12 Mrs. Evans charges assault around nine P.M.

13 Mayor Combe advises Major Penrose of the attack on Mrs. Evans; an eight o'clock curfew is established at the fort; shooting breaks out around midnight.

14 Citizens' Committee appointed at mass meeting.

18 Major Blocksom arrives in Brownsville, remains until August 29.

23 Twelve men singled out by Captain McDonald of the Texas Rangers are placed under arrest along with a former soldier, Allison.

25 Battalion leaves for Fort Reno, Oklahoma; arrives August 27.

OCTOBER 4 Inspector General Ernest A. Garlington is ordered to Fort Reno with President Roosevelt's ultimatum—all three companies will be summarily dismissed if the soldiers fail to produce the guilty men.

NOVEMBER 5 Roosevelt signs dismissal order.

6 Election day; order made public in the late afternoon.

8 Roosevelt leaves for Canal Zone.

1906

NOVEMBER 17 Taft returns to Washington.
           18 Taft suspends the dismissal order.
           20 Taft changes his mind.
           27 Roosevelt returns to the White House.
DECEMBER 3 Fifty-ninth Congress opens its second session; Senator For-
              aker offers resolution calling for an investigation of the raid.
           19 Roosevelt sends message on the raid to the Senate.
           22 Captain Macklin is shot.
           26 Purdy and Blocksom arrive in Brownsville.

1907

JANUARY 14 Roosevelt sends Purdy-Blocksom report to the Senate.
          22 Senate agrees to investigate the raid.
          26 Roosevelt and Foraker tangle at Gridiron Club dinner.
FEBRUARY 4 Senate Military Affairs Committee begins Brownsville hear-
              ings in Washington; Penrose court-martial gets under way
              in San Antonio.
MARCH 25 Penrose acquitted.
APRIL 15 Macklin court-martial begins in San Antonio.
MAY 6 Macklin acquitted.
NOVEMBER 18 Senate Military Affairs Committee resumes hearings after
              a five-month recess.

1908

MARCH 11 Senate gets committee reports and message from Roosevelt.
APRIL 14 Foraker delivers his major speech on the raid.
      16 Taft hires Browne and Baldwin as investigators.
SEPTEMBER 17 Hearst makes public Foraker's correspondence with Stan-
              dard Oil vice president.
NOVEMBER 3 Taft elected President.
DECEMBER 13 Foraker proposes a court of inquiry.

1909

JANUARY 12 Foraker makes a scathing attack on the Browne-Baldwin
              report; Theodore E. Burton is elected to succeed Foraker in
              the Senate.
FEBRUARY 23 Court of inquiry approved by Senate, passes House Feb-
              ruary 27.

MARCH 2 Roosevelt signs court of inquiry bill.
NOVEMBER 27 Court meets in Brownsville, resumes deliberations in Washington December 9.

1910

MARCH 28 Court adjourns; fourteen of the one hundred and sixty-seven discharged soldiers are found eligible for re-enlistment.

Key Witnesses

FOR THE SOLDIERS

ALLISON, ERNEST. Ex-soldier, ran Negro bar.

ARVIN, HENRY. Broke open C Co. gun racks.

ASKEW, CHARLES W. Cap with initials found in the path of the raiders.

BRAWNER, DARBY W. O. C Co. charge of quarters, failed to open the gun racks.

BROWN, ELMER. Looked after Major Penrose's horses, figured in Browne-Baldwin report.

BROWN, JOHN. Bakery worker named by Browne and Baldwin.

CONYERS, BOYD. Alleged "confession" formed the basis of the Browne-Baldwin report.

FRAZIER, JACOB. D Co. first sergeant.

GRAY, GEORGE. Ex-soldier, hired by Browne and Baldwin, called on Conyers in Georgia.

GRIER, SECOND LIEUTENANT HARRY S. Acting post adjutant, took command of C Co.

HARLEY, SAMUEL W. C Co. Acting First Sergeant, claimed he didn't hear call to arms.

HOLLOMON, JOHN. B Co. moneylender, bar owner, central figure in Browne-Baldwin version of the raid.

HOWARD, JOSEPH H. Sentry on duty between barracks and garrison wall, fired three shot to give the alarm.

JACKSON, GEORGE. B Co. charge of quarters, had keys to gun racks.

LAWRASON, SECOND LIEUTENANT GEORGE C. Company Commander, B Co.

LECKIE, SECOND LIEUTENANT HARRY G. Conducted visibility tests, disputed Mrs. Leahy's testimony.

LYON, CAPTAIN SAMUEL P. Company commander, D Co.

McCURDY, WALKER. B Co. quartermaster sergeant, responsible for guns in the storeroom.

MACKLIN, CAPTAIN EDGAR A. Company commander, C Co., on duty as officer of the day, slept through the shooting.

MILLER, WILLIE H. On pass, was in Mexican bar after paying a visit to his cousin, Mack Hamilton.

NEWTON, GEORGE W. D Co. artificer, a teetotaler.

NEWTON, JAMES W. C Co., a drinking man, head bloodied by Fred Tate, a customs officer.

PENROSE, MAJOR CHARLES W. Commanding officer First Battalion, Twenty-fifth Infantry.

REID, JAMES R. On guard duty, ordered trumpeter to sound call to arms.

REID, OSCAR W. Figured in ferry-dunking incident.

SANDERS, MINGO. B Co. first sergeant, veteran of twenty-six years' service, including Cuba and the Philippines.

TALIAFERRO, SPOTTSWOOD W. Battalion sergeant-major.

TAMAYO, MATIAS G. Post scavenger, heard shots fired on town side of the wall.

WEST, OTIS C. White infantryman who heard boy say he was collecting shells "to kill niggers with."

FOR THE TOWNSPEOPLE

BAKER, A. Y. Customs officers, dunked Reid.

BILLINGSLEY, ALBERT W. Dairyman, claimed to have heard Macklin warn of violence in Crixell bar.

COMBE, DR. FREDERICK J. Mayor.

COMBE, DR. JOSEPH K. His brother.

CONNOR, GEORGE. Police chief.

COWEN, MRS. ANNA. Lived across from the fort, house badly damaged by raiders.

COWEN, LOUIS R. Her husband, uptown at the time of the raid.

CREAGER, RENTFRO B. U.S. Commissioner.

CRIXELL, JOSEPH L. Elizabeth Street saloonkeeper, supplied Hollomon and Allison with beer.

CRIXELL, TEOFILO. His brother and partner.

DOMINGUEZ, M. Y. (Joe). Police officer, wounded in raid.

ELKINS, HERBERT. Young Leahy Hotel guest who testified he saw and heard raiders.

FERNANDEZ, VICTORIANO. Policeman, denied making threats against the soldiers.

FORSTER, WILLIAM. Fort Brown teamster, saw attempt to raid ordnance stores.

KELLY, CAPTAIN WILLIAM. Banker, head of Citizens' Committee.

LEAHY, MRS. KATE E. Widow who ran hotel near fort, claimed to have seen shots from barracks; disputed by Lieutenant Leckie testimony.

LITTLEFIELD, A. ALMAS. Police volunteer, got steady job after testifying against soldiers.

McDONALD, BILL. Texas Ranger captain who ordered arrest of Allison and twelve soldiers.

McDONNEL, JAMES P. Lived near fort, saw Tillman shortly after the shooting.

MARTINEZ, AMADA. Cowen servant girl, saw raiders.

ODIN, HALE. Miller Hotel guest; with his wife, Ethel, was a key witness in Purdy-Blocksom report.

PADRON, GENARO. Policeman, met Dominguez during raid, and then Mayor Combe.

PRECIADO, PAULINO S. In Ruby Saloon, saw Natus killed, later sued Government.

RENDALL, GEORGE W. One-eyed septuagenarian, lived across from the fort.

STARCK, FRED. Customs officer, lived next door to Fred Tate, house shot up.

TATE, FRED. Also a customs officer, attacked Private Newton.

THORN, DR. C. H. Dentist, heard Negro voices.

TILLMAN, JOHN. Ran a Jim Crow bar on Elizabeth Street.

VOSHELLE, WILBERT. Fort Brown corral master, claimed to have heard Mayor make threatening remark to Penrose before the raid.

Honor Roll

Company B, 25th Infantry

First Sergeant Mingo Sanders
Quartermaster Sergeant Walker McCurdy
Sergeant James R. Reid
Sergeant George Jackson
Sergeant Luther T. Thornton
Corporal Jones A. Coltrane
Corporal Edward L. Daniels
Corporal Ray Burdett
Corporal Wade H. Watlington
Corporal Anthony Franklin
Cook Leroy Horn
Cook Solomon Johnson
Musician Henry Odom
Private James Allen
Private John B. Anderson
Private William Anderson
Private Battier Bailey
Private James Bailey
Private Elmer Brown
Private John Brown
Private William Brown
Private William J. Carlton
Private Harry Carmichael
Private George Conn
Private John Cook
Private Charles E. Cooper
Private Boyd Conyers
Private Lawrence Daniel
Private Carolina DeSaussure
Private Ernest English
Private Shepherd Glenn

Private Isaac Goolsby
Private William Harden
Private Charley Hairston
Private John Holomon
Private James Johnson
Private Frank Jones
Private Henry Jones
Private William J. Kernan
Private George Lawson
Private Willie Lemons
Private Samuel McGhee
Private George W. Mitchell

Private Isaiah Raynor
Private Stansberry Roberts
Private William Smith
Private Thomas Taylor
Private William Thomas
Private Alexander Walker
Private Edward Warfield
Private Julius Wilkins
Private Alfred N. Williams
Private Brister Williams
Private Joseph L. Wilson

Company C, 25th Infantry

Quartermaster Sergeant George
   W. McMurray
Sergeant Samuel W. Harley
Sergeant Newton Carlisle
Sergeeant Darby W. O. Brawner
Sergeant George Thomas
Corporal Charles H. Madison
Corporal Solomon P. O'Neil
Corporal Preston Washington
Corporal Willie H. Miller
Corporal John H. Hill
Cook George Grier
Cook Lewis J. Baker
Musician James E. Armstrong
Musician Walter Banks
Artificer Charles E. Rudy
Private Clifford I. Adair
Private Henry W. Arvin
Private Charles W. Askew
Private Frank Bounsler
Private Robert L. Collier
Private Erasmus T. Dabbs
Private Mark Garmon

Private George W. Gray
Private Joseph H. Gray
Private James T. Harden
Private George W. Harris
Private John T. Hawkins
Private Alphonso Holland
Private Thomas Jefferson
Private Edward Johnson
Private George Johnson
Private John Kirkpatrick
Private Edward Lee
Private Frank J. Lipscomb
Private West Logan
Private William Mapp
Private William McGuire, Jr.
Private Thomas L. Mosley
Private Andrew Mitchell
Private James W. Newton
Private George W. Perkins
Private James Perry
Private Oscar W. Reid
Private Joseph Rogers
Private James Sinkler

Private Calvin Smith
Private George Smith
Private John Smith
Private John Streater

Private Robert Turner
Private Leartis Webb
Private Lewis Williams
Private James Woodson

Company D, 25th Infantry

First Sergeant Israel Harris
Q. M. Sgt. Thomas J. Green
Sergeant Jerry E. Reeves
Sergeant Jacob Frazier
Corporal Temple Thornton
Corporal David Powell
Corporal Winter Washington
Corporal Albert Roland
Corporal James H. Ballard
Musician Hoytt Robinson
Musician Joseph Jones
Cook Charles Dade
Cook Robert Williams
Artificer George W. Newton
Private Samuel Wheeler
Private Charles Hawkins
Private Henry Barclay
Private Sam M. Battle
Private Henry T. W. Brown
Private John Butler
Private Richard Crooks
Private Strowder Darnell
Private Elias Gant
Private James C. Gill
Private John Green
Private Alonzo Haley

Private George W. Hall
Private Barney Harris
Private Joseph H. Howard
Private John A. Jackson
Private Benjamin F. Johnson
Private Walter Johnson
Private Charles Jones
Private John R. Jones
Private William E. Jones
Private William R. Jones
Private Edward Jordan
Private Wesley Mapp
Private William A. Matthews
Private James Newton
Private Elmer Peters
Private Len Reeves
Private Edward Robinson
Private Henry Robinson
Private Robert L. Rogan
Private Samuel E. Scott
Private Joseph Shanks
Private John Slow
Private Zachariah Sparks
Private William Van Hook
Private Edward Wickersham
Private Dorsie Willis

Company A, 25th Infantry

Private James A. Simmons

Private August Williams

Company G, 25th Infantry

Private James Duncan

Unassigned, 25th Infantry

Private Perry Cisco

Troop C, 9th Cavalry

Private Alexander Ash   Private Taylor Stroudemire
Private Robert James

Troop H, 10th Cavalry

Private John W. Lewis

Bibliography

THIS ACCOUNT OF the Brownsville Raid is drawn primarily from official records, contemporary newspapers, memoirs, collected letters, and unpublished papers of some of the principal figures. The official records include War Department reports, presidential messages, and the testimony taken at the courts-martial of Major Penrose and Captain Macklin, the hearings of the Senate Military Affairs Committee, and the proceedings of the court of inquiry set up at the start of the Taft Administration.

Short-form citations have been used in the Notes for the following works, all published by the Government Printing Office, Washington, D.C. in the year indicated in parentheses:

SD Summary Discharge or Mustering Out of Regiments or Companies. Message from the President of the United States, Transmitting a Report from the Secretary of War, Together with Several Documents, Including a Letter of General Nettleton, and Memoranda as to Precedents for the Summary Discharge or Mustering out of Regiments or Companies. 59th Congress, 2d Session; Senate Document No. 155. In two parts, published by 60th Congress, 1st Session; Senate Document No. 402, Part 1 (1908).

SD-1 545 pages (contains reports by Blocksom, Lovering, Garlington).

SD-2 201 pages (contains Purdy-Blocksom report and photographs).

BA The Brownsville Affray: Report of the Inspector-General of the Army; Order of the President Discharging Enlisted Men of Companies B, C, and D, Twenty-fifth Infantry; Messages of the

President to the Senate; and Majority and Minority Reports of the Senate Committee on Military Affairs. 60th Congress, 1st Session; Senate Document No. 389 (1908).

CMP Proceedings of a General Court-Martial . . . in the Case of Maj. Charles W. Penrose. 60th Congress, 1st Session; Senate Document No. 402, Part 2 (1908).

CMM Proceedings of a General Court-Martial . . . in the Case of Capt. Edgar A. Macklin. 60th Congress, 1st Session; Senate Document No. 402, Part 3 (1908).

SMAC Affray at Brownsville, Tex.: Hearings Before the Committee on Military Affairs, United States Senate. 60th Congress, 1st Session; Senate Document No. 402 (1908). In three parts.

SMAC-1 Part 4, pp. 1–927.

SMAC-2 Part 5, pp. 927–2030 (error in pagination of 927).

SMAC-3 Part 6, pp. 2031–3411.

NEM Names of Enlisted Men Discharged on Account of Brownsville Affray, with Applications for Re-enlistment. 60th Congress, 1st Session; Senate Document No. 430. (125 pages; contains additional testimony in form of affidavits).

CI Companies B, C, and D, Twenty-fifth United States Infantry: Report of the Proceedings of the Court of Inquiry Relative to the Shooting Affray at Brownsville, Tex. 61st Congress, 3d Session; Senate Document No. 701. Twelve volumes.

CI-1 Vol. 1–3, pp. 1–815 (Testimony).

CI-2 Vol. 4–6, pp. 816–1635 (Testimony).

CI-3 Vol. 7–9, pp. 1637–1790 (Exhibits, no p. 1636).

CI-4 Vol. 10–12, pp. 1791–2361 (Summary, index).

Aptheker, Herbert, editor, *A Documentary History of the Negro People in the United States,* Vol. II (Citadel Press, 1968).

Bishop, Joseph Bucklin *Theodore Roosevelt and his Time* (2 vols., Scribner's, 1920).

Bontemps, Anna *100 Years of Negro Freedom* (Dodd, Mead paperback, 1961).

Burns, James MacGregor *Presidential Government* (Houghton Mifflin, 1965).

Busch, Noel *T. R., The Story of Theodore Roosevelt and his Influence on Our Times* (Reynal, 1963).

Bryan, William Jennings *Selections,* edited by Ray Ginger (Bobbs-Merrill, 1967).

Chessman, G. Wallace *Theodore Roosevelt and the Politics of Power* (Little, Brown; 1969).

Clark, Champ *My Quarter Century of American Politics* (Harper's, 1920).

Crissey, Forrest *Theodore Burton: American Statesman* (World, 1956).

Cullom, Shelby M. *Fifty Years of Public Service* (A. C. McClurg, 1911).

Davis, John P. *The American Negro Reference Book* (Prentice-Hall, 1966).

Du Bois, W. E. B. *The Souls of Black Folks* (Fawcett paperback, 1961).

Dunn, Arthur Wallace *Gridiron Nights* (Stokes, 1915).

Foraker, Joseph Benson *Notes of a Busy Life* (2 vols., Stewart and Kidd Co., Cincinnati, 1916).

Foraker, Joseph Benson "A Review of the Testimony in the Brownsville Investigation" (*North American Review*, April 1908).

Foraker, Julia Bundy *I Would Live It Again* (Harper's, 1932).

Fowler, Dorothy G. *John Coit Spooner: Defender of Presidents* (New York University Press, 1961).

Franklin, John Hope *From Slavery to Freedom* (Knopf, 1967).

Gerson, Noel *TR: A Biographical Novel About Theodore Roosevelt* (Doubleday, 1970).

Grant, Joanne, editor, *Black Protest: History, Documents, and Analyses, 1619 to the Present* (Fawcett paperback, 1968).

Harbaugh, William Henry *Power and Responsibility: The Life and Times of Theodore Roosevelt* (Farrar, Straus and Cudahy, 1961).

———*The Writings of Theodore Roosevelt* (Bobbs-Merrill, 1967).

Lewis, W. D. *The Life of Theodore Roosevelt*, introduction by William Howard Taft (United Publishers, 1919).

Longworth, Alice Roosevelt *Crowded Hours* (Scribner's, 1933).

McKenna, Marian C. *Borah* (University of Michigan Press, 1961).

Madden, James W. *Charles Allen Culberson* (Privately printed, Austin, 1929).

Morison, Elting E. *Turmoil and Tradition: A Study of the Life and Time of Henry L. Stimson* (Houghton Mifflin, 1960).

Mowry, George E. *The Era of Theodore Roosevelt* (Harper's, 1958).

Myrdal, Gunnar *An American Dilemma* (2 vols., Harper's, 1944).

Nankivell, Captain John H. *History of the Twenty-fifth Regiment* (Privately printed, Denver, 1927).

Ottley, Roi *Black Odyssey: The Story of the Negro in America* (Scribner's, 1948).

Paine, Albert Bigelow *Captain Bill McDonald: Texas Ranger* (J. J. Little & Ives Co., New York, 1909).

Peavey, John R. *Echoes from the Rio Grande* (Privately printed, Brownsville, 1963).

Pringle, Henry F. *Theodore Roosevelt* (Harcourt, Brace, 1931; paperback, Harvest Book, 1956).

———*The Life and Times of William Howard Taft* (2 vols., Farrar and Rinehart, 1939).

Rayburn, John C. and Virginia Kemp *Century of Conflict 1821–1913* (Privately printed; Waco, Texas, 1966).

Roosevelt, Theodore *The Rough Riders* (Scribner's, 1899).

———*Letters*, edited by Elting E. Morison, Vols. V and VI (Harvard, 1952).

———*Selections from the Correspondence of Theodore Roosevelt and Henry Cabot Lodge 1844–1918* (2 vols., Scribner's, 1925).

Ross, Ishbel *An American Family: The Tafts 1678 to 1964* (World, 1964).

Rudwick, Elliott M. *W. E. B. Du Bois: Propagandist of the Negro Protest* (Atheneum paperback, 1968).

Russell, Francis *The Shadow of Blooming Grove* (McGraw-Hill, 1968).

Sheridan, P. H. *Personal Memoirs* (2 vols., Charles L. Webster Co., 1888).

Simkins, Francis Butler *Pitchfork Ben Tillman* (Louisiana State University, Baton Rouge, 1944).

Stoddard, H. L. *As I Knew Them* (Harper's, 1927).

Sullivan, Mark *Our Times*, Vols. II and III (Scribner's, 1943 and 1930).

Texas: A Guide to the Lone Star State (Hastings House, 1940).

Thornbrough, Emma Lou "The Brownsville Episode and the Negro Vote" (*Mississippi Valley Historical Review*, December 1957).

Tinsley, James A. "Roosevelt, Foraker, and the Brownsville Affray" (*Journal of Negro History*, January 1956).

U.S. Commission on Civil Rights, *Freedom to the Free: Century of Emancipation* (Government Printing Office, 1963).

Walters, Everett *Joseph Benson Foraker: An Uncompromising Republican* (Ohio History Press, Columbus, 1948).

Watson, James Eli *As I Knew Them* (Bobbs-Merrill, 1936).

Webb, Walter Prescott *The Texas Rangers* (Houghton Mifflin, 1935).

Wood, F. S. *Roosevelt as We Knew Him* (Winston, 1927).

Woodward, C. Vann *Origins of the New South 1877–1913* (Louisiana State University, 1951).

——*The Strange Career of Jim Crow* (Oxford paperback, 1966).

Along with the sources listed in the Bibliography, material has been drawn from the Cincinnati Historical Society (the papers of Joseph Benson Foraker); the Eugene C. Barker Texas History Center, University of Texas (papers of Walter Prescott Webb and James B. Wells); the Texas State Library Archives (the papers of Harbert Davenport and S. W. T. Lanham, and the Adjutant General file which contains the records of the Texas Rangers); National Archives (Old Military Records and Department of Justice files); and the Library of Congress (the papers of Charles W. Anderson, Theodore Roosevelt, William Howard Taft, Mary Church Terrell, and Booker T. Washington).

These additional short-form citations are also used in the Notes:

BDH Brownsville *Daily Herald*
BTW Booker T. Washington
ConRec *Congressional Record*
IWLIA *I Would Live It Again*, by Julia Foraker
JBF Joseph Benson Foraker
NBL *Notes of a Busy Life*, by Joseph Benson Foraker
NYT New York *Times*
TR Theodore Roosevelt
WHT William Howard Taft

References

The Mystery

I

JBF-TR on men's guilt, IWLIA, pp. 276, 277.

The Soldiers

2

Hoyt and Steward fear Texas, CI-2, pp. 1391, 1390.

Lincoln on Fort Brown, footnote, Sandburg, *The Prairie Years*, I, p. 372. Sheridan on Texas Negroes, *Memoirs*, II, pp. 261, 262. Kelly on Negro soldiers, SMAC-3, pp. 2525, 2551; "less race prejudice," SD-1, p. 241; on local blacks, SMAC-3, pp. 2540–2541. Customs officer, Fred Tate, on local constabulary, CMP, p. 395.

Edger on the coming of black troops, letter to JBF, February 16, 1907, JBF Papers; also SMAC-2, p. 1100. Departing first sergeant, Nelson Huron, SMAC-2, p. 1117. Fernandez denial, SMAC-3, p. 2245. Corroborating white soldier, William J. Rappe, SMAC-2, p. 1192. Cook, Frank Fisher, SMAC-2, p. 1185. WHT on "race prejudice," SD-1, p. 301.

Penrose on cold reception of troops, SMAC-2, 1945–1946. White sergeant, "good showing," Francois Oltmans, SMAC-1, p. 765. Artificer Newton on "niggers' trade," CI-1, p. 724. Captain Lyon's cook, William E. Jones, CMP, p. 1090.

Levie, "first crooked move," SMAC-3, p. 2941; "wildcat niggers," pp. 2949, 2550; Padron, "for cutting purposes," p. 2942.

3

Crixell on segregated bars, SMAC-3, pp. 2484, 2502. Williams-McGuire incident, SD-1, pp. 507–508. Newton-Tate incident, SMAC-3, pp. 2960, 2962, 2371. George Newton on James Newton, footnote, CI-1, p. 723. Taliaferro on Newton, SMAC-2, p. 1552; Newton admission, SMAC-3, p. 2974.

Adair's story, SD-1, p. 479. Reid dunking, SD-2, p. 118; Macklin on, SMAC-3, p. 1787.

Allison-Hollomon bar opens, CI-1, pp. 360, 379, 399; Crixell on, SMAC-3, p. 2486. Fernandez, "quietest pay day," SMAC-3, p. 2257; saw no drunks, p. 2258. "No arrests," SMAC-1, p. 765.

Combe-Evans, SMAC-3, p. 2381. Penrose-Combe-Evans, CMP, pp. 1146–1147; Mexican prostitutes, p. 1147; decided on curfew, p. 1148.

Taliaferro, "all passes cut off," SMAC-2, p. 1497; mail orderly, *ibid.*

Daniels, "directly after supper," NEM, pp. 109–110. Hollomon on betting, CI-1, p. 375. English, "no excitement," NEM, p. 7.

Macklin, "men laughing and joking," CMM, p. 196; talks to Corporal Wheeler, p. 66; reports on Evans incident, p. 179.

4

Macklin, "all the men were in," CMM, p. 178. Thomas and Lee, footnote; SD-1, p. 117 and CI-1, p. 352. Macklin, dog incident, CMM, p. 181; retires, p. 182.

Penrose, "worse than fire," CMP, p. 1152; sentry, p. 1153; Tamayo, "first shot in town," p. 824.

Howard, "shots down the road," CMP, p. 1058. Artificer Rudy, "shot right up in the air," SMAC-1, p. 792; "Come out, all you black nigger sons of bitches," p. 799.

In SMAC-1, p. 286, Sanders said it was Sergeant Brawner's wife who awakened him; in CI-2, p. 1104, he corrected his testimony. Sanders on mixed fire, SMAC-1, pp. 300, 323, 332. Lawrason, who reached B Company ahead of Sanders, said firing had ceased, NEM, p. 3. Cf. Sanders, CI-2, pp. 1045, 1059.

Frazier and Lyon on D Company response, SMAC-1, pp. 59, 61, 62 and CMP, p. 1073.

Mapp, "shooting still going on," SMAC-1, p. 530. Harley, "I was woke up," SMAC-1, p. 437; thought post under attack, CI-2, p. 1300.

Penrose fears for Macklin, CMM, pp. 226–227 and CMP, p. 1156. "Officers of the law!," CI-1, p. 717.

THE TOWNSPEOPLE

5

Police preying on soldiers, SMAC-2, pp. 1006, 1038, 1084. Similarity of uniforms, p. 1073. Police on duty August 13, SMAC-3, pp. 2148–2149. Combe awakens, p. 2383. Padron meeting, p. 2384. Garza gun, p. 2384 and Crixell's explanation, p. 2515.

Crixell, "quiet night," SMAC-3, p. 2488. Shannon's bicycle, SD-2, p. 140.

Preciado on Natus' death, SMAC-3, p. 2301.

Crixell-Cowen, "I want to go home," SMAC-3, p. 2488; Kibbe calls, ibid.

Dominguez meets Padron, SMAC-3, p. 2120. Padron, "yellow uniforms," p. 2140. Dominguez, "I saw them," p. 2116. JBF, "dark night," BA, p. 78. Dominguez route, pp. 2114, 2115.

6

Cowen party, SMAC-3, p. 2799. Mrs. Cowen, "get me sandwiches," p. 2816. Cowen's version of Leahy talk, p. 2817; her version, p. 2911. Porter meeting, p. 2816. Cowen-Natus meeting, pp. 2818–2819.

Mrs. Cowen, "alone with children," SMAC-3, pp. 2791, 2792. Amada Martinez, pp. 2803–2805. Mrs. Cowen quotes Amada, p. 2794.

Kowalski story, SMAC-3, pp. 2835, 2834, 2837.

Mrs. Leahy, when shooting started, SMAC-3, pp. 2894–2896; two policemen, pp. 2909–2910; sees raiders, pp. 2896, 2905, 2906; takes in Mrs. Cowen, p. 2916; Lyon patrol, p. 2898. Elkins, "We will come back tomorrow," CMP, p. 467.

7

Combe, when shooting ended, SMAC-3, pp. 2385–2386. Mrs. Leahy, "I do not know what fear is," p. 2918; frees two policemen, p. 2914.

Cowen pleads for gun, SMAC-3, p. 2826; talks of suing Government, p. 2917; examines his house, p. 2827. Mrs. Leahy, "Did you put him on guard?" p. 2919.

Combe calms mob, SMAC-3, p. 2886; reply to Lyon, p. 2387. Penrose-Combe meeting, CMP, p. 1157. Macklin reports, SMAC-3, p. 2388.

Penrose orders, CMP, p. 1158; picks up wife, examines garrison, p. 1159.

Reveille, Penrose on rifle inspection, CMP, pp. 1160–1161; Macklin, CMP, p. 552; Lyon, CMP, p. 1078. Penrose fears "our men" did it, SMAC-2, p. 1933.

THE INVESTIGATORS

8

Creager learns of raid, SMAC-3, p. 2840. Mrs. Cowen "unjointed," p. 2797.

Creager-Penrose, SMAC-3, p. 2841; CMP, pp. 1162, 1163. Combe-Penrose, SMAC-3, p. 2392. Crixell "peddling cartridges," SMAC-3, p. 2517. West on shells "to kill niggers with," CMP, p. 806.

Kelly's cartridge, SMAC-3, p. 2534; soldiers' guilt, p. 2529; newcomers from South, p. 2530; talk of marching on fort, p. 2529. Combe-Billingsley, p. 2391; Wreford, pp. 2391–2392. Kelly on citizens' mass meeting, p. 2530. Combe's account, p. 2393. Kelly-Penrose, p. 2531. Combe-Penrose, pp. 2394–2395.

Jackson record, SD-1, p. 246; affidavit, p. 73. Brawner record, p. 256, affidavit pp. 73–74. Powell record, p. 267, affidavit p. 74. Penrose's first telegram, SD-1, p. 66; second CI-2, p. 1345.

9

Kelly's method of interrogation, SMAC-3, p. 2533. Canada, SD-1, pp. 82, 81; Madison, p. 84; Thorn, p. 84 and SMAC-3, p. 2105; Martinez, SD-1, p. 78, Rendall, p. 76.

Fernandez disavows testimony, SD-1, p. 83 and SMAC-3, pp. 2250–2255. Padron, SD-1 p. 87 and SMAC-3, p. 2140. McDonnel, SD-1, p. 84. BDH, "dastard outrage," August 15, 1906.

Citizens' Committee telegram, SD-1, pp. 20–21.

Ainsworth telegrams, SD-1, pp. 26–27. Penrose reply, p. 28. Blocksom, pp. 28, 34.

Ainsworth-WHT, SD-1, pp. 52–53. Texas senators, pp. 19, 23. Texas commanding general, p. 24.

Citizens' appeal; SD-1, p. 26. "All is quiet," BDH, August 16, 1906; verse, August 22.

"Planned to have a band," BDH, August 22, 1906. Closing of Fort Brown, SD-1, pp. 38–39; Culberson-Ainsworth, p. 45.

10

"Incredible folly," NYT, August 27, 1906; "If there must be Negro troops," August 20. "The guns he carried," letter from A. Wayne Wood to Harbert Davenport, in Davenport Papers. Paine, *Captain Bill McDonald: Texas Ranger*. Webb MS of *The Texas Rangers* in Webb Papers. Davenport on McDonald, "troublemaker, advertiser," p. 875 of Webb MS.

McDonald, "them hellions" and meeting with Welch, Paine, p. 324. Welch, loss of arm, SMAC-3, p. 2430. Delling, SD-1, p. 88 (misspelled

"Dalling"); soda water man, G. W. H. Rucker, SD-1, p. 88. McDonald-Hamilton-Miller-Sheriff, in McDonald's report to the governor, Texas Rangers file.

McDonald, "Put up them guns!," Paine, p. 328; "a fox," p. 330. Miller-Askew, from McDonald report. Askew's explanation of cap, SMAC-1, p. 560. McDonald on Macklin, from report. McDonald-Penrose exchange, Paine, pp. 336, 337.

McCaskey on "unbiased trial," SD-1, p. 46. TR told "unsafe" to leave prisoners and his approval of proposed action, SD-1, p. 50. Telegram leak, SD-1, pp. 103–104; text, pp. 50–51.

McDonald-Welch on "those niggers," Paine, p. 345. McDonald telegram, Texas Rangers file. McDonald-Penrose confrontation, McDonald report, Meeting in Welch's office, SMAC-3, pp. 2397, 2398. "Feeling ran very high," BDH, August 25, 1906. Kelly on McDonald, SMAC-3, 2545; Combe, p. 2431. Wells telegram to governor, November 6, 1906, in Wells Papers.

II

Soldiers' departure, SD-1, p. 55; SMAC-3, p. 2404. Combe-Penrose, SMAC-3, p. 2405. "Not a word," BDH, August 25, 1906. Troops reach San Antonio, SD-1, p. 55; reach El Reno, p. 59.

"Diabolical plot," BDH, August 27, 1906. Forster, "three men at the arsenal," SMAC-3, p. 2657; on Voshelle, p. 2658.

Blocksom Report, SD-1, pp. 60–65. Penrose on prostitutes, p. 69. "Too preposterous," BDH, August 27, 1906.

Howard on Penrose, SMAC-2, p. 956. McCaskey on twelve prisoners, SD-1, p. 57. Lovering, "eight can prove an alibi," SD-1, p. 110. McCaskey, "dragnet proceeding," SD-1, p. 66. Welch charge to jury, SMAC-3, pp. 3297–3298. Creager, "insufficient evidence," p. 3242. Welch, "entitled to release," SD-1, pp. 107–108. Athens, Ohio, episode, SD-1, pp. 414–418; ConRec, January 12, 1907, p. 1035.

Penrose on men's conduct, SMAC-3, p. 3026; on Corporal facing charges, SMAC-2, p. 1943. Penrose suggestion to lift restrictions, SD-1, pp. 105–106; McCaskey reaction, p. 106; Garlington ultimatum, p. 109.

Garlington assumption of guilt, SMAC-3, p. 2741. Garlington Report, SD-1, pp. 178–183. Garlington, "I lived with them," SMAC-3, p. 2733. "Secretive nature," SD-1, p. 180. Foraker questioning, SMAC-3, p. 2733.

Foraker on "conspiracy of silence," SMAC-3, p. 2723. Sanders record and interview, SMAC-1, pp. 302–307; quote, p. 306. Garlington rejoinder, SD-1, p. 182. English, "the men of long service," NEM, pp. 8–9. Garlington on Negro veracity, SMAC-3, p. 2747.

12

Garlington, "beyond reasonable doubt," SD-1, p. 182. TR to son, "killed it dead," TR Papers. WHT-Mrs. Taft-TR on Hughes's candidacy, Pringle, *WHT*, I., pp. 314, 318. TR to WHT, *TR Letters*, V, p. 486. TR to War Department on Garlington recommendation, BA, pp. 8–10. Election results, Washington *Post*, November 22, 1906; N.Y.*Age*, November 15.

"Negroes not fools," N.Y.*Age*, *op. cit.*; Waterville, Maine, *Sentinel*, quoted, Thornbrough, *The Brownsville Episode and the Negro Vote*, p. 471. TR defends his action, *TR Letters*, V, p. 489. Richmond *Planet*, reprinted in N.Y.*Age*, *op. cit.* TR, "if troops had been white," Bishop, *Theodore Roosevelt and his Time*, II, p. 29; "cannot be tolerated," *TR Letters*, V, p. 509. BTW, "blunder," Tinsley, *Roosevelt, Foraker, and the Brownsville Affray*, p. 48; letter to WHT, Thornbrough, pp. 474–475. Morriss, TR "our Judas," Tinsley, *op. cit.* TR-BTW dinner, "damnable outrage," *Literary Digest*, October 26, 1901, p. 486; "Negroes shall mingle freely," Sullivan, *Our Times*, III, p. 134. New Orleans *Times-Democrat* and Ben Tillman on the incident, Sullivan, p. 136; JBF on it, NBL, II, pp. 106, 107. Atlanta *Constitution*, "TR is right," N.Y.*Age*, op. cit. TR, "respectable colored people," ConRec, December 4, 1906, p. 24. Boston *Guardian*, N.Y.*Age*, *op. cit.* TR, Jr. episode, NYT, October 4, 5, 1906; case dismissed, November 11.

Army officers, "men have themselves to blame," NYT, November 8, 1906. Pitcher, statement and denial, Washington *Post*, November 24; NYT on authenticity, November 8; TR, "intention to be fair," Washington *Post*, November 7. Pillsbury, N.Y.*Age*, November 29. Sickles, "foundation of all discipline," Washington *Post*, November 21. Oliver, "if affair had gone unpunished," *ibid.*, November 20. "Turned loose like mangy curs," N.Y.*Age*, November 17.

THE POLITICIANS

13

TR goodbye, NYT, November 9, 1906. WHT gets bad news, NYT, November 21. N.Y.*Age* on county committee's action, November 22. "Dreyfus affair echoed," N.Y. *World*, November 16.

Mrs. Terrell, from *A Colored Woman in a White World*, unpublished memoirs, Library of Congress.

WHT, "I do not think he realizes," Pringle, *WHT*, I, pp. 324–325. Confidential message, WHT to TR, TR Papers. WHT telegrams, WHT Papers. "Mr. Taft has enlisted zealously," NYT, November 20, 1906. TR, "Discharge is not to be suspended," *TR Letters*, V, p. 498. "He is too big to play the lackey," quoted, N.Y.*Age*, December 13. TR to Richard Harding Davis, "order sustained by facts," National Archives. NYT, documents are "surprising," November 22. Stewart to WHT, "no conspiracy," National Archives. Soldiers on Garlington inquiry, N.Y.*Age*, November 15.

"Discreet officer," SD-1, p. 185. "I feel sorry for them," N.Y.*Age*, November 15, 1906. "Very neat, very soldierly," CMP, p. 1141. "Such sadness," Conyers, CI-2, p. 1380. "Orderly and well behaved," NYT, November 20. Clarke testimony, CMP, pp. 1141–1142.

"Great pressure," TR Letters, V, p. 509. JBF "writing, wiring, sending men," IWLIA, p. 277. TR to WHT, *TR Letters*, V, p. 517.

14

"Far pleasanter," Walters, *JBF*, p. 1. Newspaper reaction, *ibid.*, p. 224, muckraker; p. 254. TR to Lodge, *TR Letters*, V, pp. 428–429.

JBF reaction to news of raid, NBL, II, 234. Wife hears mutterings, IWLIA, p. 277. JBF resolution, ConRec, December 3, 1906, p. 2. Dayton clipping, December 18, 1906, JBF Papers. WHT's "judicial lobes," Pringle, *WHT*, I, p. 325. WHT concurs with TR, SD-1, p. 305. Sickles, "This country is not Turkey," Washington *Post*, November 21.

JBF reaction to TR message, NBL, II, p. 236. "More in this contest," Washington *Post*, December 20, 1906. "Negro vote," NYT, December 25. TR message, SD-1, pp. 1–9. JBF on Blocksom, ConRec, December 20, 1906, p. 573. TR-JBF on "eyewitnesses," SD-1, p. 2 and ConRec, p. 572. TR, "horrible atrocity," SD-1, p. 3.

JBF, "Does any man believe?" ConRec, December 20, 1906, pp. 575–576. TR-JBF on "punishment," SD-1, p. 6 and ConRec, p. 570.

Precedents: "none," SD-1, p. 313; "plenty," *ibid.*, p. 6. TR-JBF on Sixtieth Ohio, SD-1, p. 7 and ConRec, December 20, 1906, p. 578.

"Case needs bolstering," reprinted in Washington *Post*, December 27, 1906. Smyser, "flimsy evidence," *ibid.*, December 26. Letter to JBF on Secret Service from C. S. Watts, JBF Papers. Grimke letter, *ibid.* JBF reminded of Festus, ConRec, January 17, 1907, p. 1256.

15

TR's "astonishing frame of mind," NYT, December 24, 1906. Senator Scott on Tenth Cavalry, ConRec, December 20, 1906, p. 592. TR reply, TR Papers. TR orders "two first class colored men" from BTW, *ibid.*; footnote, TR disavows political motives, IWLIA, p. 294.

TR on equal treatment, SD-1, p. 6. TR-WHT, "have both assumed," WHT letter to Purdy, Justice files, National Archives. Penrose, "They were excellent," SMAC-2, p. 1937; Burt concurs, SMAC-3, p. 3190. "Will those niggers really fight?" anecdote told by Mrs. Terrell in her memoirs. Burt-Sanders, SMAC-3, pp. 3192, 3190.

Harley, "well set up and soldierly," NYT, December 10, 1906.

"If President is wrong," WHT to Purdy, SD-2, vii. WHT-Purdy regarding Odins' "opportunity for distinguishing the soldiers," memo in

Justice files. Also, Purdy letter to WHT, December 30, 1906, and Purdy on Judge Parks letter, January 6, 1907. Combe on Parks's death, SMAC-3, p. 2423. Text of Parks letter, SD-2, pp. 48–49. Elkins affidavit, SD-2, pp. 50–54. "Remarkably quiet," BDH, August 17, 1906. Elkins, "sounded like a Negro's voice," SD-2, p. 51.

Odin affidavits, SD-2, pp. 75-88; Mrs. Odin, "to raised window," p. 86. Purdy to WHT on Odins, January 4, 1907, Justice files. "I counted six Negro soldiers," SD-1, p. 76.

WHT to TR on Odins, SD-2, xvii; heard shooting at the "barracks," *ibid.*, xiv.

TR, "very few, if any" innocent, SD-2, v. TR message accompanying Purdy-Blocksom Report, i–vi. Text of report, SD-2, pp. 7–201. Martinez, "they were soldiers," p. 64. Rendall, "talking low," p. 15. Martinez, "I hear the noise," SD-1, p. 78. Sanborn, "firing so near me," SD-2, p. 11.

16

JBF, "their day in court," Washington *Post*, January 15, 1907. TR "not always as bold at end," ConRec, January 16, 1907, p. 1206. TR woos Spooner, Fowler, *John Coit Spooner*, pp. 360–362, also Spooner Papers, Library of Congress. "Discharge without honor," ConRec, January 14, 1907, p. 1082, and December 20, 1906, p. 570.

Spooner speech, ConRec, pp. 1130–1143. "John was the hero," Fowler, *op. cit.*, p. 362.

TR has "comic time" and "sorry that Foraker," *TR Letters*, V, pp. 559–560. TR meeting at Lodge home, Washington *Post*, January 21, 1907. JBF thinks TR "would undo the wrong," NBL, II, 249.

17

Gridiron jingles, in Dunn, *Gridiron Nights*, pp. 179, 180. Footnote, Irish sagas, Bishop, *Theodore Roosevelt and His Time*, II, 30–31. Watson, "bright young fellows, *As I Knew Them*, p. 70. Footnote, White House approves correction, NBL, II, p. 251.

Foraker's letter to son, NBL, II, pp. 249–254. Champ Clark, "white as a sheet," *My Quarter Century of American Politics*, p. 446.

JBF, "I did not come to the Senate," Clark, p. 447. "Scant applause," Watson, p. 72. "Bloody butchers," Clark, p. 447. Cannon, "What in hell?", Watson, pp. 72–73.

Beveridge, "altogether thoroughbred," NBL, II, p. 252. TR's version, footnote, *TR Letters*, V, p. 571. Clark, "ended in a draw," p. 443. TR, "only a quart of sauterne," letter to JBF from Edward G. Riggs, March 7, 1916, JBF Papers.

JBF, "white and fagged," IWLIA, pp. 3–4. JBF, "no happiness in politics," Walters, *JBF*, p. 288. Mrs Foraker to son, "town full of it," JBF Papers.

THE HEARINGS

18

Penrose defense, "falsehood and fabrications," BDH, December 19, 1906. Charges, CMP, p. 4. Rendall, pp. 6–25, 43–45. Thorn, "I know nothing," SD-1, p. 84; on Negro voices, CMP, pp. 363, 371. Arsenal of shotguns, revolvers, etc., W. F. Dennett, CMP, p. 321.

Littlefield, age, CMP, p. 343; police work, p. 344; "twenty feet" from black man, pp. 340, 354. Lawrason, "three feet" needed for recognition, p. 495; Grier, pp. 726, 745. *Daily Express* on Elkins, February 22, 1907. Elkins sees "small black Negroes," SD-1, p. 85.

Defense counsel on Mrs. Leahy's "positiveness," CMP, p. 1230. Edger on Mrs. Leahy, letter to JBF, February 10, 1907, in JBF Papers; "used to speak with her," SMAC-2, p. 1105. Mrs. Leahy, "preparing to retire," CMP, p. 73. Tamayo, shots "in town," p. 824. Howard on "first shots," p. 1058. Mrs. Leahy positive about time, pp. 91–92. Lackie on view from Leahy Hotel, p. 1110. Mrs. Leahy, "I saw through the leaves," SMAC-3, p. 2902.

Stucky, "They led us out back," CMP, p. 983; could make out no figures, p. 984. Harbold, "nothing whatever," p. 1030; Blyth unable to see clothing, p. 1013. Wiegenstein, on test with Negro sergeant, p. 995. Blyth, "Then we went downstairs," p. 1015.

Mrs. Leahy sees Negroes by "flash of their guns," CMP, p. 79; Elkins agrees, p. 462. Stucky disputes the point, p. 984. JBF to Penrose on testimony, May 18, 1907; Penrose reply, May 25, both in JBF Papers.

Dominguez confused, CMP, p. 116; saw soldiers, p. 117; on voices, p. 152; "I was shot by Government colored soldiers," p. 120; "How do you know?" p. 128; "I get so confused," p. 131. "Contemptible," BDH, February 18, 1907; BDH chips in two dollars, October 9, 1906.

19

Blocksom, "interviewed quite a number," CMP, p. 614; no clues, p. 635. Blocksom on Penrose's lack of "proper effort," SD-1, p. 64; missed "valuable information," CMP, p. 616; on "keeping them in solitary confinement," p. 618; "justified in threatening them," p. 619. Blocksom on Jackson, "several witnesses," pp. 615–616; McDonnel on Jackson, pp. 62, 66. Penrose and call to arms, pp. 613, 614; Foraker on call to arms, SMAC-3, p. 2609. Blocksom on Howard, p. 613; took no affidavits from townspeople, p. 645. General Burt, "simply an impossibility," SMAC-3, p. 3192.

Penrose on battalion's discipline, CMP, p. 1143. Combe on Penrose, p. 168; Penrose's version, p. 1148. Voshelle's story, BDH, December 15, 18, 1906; SD-1, p. 223; SMAC-1, p. 714.

Penrose, "instructions as to firing," CMP, p. 1159. Combe-Penrose, p. 174. Crixell, "Negroes are shooting on the town," SMAC-3, p. 2384. Combe-Penrose, CMP, pp. 174, 1177. Penrose, on cleaning shotguns, p. 1177. Preston on rifle-cleaning experiment, p. 811.

Penrose, "damaging evidence," SD-1, p. 432; changes mind, SMAC-2, p. 1944. Penrose verdict, CMP, p. 1248.

Penrose trial a "whitewash," BDH, March 25, 1907. Penrose on BDH, footnote, CMP, p. 1184. Tamayo "the blackest perjurer," BDH, March 11, 1907. Tamayo to JBF, April 28, 1907, in JBF Papers. Kilburn, "low order of intelligence," SMAC-2, p. 1026; skating rink, p. 1038. "Depravity," BDH, March 14, 1907.

Accusations against Macklin, CMM, p. 4. Penrose, "a hard sleeper," p. 19. Lawrason, "very sound sleeper," p. 202. Dr. Brown, "I have pounded on the wall," p. 214. Macklin, "very much tired," p. 183; leaves call for reveille, p. 181; "thought I heard a knock," pp. 183–184. Hairston's story, p. 79; Lyon's, p. 33. Penrose greets Macklin, "My God, Ed," p. 15.

Penrose on Macklin's conduct, CMM, p. 19. Headline, "Second Military Whitewash," BDH, May 4, 1907. Penrose to JBF on verdict, May 7, 1907, in JBF Papers. Text of verdict, CMM, p. 1248.

20

Senators refer to "trial," Washington *Post*, February 5, 1907. JBF questions Harris, SMAC-1, p. 46; Frazier, p. 78. Frazier described, Washington *Post*, February 7, 1907; first impression of shooting, SMAC-1, p. 94; why changed mind, p. 89; queries men, p. 74; soldier will "make his brags," p. 78; "I never seen General Garlington," p. 68.

"Soldiers swearing to their innocence," BDH, February 18, 1907; gossip regarding Macklin, March 15. Penrose, "absolutely false," JBF Papers.

Crixell quotes Macklin on "nigger being hit," SMAC-3, p. 2485; Billingsley's version, pp. 2475–2476; his parting words, as Crixell remembered, p. 2485.

Macklin denies remark, SMAC-3, p. 3122. Lyon fixes time, pp. 3151–3152. Macklin on Lyon's printing job, p. 3122.

Crixell on Combe's visit, SMAC-3, p. 2513. Crixell, "It was in the paper," SMAC-3, p. 2495; BDH an evening paper, SMAC-2, p. 1040 and SMAC-3, p. 2831. Crixell murder, footnote, BDH, August 10, 1912 and Peavey, *Echoes from the Rio Grande*, p. 48.

T. Crixell and Leckie, bullet hole, SMAC-2, p. 1893; "all lead," p. 1894. Soldiers dislike lead bullets, BA, p. 76.

Penrose, "Frankford arsenal shells," SMAC-3, p. 3076; bullets recovered in the area, ConRec, May 4, 1908, pp. 5661–5662.

Four guns, BA, pp. 94 ff.; SMAC-2, pp. 1309–1326, 1365–1370, 1439, 1441, 1443, 1453, 1462, 1473, 1581–1582; SMAC-3, pp. 3025, 3042–3043, 3116–3119; CI-2, pp. 1361–1372, 1419–1445, 1566. McCurdy unlocks storeroom, SMAC-2, p. 932; Lawrason corroborates, pp. 1581–1584; rifles undisturbed, p. 1582.

Burt on McCurdy, SMAC-3, pp. 3189, 3191.

Double indentations, Lyon and Lawrason, SMAC-2, pp. 1597–1598, 1858–1859. Lawrason traces shells to Niobrara, pp. 1598–1599.

McCurdy explains shells, SMAC-2, pp. 1662–1664, 1666, 1667; "clips in box," p. 1686.

THE VERDICT

21

Majority Report, BA, pp. 23–27; minority, pp. 27–106; JBF on majority, NBL, II, p. 264. Kelly Miller on report, letter to JBF, in JBF Papers. TR, "the only conclusion," TR Letters, VI, pp. 966–967. TR message on re-enlistments, BA, p. 22. Fulton, "How prove their innocence?" ConRec, May 6, 1908, p. 5784. NYT on difference between two reports, March 12, 1908. TR, "proposal to condone murder," TR Letters, VI, p. 967.

JBF speech, The Black Battalion, ConRec, April 14, 1908, pp. 4709–4723.

Schurman letter, April 27, 1908; JBF reply, April 29, both in Foraker Papers. TR-Borah, McKenna, Borah, p. 100; Borah speech, ConRec, April 20, 1908, pp. 4962–4970. Bacon, "You are a lawyer," McKenna, p. 101.

TR to Smith on soldiers' guilt, TR Letters, VI, p. 1017. N.Y. World on TR's "vindictiveness," April 16, 1908.

22

WHT reply to JBF, mentioned in Pringle, WHT, I, p. 327; document in Taft Papers, Vol. 46, Letter Series 8, pp. 122–243. Letter, Browne to WHT, April 13, 1908, National Archives. WHT to TR on Browne-Baldwin, ConRec, January 12, 1909, p. 795.

Browne and JBF, CI-2, pp. 1393 ff.

Judge Advocate General on Browne and Baldwin, telegram of April 20, 1908, National Archives. Browne poses as "sympathetic newspaperman," CI-1, p. 418. Browne "have located 118 members," National Archives. May-June reports, ConRec, December 14, 1907, pp. 186–191.

Browne, "Conyers has confessed;" TR "will be glad to hear;" "sufficient evidence to convict and hang;" report is "full and satisfactory," all in Old Military Records, National Archives.

Lawson's affidavit, ConRec, December 14, 1908, p. 187. Browne "evidence is conclusive;" would like to continue work, National Archives. JBF on absence of Baldwin's name, footnote, ConRec, January 12, 1909, p. 796. TR, able "to fix with tolerable definiteness," ConRec, December 14, 1908, pp. 185–186; Browne "every reason to believe" Conyers confession, p. 186.

23

Conyers, "I love my wife," CI-1, p. 133; first hears of his "confession," p. 135; sheriff "wanting to investigate him," p. 244. Conyers to JBF, "I am innocent," ConRec, December 14, 1908, p. 192. JBF recalls Conyers' "open, manly face," ConRec, January 12, 1909, p. 802. Conyers testimony, quoted, SMAC-1, pp. 704, 705, 706.

Conyers to JBF on Gray-Baldwin, ConRec, December 14, 1908, pp. 192–193.

Conyers on meeting with Browne and Arnold, ConRec, December 14, 1908, pp. 193–194; JBF letter to Conyers, footnote, p. 192.

JBF, "Oh, shame," p. 195.

24

JBF arouses TR's "virulent hostility," IWLIA, p. 270; "haunted house," p. 289; detective, p. 287; "Poor Mrs. Fairbanks," p. 288. Tyler appointment, Walters, JBF, p. 241 and Thornbrough, The Brownsville Episode and the Negro Vote, pp. 479–480. JBF on BTW, "Ohio's third senator," Washington Post, February 8, 1907. Mrs. Foraker, JBF "almost alone," IWLIA, p. 293. Grover Cleveland, JBF's "display of courage," quoted, NBL, II, p. 327.

Mrs. Foraker, "too much for Foraker's sense of justice," IWLIA, p. 277. WHT says TR "impatient" at law's delays, introduction to Lewis' Life of Theodore Roosevelt (1919), viii. TR on "substantial justice," Pringle TR, p. 314. TR truce terms, IWLIA, p. 295.

JBF's re-election, Walters JBF, p. 272. WHT, JBF can help with "colored vote," Pringle WHT, I, p. 371; "peace pact," Walters, p. 272. JBF-Hearst, Standard Oil letters, NBL, II, pp. 328–354. JBF to WHT, Walters, p. 277. Dick-Crane report WHT "disturbed and embarrassed," and JBF "surprised and mortified," NBL, II, p. 396. TR to WHT, would not "appear with JBF," TR Letters, VI, p. 1244. WHT, "If it would win me every vote," NYT, September 21, 1908. TR to Lodge on "ugly revelations," Letters of Theodore Roosevelt to Henry Cabot Lodge, II, p. 316.

TR at funerals and weddings, quoted, IWLIA, pp. 204–205. TR's advice to WHT on golf, TR Letters, VI, p. 1234; on smiling, Pringle TR, p. 355. TR decides to put vim in campaign, ibid., p. 356. TR attacks JBF opposition to policies, NYT, September 22, 1908; Harper's Weekly replies, October 3, 1908, p. 4. TR, "JBF is a brilliant man," footnote, TR Letters, VI, p. 1257. Cincinnati Enquirer, "political epitaph," Walters JBF, p. 279. "Vigorous, vitriolic valedictory," NYT, January 13, 1909.

25

JBF speech on Browne and Baldwin, ConRec, January 12, 1909, pp. 792–809. Conyers on George Gray, *ibid.*, December 14, 1907, p. 193.

JBF, "atrocious, disreputable," ConRec, January 12, 1909, p. 798; on Supreme Court decision, p. 799. Lodge, "Pendulum has swung," footnote, ConRec, December 16, 1908, pp. 307–308. Clay on Arnold, ConRec, January 12, 1909, p. 800.

Lawson affidavit, ConRec, December 14, 1907, pp. 186–187. Giles, ConRec, January 12, 1909, pp. 801–802; Mayfield, p. 801; Blassingame and Arnold, p. 800.

Garrity affidavit, ConRec, January 12, 1909, p. 801. Conyers to JBF on excursion, ConRec, December 14, 1908, p. 194. Hinton, CI-1, pp. 252–253; cf. CI-3, p. 1646.

Browne finds Conyers "disturbed," ConRec, December 14, 1909, p. 187. The "careful and persistent questioning," ConRec, January 12, 1909, pp. 800–801.

Browne and Baldwin on Elmer Brown, ConRec, December 12, 1908, p. 188. Penrose on Elmer Browne, SMAC-2, p. 1943. Foraker questions him, SMAC-1, pp. 687–688. Elmer Browne's affidavit, ConRec, January 12, 1909, pp. 802–803.

JBF, "Oh, such plotting," ConRec, January 12, 1909, p. 801. NYT, "solemnity," January 13, 1909.

The Face-Saving

26

Tillman, "Jedwood justice," ConRec, February 23, 1909, p. 2948. JBF told "it's packed," IWLIA, p. 296. Taft rules out Lyon for defense, Old Military Records, National Archives. Daggett to JBF, November 16, 1909, JBF Papers. Daggett's attitude toward case, CI-1, p. 98; War Department's stance, National Archives. Daggett to JBF, November 16, 1909; JBF reply November 22; both in JBF Papers.

Only "new evidence," CI-1, p. 18. Court reaches Brownsville, BDH, November 26, 1909. Location of streets, SMAC-2, p. 1890. Reservation open to public, CI-1, p. 24. Crixell on quantity of beer, p. 62.

Conyers visited Negro bar, CI-1, p. 132; how treated, p. 145; wants to call Browne, p. 159.

Browne's new version of Conyers "confession," CI-1, p. 413; "Negroes will kill me," p. 408; how "we got cartridges," p. 409; "Conyers told the rest," p. 414. Browne, cross-examined by Marshall, pp. 449–450.

Conyers on Mr. Lancaster, CI-2, p. 1231. Browne, "barely time to catch train," CI-1, p. 413. "It left on time," Rufus Jackson, CI-3, p. 1697; Baker, "about a minute," p. 1703; Cook looks at watch, p. 1705.

Browne puts hypothetical question to Conyers, CI-1, p. 411; found sheriff "obstructive," p. 447. Conyers gun jammed in Cowen alley, footnote, ConRec, December 14, 1908, p. 186.

Arnold on Conyers' reaction, CI-3, p. 1688, 1690. Conyers-Arnold on sending for the picture, CI-2, p. 1231 and CI-1, p. 245. Browne says Conyers told about Holloman; CI-1, pp. 406–407; earlier reference, May 9, 1908, Old Military Records, Box 4504, National Archives.

27

Hollomon, "chief conspirator" and "known to very few," ConRec, December 14, 1908, p. 190. Hollomon-Reid travels, Hollomon affidavit, January 8, 1909, National Archives; cf. CI-1, p. 357.

Hollomon, "why called financial man," CI-1, p. 361. Sanders, "common occurrence," footnote, CI-2, p. 1054. Hollomon, on "being a money lender," CI-1, p. 389; will get "a warm reception," p. 387; men "didn't like" Jim Crow bars, p. 389; had plans for saloon, p. 399. For details of opening saloon, cf. SMAC-3, pp. 2486, 2497–2499; CI-1, p. 384. Hollomon's activities on August 13, in January 8, 1909, affidavit. Mrs. Hollomon, affidavit of January 7, 1909, also in National Archives.

Hollomon on his "rake-off," CI-1, p. 382; no "unusual irritation," p. 388; "effect of liquor," p. 390; "went up to my bunk," p. 358; firing going on, ibid. Sanders-Hollomon colloquy, SMAC-1, pp. 317, 328, 329; Hollomon's version, CI-1, p. 377; on giving first sergeant orders, p. 378.

Hollomon on John Brown, CI-1, pp. 361, 385, 386. Hollomon, "would have tried to prevent crime," p. 361.

Howland on Sanders, "controlling hand," CI-2, pp. 1548–1549; cf. also pp. 1040, 1048, 1547, 1584. Daggett on Sanders, CI-3, p. 1684. Sanders' one infraction, memorandum, Old Military Records, Box 4503, National Archives. Penrose, "exceptionally good man," NEM, p. 3; "strict disciplinarian," pp. 3–4; "company in excellent condition," p. 4. Why Grier changed mind, SMAC-2, p. 1723; Conyers gets same notion, CI-2, pp. 1379–1380. Sanders' farewell address, CI-2, pp. 1111–1112.

TR on Sanders, "dangerous, unprincipled," Adjutant General file, National Archives. Holman, ibid. WHT uses Sanders, 1912, Taft Papers.

28

Marshall protests court's procedures, CI-3, p. 1684; Howland distressed, CI-2, p. 1468; "suspects not arrested," p. 1622; "conspiracy as broad as the garrison," p. 1615. Daggert, "Who were they?" CI-3, p. 1682. Howland finds Conyers confession "bona fide," CI-2, p. 1589.

"Successful farce," quoted, NBL, II, p. 320. Decision of court of inquiry, CI-2, 1624–1635. Coltrane "asleep," SMAC-1, p. 846; Daniels, p. 829. Winter Washington on "Mexicans and greasers," SMAC-1, p. 172.

Lodge questions Kelly, SMAC-3, p. 2563. Garner, "preposterous,"

BDH, January 10, 1907. Tillman, "will run Negro troops out of town," SMAC-2, p. 1003; on his segregated bar, SD-2, p. 100. Tillman-McDonnel, SMAC-2, p. 1353; SMAC-3, p. 2639, 2569; and SD-2, p. 99.

Meeting of townspeople, SMAC-3, pp. 2497, 2487. Crixell on visit to Allison, SMAC-3, 2487; Allison "decent, orderly," p. 2503.

Allison tells Crixell he is leaving town, SMAC-3, p. 2506. Leckie visits Allison in jail, SMAC-2, p. 1896. Dewalt affidavit, Wells Papers. Allison's sanity, cf. CI-2, pp. 911–912, 940, 1445–1446.

29

Marshall on Mack Hamilton, CI-2, p. 980–982. Garza advised to "just ask Mack Hamilton," grand jury affidavit, September 20, 1906, in Wells Papers. McDonald, "I then went to the jail," report to governor, Texas Rangers file. Miller on Hamilton talk, CI-1, pp. 341–342.

"If Brownsville people did it," CMP, p. 1238; "very poor marksmen," CI-2, p. 983. "There goes the son of a bitch!" SD-1, p. 446; "Give it to him," p. 450.

Rendall on soldiers' motive, SMAC-3, p. 2052. Cowen on kindness of black sergeant, interview, April 28, 1969; Senate version, SMAC-3, p. 2924; mother's version, footnote, p. 2802. "What grudge?" SMAC-3, pp. 2796, 2810. "Kitchen was open," p. 2792. "They meant murder," p. 2801. Odins' light, SMAC-3, p. 2934. Starck light, CMP, p. 154. JBF on smugglers, BA, p. 105.

JBF, "No one hundred and sixty-seven men," NBL, II, p. 327. "All of us were armed," undated letter to Harbert Davenport, Davenport Papers, Texas Archives. Neale's account in Rayburn, *Century of Conflict*, pp. 143–144. Lunkenheimer story, SMAC-3, pp. 2927–2929; cf. p. 3015 for Penrose rebuttal. "They shot at advertising signs," *Century of Conflict*, p. 136. Mrs. Lyon to JBF on the black regiment, March 6, 1909, in JBF Papers, F692, Box 92.

Daggett to JBF on Lyon trial, JBF Papers. Daggett addresses men in Cuba, Nankivell, *History of the Twenty-fifth Regiment*, p. 84. Daggett obituary, NYT, May 15, 1938. TR to JBF, "no use raking up the past," June 28, 1916, JBF Papers.

THE CODA

30

Du Bois on Jim Crow cars, Aptheker, *A Documentary History of the Negro People in the United States*, Vol. II, p. 903; "right to vote," p. 908. BTW on the ballot, quoted in Bontemps, *100 Years of Negro Freedom*, p. 202. BTW, "remedy lies in education," *Harper's Weekly*, September 15, 1906, p. 1319. BTW, "make the Negro humble," quoted in Woodward, *The Strange Career of Jim Crow*, p. 95. TR to Tuskegee students, Harbaugh, *The Writings of Theodore Roosevelt*, pp. 199–204. TR, "occasionally they produce noncommissioned officers," *The Rough Riders*, p. 143. "They *know* we are soldiers," footnote, ConRec, January 17, 1907, p. 1263.

Negro refuses to "assent to inferiority," Aptheker, p. 902. Wells, "victims of prejudice," September 15, 1906, p. 1318. White men's fears, Myrdal, *An American Dilemma*, II, p. 1356; Cash, *The Mind of the South*, p. 116. Tillman, "I have three daughters," ConRec, January 21, 1907, p. 1441. "Lynch law is all we have left," *Afro-American Ledger*, December 1, 1906. TR on lynching, ConRec, December 4, 1906, p. 24. "Executive lynching," quoted *Literary Digest*, November 17, 1906, p. 710.

Patterson on disenfranchisment, ConRec, January 12, 1907, p. 1047. Tillman, "I believe they are men, but . . ." January 21, p. 1440; "move where they please," p. 1443. Spooner, "a right sacred as the ark," p. 1445; Tillman "kill! kill! kill!" p. 1441. Patterson's statistics, January 12, p. 1045; Tillman's rejoinder, "will continue to lynch them," p. 1047. Slayden on West Coast prejudice, January 8, 1907, p. 777; Gearin, January 7, p. 680. "This is a white man's country," January 12, p. 1040.

"Register and vote," Thornbrough, *The Brownsville Episode and the Negro Vote* (unless otherwise stated, all direct quotes in this section are from this source). BTW, "I have the strongest faith" and Villard reply, BTW Papers. TR, "swaggering roughshod," Aptheker, p. 913. "The bulk of the Negro people," BTW quoted in Tinsley, *Roosevelt, Foraker, and the Brownsville Affray*, p. 49. Bryan, "white men are lynched," *William Jennings Bryan: Selections*, edited by Ginger, p. 71. TR, "white men are lynched," ConRec, December 4, 1906, p. 24. Du Bois, "more Negroes voted against Mr. Taft," quoted in Rudwick, *W. E. B. Du Bois: Propagandist of the Negro Protest*, p. 114.

Du Bois, "The Negro is a sort of seventh-son," *The Souls of Black Folks*, pp. 16–17. WHT, on Negro jobs, Pringle *WHT*, I, p. 390. "We believe in taking what we can get," Rudwick, p. 95; "full exoneration," Aptheker, p. 914.

INDEX

New Afterword

AFTER READING *The Brownsville Raid*, Representative Augustus F. Hawkins, a black Los Angeles Democrat, called on his colleagues in Congress to join him in seeking to right this "grievous wrong." His bill, H.R. 6866, introduced on March 29, 1971, evoked a sympathetic response in the Department of Defense, but no action was taken until September 28, 1972, when Secretary of the Army Robert F. Froehlke announced that the 167 black soldiers dismissed without honor in 1906 were to be granted honorable discharges.

No mention was made of the two presidents involved in their discharges without honor, and army spokesmen made it clear that "no back pay, allowances, benefits or privileges shall accrue by reason of the issuance of this order to any heirs or descendants." Nothing was said about any of the soldiers or their widows who might still be alive.

Later, however, thanks to Congressman Hawkins's campaign to locate survivors and their families, two members of the black battalion surfaced. Edward Warfield of Company B was living in Mr. Hawkins's congressional district and turned out to be one of

the fourteen men the 1910 court of inquiry had permitted to re-
enlist. He had served in the first world war and received an honorable discharge in 1919, along with all the benefits to which a
soldier of his time was entitled. He died in September, 1973, shortly
before his ninetieth birthday.

The other survivor, Dorsie W. Willis of Company D, had borne
the full burden of the "gross injustice." For nearly sixty years he
had swept floors, shined shoes, and brushed coats in the North-
western Bank Building barber shop in Minneapolis. In failing
health, his hands crippled by arthritis, he had given up his job
only a few weeks before the army announced its exoneration order.

"Some people feel the world owes them a living," he told Andrew Malcolm of the New York Times. "I never thought that. And
I never took a dime in welfare. I did figure the world owed me an
opportunity to earn a living myself. But they took that away from
me. That dishonorable discharge kept me from improving my station. Only God knows what it did to others."

On Sunday, February 11, 1973, when Major General DeWitt
Smith, Jr., offered the army's official apology in an emotional ceremony at Zion Baptist Church in Minneapolis, ex-Private Dorsie W.
Willis represented the men of Companies B, C, and D, Twenty-
fifth Infantry, who had lived out their lives under the cloud of
their dismissal without honor.

"We are trying to substitute justice for injustice, to say how
much we of this generation—white men as well as black—regret
the errors and injustices of an earlier generation. . . . Mr. Willis,
you honor us by the quality of the life you have led, by your out-
standing citizenship, by the faithful service you rendered the
United States Army."

Accompanied by his wife Olive and his son Reginald, the old
man leaned on a wooden cane as the general handed him an honorable discharge certificate backdated to November 25, 1906. The
congregation gave him a standing ovation. The choir sang "The
Battle Hymn of the Republic" and, the New York Times reported,
"grown men wept." It was Mr. Willis's eighty-seventh birthday.

A year later, thanks to the persistence of Gus Hawkins and
Hubert Humphrey, Dorsie deposited a tax-free government check
for $25,000 in his Minneapolis bank and flew out to Los Angeles

to receive the keys to the city from Mayor Tom Bradley, who pointed out that Dorsie's birthday coincided with the start of Black History Week.

"The trials and tribulations of Dorsie Willis and all of the other members who were involved in that gross miscarriage of justice are a part of the history of this country," the mayor said, "and the fact that justice finally was done in terms of absolving them of the charges made against them is at least some help. The money obviously is not enough to ever repay him for the suffering that he went through, or that others went through."

"No," Dorsie said when a young black reporter asked if he were bitter, but he added, "They can't pay me for the sacrifice I've made, the sacrifice that my family had to undergo. You can't pay for a lifetime."

A respectful hush fell over the room; even the television crews stood silent for a moment as they watched Dorsie sitting in his wheelchair, at peace with himself and his fellow men, secure in his personal conviction that Providence had some reason beyond human understanding for reaching down into the rear ranks of Company D, Twenty-fifth Infantry, and picking Private Dorsie W. Willis to be the black battalion's last survivor.

He died August 24, 1977, at the age of ninety-one and was given a soldier's burial at Fort Snelling National Cemetery.

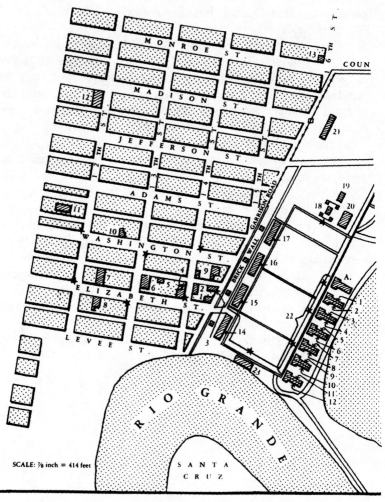

SCALE: ⅞ inch = 414 feet

1	Western Union office	8	Crixell's saloon	15	B Co. barracks
2	Louis Cowen house	9	F. Yturria house	16	C Co. barracks
3	Martinez cottage	10	Fred Starck house	17	Vacant barracks
4	Leahy Hotel	11	Police station	18	Guard house
5	Dr. C. H. Thorn house	12	County jail	19	Noncommissioned officers' quarters
6	Miller Hotel	13	Allison's saloon	20	Post exchange
7	Tillman's saloon	14	D Co. barracks	21	Sergeants' quarters

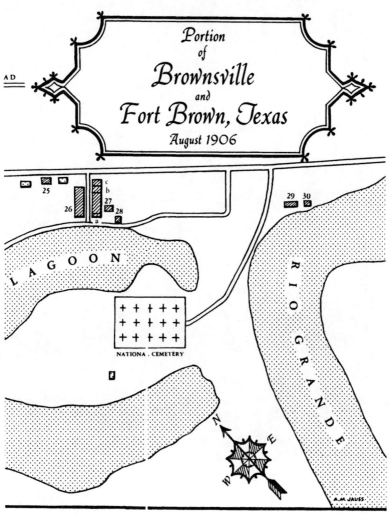

Portion
of
Brownsville
and
Fort Brown, Texas
August 1906

A D

25

26   27
      28
    a
    b
    c

29 30

L A G O O N

+ + + +
+ + + +
+ + + +

NATIONA CEMETERY

R I O   G R A N D E

N
W   E
S

A.M. JAUSS

22	Officers' quarters. Penrose in A, Lyon in 3, Grier in 5, Lawrason in 10, Macklin in 11.	26 Q.M. stable
23	Administration building	27 Wagon shed Penrose barn Teamsters' quarters Teamsters' quarters
24	Hospital	28 shed
25	Bakery	29 Ordnance storehouse
		30 Ordnance sergeant's quarters

★ Street lamps

Adapted from map drawn by draftsmen in the Office of the Quartermaster General, for the Court of Inquiry, December 1909.

CPSIA information can be obtained at www.ICGtesting.com
Printed in the USA
LVOW08s0833110214

373219LV00001B/106/A

9 780890 965283